PRAISE FOR *SELLING T*

From the Silk Road to Sony and Starbucks, Philip Squire examines attributes that are crucial in creating and sustaining a positive selling and buying experience. *Selling Transformed* clarifies and reminds us of the human basics and values essential to effective selling – then, now and in the future.
Frank Cespedes, Senior Lecturer, Harvard Business School, and author of *Sales Management That Works*

This is not just another book on selling. This is the definitive handbook for people who truly believe that sales is a profession worth investing a lifetime in. Dr Philip Squire could not have picked a better time to bring out a guide to selling where both values and ethics are foundational elements. This is certainly a new reference book for anyone taking a career in B2B sales seriously.
Simon Dale, Managing Director, South East Asia, Adobe

Organizations have always had to 'manage' their way through crisis and opportunity. Academics in their research of these 'events' develop interesting but theoretical hypotheses designed to explain and suggest ways to manage these events. Often these hypotheses lack practical strategies for implementation. Sales is the link between strategy and frontline execution. Providing research-led insights into sales has huge value. Dr Philip Squire's *Selling Transformed* is as applicable to those selling in Asia as it is in other parts of the world. This book will create future impact for senior management!
Professor Yong Joo Choi, Vice Chancellor, Seoul Business School, aSSIST

Selling Transformed is a very inspiring book. It clearly describes how selling has changed so much and is still in a continuous transformation process. I felt confronted by recognizing old habits at a personal and organizational level, but I felt proud recognizing significant improvements have been made. I was inspired by all the practical stories and reflecting that there is still a lot to learn. *Selling Transformed* has helped me to realize that the reason why I like being a sales professional is because of the importance of values. It has helped me to recognize this, to reflect, to learn and to work on it. If your ambition is to improve as a sales professional, this is a must-read book, with theory, practice and tools combined.
Monic van Aarle, Chief Commercial Officer, SAP Nederland BV

Selling Transformed offers an in-depth look at the journey in professionalizing sales through the lens of Dr Philip Squire's revolutionary global sales research. A viewpoint through time illustrating proof that sales as an artform and career has always been deeply rooted in society and that certain expectations, mindsets and behaviours must be a part of sales excellence. A must-read and notable investment in any salesperson's advancement towards professionalism.
Grant Van Ulbrich, Sales Transformation leader, Royal Caribbean Group

Philip Squire takes the reader on a fantastic journey from the Silk Road to modern-day sales, expertly weaving world-class research with many examples of companies who transformed their mindset and their approach. In a world of constant change, for any C-Suite, salesperson or sales leader, whatever their experience, this book will challenge your thinking, your practice and in the end your results.
Paul Devlin, Chief Customer Officer, SUSE

A cracker of a sales book, which redefines the scope of what good selling is, and manages to be both academic and practical whilst nodding both to history and the future. Game-changing.
Simon Harrison, Group Strategic Development Director, Mott MacDonald

Selling Transformed

Develop the sales values which deliver competitive advantage

Philip Squire

KoganPage

Publisher's note
Every possible effort has been made to ensure that the information contained in this book is accurate at the time of going to press, and the publishers and authors cannot accept responsibility for any errors or omissions, however caused. No responsibility for loss or damage occasioned to any person acting, or refraining from action, as a result of the material in this publication can be accepted by the editor, the publisher or the author.

First published in Great Britain and the United States in 2021 by Kogan Page Limited

Apart from any fair dealing for the purposes of research or private study, or criticism or review, as permitted under the Copyright, Designs and Patents Act 1988, this publication may only be reproduced, stored or transmitted, in any form or by any means, with the prior permission in writing of the publishers, or in the case of reprographic reproduction in accordance with the terms and licences issued by the CLA. Enquiries concerning reproduction outside these terms should be sent to the publishers at the undermentioned addresses:

2nd Floor, 45 Gee Street	122 W 27th St, 10th Floor	4737/23 Ansari Road
London	New York, NY 10001	Daryaganj
EC1V 3RS	USA	New Delhi 110002
United Kingdom		India
www.koganpage.com		

Kogan Page books are printed on paper from sustainable forests.

© Philip Squire, 2021

The right of Philip Squire to be identified as the author of this work has been asserted by him in accordance with the Copyright, Designs and Patents Act 1988.

ISBNs

Hardback   978 1 78966 537 6
Paperback   978 1 78966 535 2
Ebook   978 1 78966 536 9

British Library Cataloguing-in-Publication Data

A CIP record for this book is available from the British Library.

Library of Congress Cataloging-in-Publication Data

Names: Squire, Philip, author.
Title: Selling transformed: develop the sales values which deliver
  competitive advantage / Philip Squire.
Description: 1st Edition. | New York: Kogan Page Ltd, 2020. | Includes
  bibliographical references and index.
Identifiers: LCCN 2020041847 (print) | LCCN 2020041848 (ebook) | ISBN
  9781789665376 (hardback) | ISBN 9781789665352 (paperback) | ISBN
  9781789665369 (ebook)
Subjects: LCSH: Selling. | Customer relations.
Classification: LCC HF5438.25 .S719 2020 (print) | LCC HF5438.25 (ebook)
  | DDC 658.85–dc23
LC record available at https://lccn.loc.gov/2020041847
LC ebook record available at https://lccn.loc.gov/2020041848

Typeset by Integra Software Services Pondicherry
Print production managed by Jellyfish
Printed and bound by CPI Group (UK) Ltd, Croydon CR0 4YY

My Louise and Emma, Laura and Wills

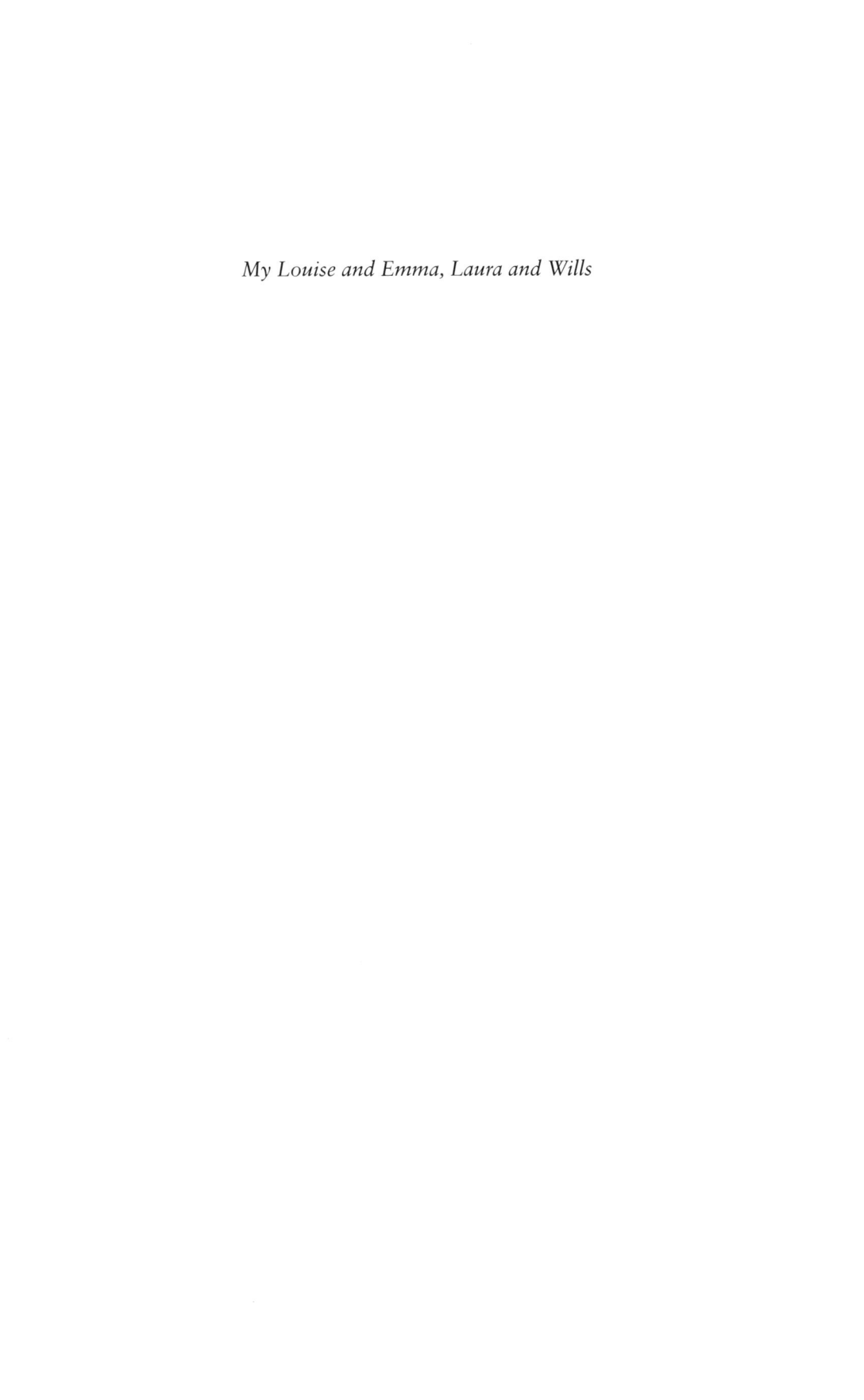

CONTENTS

About the author xi
Foreword xii
Acknowledgements xv

Introduction 1

01 How history informs current sales practice 5

How long has selling been around? 5
Zhang Qian: opening up the overland Silk Road 6
History repeats itself 8
What selling attributes did Zhang Qian possess? 9
Zheng He: opening up the Maritime Silk Route 9
Little research exists on sales and selling 13
Why has sales been so poorly served in terms of research? 13
Some good news for the sales profession – but still a long way to go 14
Continued curiosity 15
Endnotes 16

02 Sales psychology and the pressure of time 17

03 Changing sources of competitive advantage require a new selling paradigm 23

Sources of competitive advantage when selling in the industrial era 23
Sources of competitive advantage when selling in the knowledge era 26
Sources of competitive advantage when selling in the post-knowledge era 30
So what's the new norm? 32
Concluding comments 35
Endnotes 36

04 A new paradigm of selling based on values: the research journey 39

The spark that ignited the research – '95 per cent of salespeople are a complete waste of time' 39
The research demographics 40
First attempts at solving the problem – how to make it into the winner's circle 42
Yet the platform still burnt 43
What enabled a breakthrough 44
Popular books on selling 48
Back to the central question: why do so few salespeople sell in a way customers want? 57
Paradigm shift in research approach 58
Creating a new vernacular: values for selling 61
To conclude 63
Endnotes 63

05 Values creating a positive or negative selling experience 67

Manipulation 67
Supplier-centricity 68
Complacency 69
Overt arrogance 69
Authenticity 75
Client-centricity 76
Proactive creativity 76
Tactful audacity 76
Starbucks 79
Innovation in Compaq's response 82
Let's now consider the underpinning values that led both parties to this deal 84
Emerging conclusions from our research at this stage 86
Endnotes 88

06 Values that are an antecedent to trust 89

Pre-call planning: making that first contact 89
Opening the call 91
Understanding the need – what does the customer *really* care about? 91

Product discussion/presentation of solution 92
Handling objections 93
Gaining commitment 93
Post-call review 93
But what about the buying cycle? 94
The connection between values and trust 95
Hewlett-Packard case study – evidence linking values to sales performance 103
Values for selling: as guiding principles 106
Endnotes 107

07 Principle one: the value of authenticity 111

People's reliance on intuition to make decisions 112
Authentic self 114
How best to assess your lived values 114
Critical reflection – a core competence for salespeople 117
Code of ethics 122
Mental health and stress 123
Endnotes 124

08 Principle two: the value of client-centricity 125

A global mining business study – using a client-centricity mindset to win a new account 125
Cracking the industry code 129
Tool 1: for cracking the code 131
Tool 2: the customer pulse check 132
Professional services technical consultancy group (ConstructXion) 137
Endnotes 144

09 Principle three: the value of proactive creativity 147

Tool 3: the third place from the seller's perspective 150
Tool 4: customer strategy grid 155
Tool 5: whitespace analysis 159
To what extent can a national culture be encouraged to live the positive mindsets? 160
Endnotes 163

10 Principle four: the value of tactful audacity 165

Sony Mobile: how can you increase market share from 8.7 per cent to 17.4 per cent in less than two months? 167
Win themes 171
Trust the foundation for tactful audacity 172
Tactful audacity requires conviction, a 'just do it' attitude 173
The five key tactful audacity moments 177
Tactful audacity applied internally 178
Endnotes 179

11 Royal Caribbean International case study: turning a potential disaster into an opportunity 181

Royal Caribbean International: how mindsets applied turned 'terminal' decline into 282 per cent growth within 18 months 181
So what was in it for the ships' hotel directors? 184
Further reflections 187
The element of time 190

12 The role of leadership in transforming sales 193

So what mindsets/values are required of great sales leaders? 194
Sales management systems 196
Coaching to the mindsets 204
Organization support for a client-centric culture 207
Concluding comments 208
Endnotes 209

13 Looking to the future 211

The emerging Cx focus: purpose-driven value-creation 211
The future of capitalism: implications for sales 213
Capitalization of sales relationships: where value and values intersect 216
The final frontier: the professionalization of sales? 222
Endnotes 230

Appendix 233
Index 241

ABOUT THE AUTHOR

Dr Philip Squire is the co-founder and CEO of Consalia, a UK- and Singapore-based specialist sales business school. Philip has been educating companies such as BT, Hewlett-Packard, Microsoft, Royal Caribbean Cruises, Santander, SAP, Sony and many others, in leading and executing sales transformation approaches for four decades. He is one of just a handful of sales professionals internationally to have a research doctorate in sales. His passion for professionalizing sales led him to create the world's first sales consultancy delivering university-accredited undergraduate and postgraduate degrees in sales. He sat on the 2018 UK government-initiated Trailblazer group, created to set standards of sales practice in the UK, which has led to government-recognized sales apprenticeship degrees. He is a Visiting Professor at the Seoul School of Integrated Sciences and Technologies. In 2016 he co-founded the *International Journal of Sales Transformation* to bring practitioner and academic research to the global sales community and is also a trustee of the Association of Professional Sales, a not-for-profit body responsible for promoting ethical sales practice.

Philip spent the first years of his life moving around the Middle East, Africa and the Caribbean with his parents and brother. This sparked a lifelong love of learning about people and cultures and inspired his fascination with global sales techniques. He enjoys playing real tennis – arguably the best racquet sport ever invented though least known – fly fishing in the summer and road biking in and around the Surrey Hills, where he now lives.

FOREWORD

Ten years ago, I was asked to create an enablement curriculum for our European front-line sales managers to improve the way they lead, managed and coached their sales teams. At that time, it was clear that traditional 'shoot and forget' training sessions would not be effective enough to drive the magnitude of change that was requested, as we had to support the massive transformation that our organization was undergoing, namely the move from an on-premise to a cloud selling motion.

I intuitively sensed that we needed to create something new, a programme so innovative that it would provide sales managers with a deep and long-lasting shift in the way they perceived their roles and drove innovation. From my point of view, the best way to achieve this goal was to create an academically accredited programme – an MSc master's degree in fact – focused on Leading Sales Transformation. The issue was that, after weeks of market analysis, no university could provide a master's degree dedicated to sales, let alone sales managers. And the reason was quite simple: sales was not a profession and there seemed to be very little appetite from academia to investigate sales at depth.

Refusing to let go of my initial idea, I approached Dr Squire to discuss the options available to us. Although there were no master's programmes out there, Dr Squire and his company, Consalia Ltd, had the competencies to design such a master's programme from scratch. Our vision was to merge two totally opposed cultures, sales and academia, into one comprehensive and accredited framework. But we were still missing an important element: the university. We decided to reach out to Middlesex University, which was leading the way in terms of Action Based Research, an academic yet extremely pragmatic approach in which research was generated by professionals during their daily activities.

It took us 18 months to design the SAP master's programme. The journey was a real rollercoaster, you can trust me! Yet, on a nice day in July 2010, we successfully launched our first cohort, with Dr Squire being our host and facilitator. I was amazed to see the results; can you imagine a two-year programme tailor-made for sales professionals based upon academic principles, within which sales managers are turned into researchers, inviting them to reflect on their mindsets and values, revisiting their practices, investigating new ways to solve complex sales and customer issues and generating new researches on a quarterly basis. What a revolution!

The good news is that you do not need to create a master's programme to move ahead with the transformation of your sales organization. Instead, let *Selling Transformed* become your co-pilot. I cannot reinforce enough the true power of a mindset and values based model to infuse a sustainable shift in the way sales professional behave and operate. By applying the four mindsets presented in this book: authenticity, customer-centricity, tactful audacity and proactive creativity, you will help your sales team raise their game to a totally different level and in a sustainable manner.

A fact is that, in a time of accelerated change and uncertainty, we have to reflect on how sales should transform to help customers thrive, not only survive. It is our responsibility to ensure that sales teams deliver against customers' expectations and *Selling Transformed* provides a pragmatic blueprint for it. Putting ourselves in the shoes of the customers and their customers via third-box thinking, while coming up with new strategic initiatives and value proposition thanks to the strategy grid, should become the new norm.

I can only agree with Dr Squire when he reinforces the importance of coaching towards the mindsets. Driving transformation within sales requires a systemic and orchestrated approach and relies on the proactive involvement of first-line and second-line sales managers to coach their team members, otherwise the pressure of the 'quarter' will freeze the transformation process and inevitably push your sales organization back to the collective transactional behaviour.

Selling Transformed invites us to think about the future and assess the importance of purpose. Blackrock and numerous financial investors start placing their bets on companies that have clearly defined sustainability and inclusion strategies. Customers prioritize sellers who share the same values and drive solid environmental and social agendas. There is little doubt that sales professionals should understand this new tectonic shift and start integrating the greater good into their engagement model. But to be effective, the purpose-led sales approach will have to be genuine at the core, otherwise it faces the risk of becoming yet another non-authentic approach that customers will not adhere to.

The time has come to professionalize sales and give sales professionals back their *lettres de noblesse*. I fell into sales by chance, not by choice. This must change. I would like to thank Dr Squire and the entire Consalia team for their ongoing contribution towards sales professionalization. I am convinced that *Selling Transformed* represents a cornerstone upon which many organizations and governmental bodies will find inspiration and the energy to move towards that goal.

I wish you a great reading of *Selling Transformed* and maybe, more importantly, a deep reflection upon it.

Axel Ferreyrolles
Head of Innovation and Sales Digital Learning Strategy at SAP

ACKNOWLEDGEMENTS

This journey, the writing of *Selling Transformed*, started in the club gardens of that ancient sport, real tennis, at Hampton Court Palace. This was where Geraldine Locke (to whom I am indebted for many reasons) introduced me to Dr Peter Critten, one of the UK's thought leaders in 'work-based learning'. There are not enough words I can use to describe my appreciation of the support that Peter as my coach gave me during the highs and lows of trying to figure out what my doctorate research was telling me. He was both a harsh and enthusiastic critic, and being a Latin scholar, very picky on grammar and words! Through him I began to appreciate the influence of work-based research and the written word.

The powerful and combined intellect of David Hennessey, Professor of Marketing at Babson College, USA, and Roger Scarlett Smith, then Marketing Director and CEO of various GlaxoSmithKline businesses, also provided sage advice as mentors as I completed the academic journey that is the foundation of this book.

One of the best recruitment decisions I have ever made has been Libby Drake, our instructional designer. Libby is my 'opposite'. She has the unique ability to take my semi-formed ideas and make them come alive in structured content. She has been there from the beginning during the doctorate and then helping us build the future that is now Consalia. Her Australian sense of humour has kept me honest, particularly when she felt I was getting too academic in my writing.

In the corporate world I am truly indebted to Michael Hurley, William Mills, Alan Coffey, Birgitte Pingel, all then at Hewlett-Packard's managed services large deal bid team, who encouraged and participated in the research. The way they embraced the research ideas, but then extended the application of these ideas in practice, hugely helped in defining the mindsets framework referred to in the book.

Professor Garnett, at the time the Head of the Institute for Work Based Learning at Middlesex University (MU), was to become a great advocate of the special partnership we began to develop that is now thriving through the entrepreneurial support of its Pro Vice Chancellor and Executive Dean Anna Kyprianou and Professor Darryl Bravenboer, Head of Apprenticeships. The joint venture between Consalia and Middlesex is a great exemplar of how academia and business can co-exist and, by doing so, provide enormous value to the fast-growing number of students attending the undergraduate and postgraduate programmes we are running in the UK and globally for many of our coveted international clients. A special mention goes to Dr Christine Eastman, a senior lecturer at MU and author, who introduced me to 'writing for publications'. Her infectious enthusiasm and expertise in writing was a key factor in my completing the book.

Without our clients we would not be here. Axel Ferreyrolles, now Head of Digital Learning at SAP and maverick, said 'let's build it' and see what happens. So we did, and the journey towards professionalizing sales began in earnest with the MSc in Leading Sales Transformation. Thanks to SAP for being such great sponsors and believers in this new approach to sales education. Thanks also to Carl Day, now Sales and Marketing Director of Apogee, who, like me, did not start his career with a strong academic background but who has been such a huge advocate of sales education. The extraordinary performance that he and his dealers achieved whilst at Toshiba as they did their master's programme is described in this book and is testament to the synergies between commerce and academia. This leads me on to Louise Sutton, then at Sony Mobile, who brought us in to run the master's for a group of their most amazing key account executives. Special mention goes to Brian Tilley, who introduced to us Royal Caribbean Cruises, who have been, through Grant Ulbrich, such great supporters of our ideology; and Michael Crean of SKF, whose belief in what we are doing has led to the growing body of postgraduate research. These early clients have provided the values-based evidence for us to be confident that the direction we were taking was and is right at many levels.

I am deeply grateful to Louise Sutton, now our Academy Director; she has built on the great work Geraldine started in developing the master's and led us through the highs and lows of apprenticeship validation, with us being the first UK-based business to launch and run the BSc sales undergraduate apprentice programmes. Her uncompromising approach to student experience and passion for seeing students develop and the team she has now built at Consalia are testament to her leadership skills.

I must thank the fellow international shareholders of Consalia: Vito Crosetto and Maite Fuentes, who have tolerated and supported the shift in our vision to help make sales the world's most sought after profession, and have supported the sacrifices the business has made in the achievement of those goals. To Ian Helps, fellow shareholder: he has been amazingly supportive of our vision and has brought an encyclopaedic knowledge of corporate frameworks and processes – he has been such a great mentor and coach to me at a personal level. Together they have allowed us the space to experiment, try new ideas and build what we really believe in.

Of course, none of this would have happened without the support of all the team at Consalia, to whom I report. They, like Libby, have been incredibly loyal, professional and supportive of the uncharted waters into which we have navigated.

If the start was the chance meeting at Hampton Court Palace, the beginning of the end of the completion of the book was a chance meeting with Tim Godfrey at Twickenham rugby ground – a friend of many years, who, unbeknown to me, was so very well connected in the publishing world. When he heard of my desire to approach Kogan Page, he made the introductions. Thank you to Chris Cudmore and Helen Kogan for your initial support, and to Stephen Dunnell, my editor, whose calm, objective advice has been exceptional. It's been an education.

Finally, to my wife Louise, to whom the book is dedicated alongside my family. Our shared interest in the Silk Route, hers through the conservation of ancient textiles and mine through trade, was an important source of the connection between trade and culture referred to in the early chapters of the book. The book could not have been completed without her patient and tolerant support.

Introduction

Many think that transforming sales is implementing a new customer relationship management (CRM) system or introducing a sales process and expecting that sales performance will be transformed as a result – a bit like moving furniture around a room and saying it's transformed – this is not the case. Transformation requires a complete mindset change. Unlike furniture, which can be moved back, transformation is permanent, irreversible and involves a fundamental shift in the core values and belief systems of the sales organization.

My concern with 'what works and does not work in sales' has taken me on a personal learning journey that started in earnest with a doctorate in sales. This involved interviewing many buyers of products and services around the world and then working with many hundreds of salespeople in testing and trialling different approaches to selling and evaluating sales performance. The outcomes of this research are detailed in Chapter 4.

In conducting my research, I have met some extraordinarily great salespeople. Many have been enthusiastic supporters of my journey, happy to take on board and co-develop new ideas and provide great case studies – some of which I refer to in this book. To them I am extremely grateful.

So what can you expect from *Selling Transformed*? The book:

- Considers the role selling has played in the context of world history and suggests that its contribution to global economic and cultural development is both profound and unrecognized (see Figure 0.1).
- Explores how selling has had to adapt to the changing sources of competitive advantage in the industrial, knowledge and post-knowledge era. A new paradigm for selling is suggested – one based on values and belief systems and formed as a result of my doctoral research. It is very relevant in the post-knowledge era that we are now entering and contrasts with current practice that focuses on behavioural approaches to sales training.

FIGURE 0.1 Pivotal moments in history

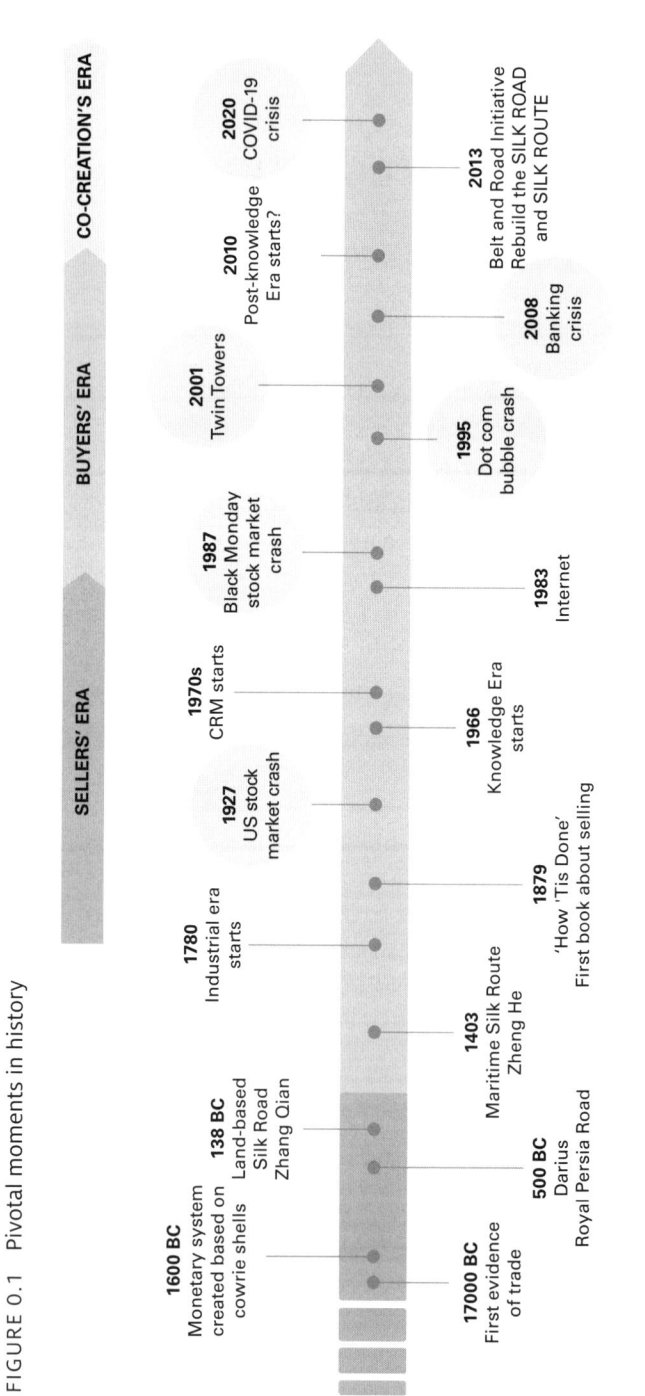

- Argues that sales management systems for transforming sales teams are different from the sales management systems for transactional sales. A transformational sales manager is required to be aware of both systems and apply that which is most relevant to individuals and teams.
- Considers the future initiatives that can elevate sales into the profession it fully deserves to be and the alignment of sales to purpose-led organizations, an emerging phenomenon of the world in which we now live, at a time where traditional economic models are being challenged. It explores the potential to connect professional sales practice with relationship capitalization and with shareholder value. It describes the emerging numbers of not-for-profit bodies that have the potential to set new standards of ethical sales practices supported by professional graduate qualifications.

01

How history informs current sales practice

By choice, 'history' did not feature in my student past – I questioned then its relevance for the future. I find now that the more my sales career has developed, 'history' does inform current and future practices of sales. I realize now how naïve it was then to have been so dismissive of history's relevance. But that transformation of perspective *in* oneself, in pursuit of a focused purpose – in my case learning about what works and does not work in sales – is a central tenet of this book.

How long has selling been around?

In historical terms, 'sales' as defined by trading has been around a long time; however, it has only been since the 1930s that books have been written specifically about how to sell. We have much to consider and learn from those in the past – particularly from those who helped to create the great financial systems and trade routes that exist today, albeit with a changed context.

Evidence of monetary systems to buy, sell, repay or mark debt, and bartering, predate written history. Earliest records indicate that gold and silver were used as currency as far back as 600 BC for high-value items and are still used as currency today. From around 1600 BC cowrie shells from the Maldives were used extensively as currency in India and China, and if we include Yunnan, a newer province of China, their use ended as late as the 1600s.[1]

In Africa cowries from the Maldives were used as a main unit of currency until 1900. Indeed, in 1845, an entrepreneurial German firm from Hamburg began to buy cowries from Zanzibar, which precipitated the cowrie currency collapse and high inflation. Interesting to think that the Maldives, now considered mainly as a prime tourist destination, was once the global centre of currency and that Sri Lanka was where these units of value were shipped and traded internationally.[2]

European trade ships often used cowrie shells as ballast as they sailed to and from Europe. Millions of cowrie shells were imported and exported internationally. A sophisticated, multi-tiered gold, silver, copper and cowrie monetary system was created to 'service' the great trade routes of the East, both at a local and a regional level.

Evidence of trade[3] is first attributed to South West Asia in 17000 BC. Humankind clearly has in its DNA a requirement and propensity to trade, to buy and to sell! As new modes of transportation and communication developed, trade moved from local to regional and then global, and more sophisticated mechanisms of buying and selling have been developed over many millennia.

The term 'globalization' found its way into the Oxford Dictionary in 1930 but became widely linked with the digital and internet economy[4] in the 1980s.

Zhang Qian: opening up the overland Silk Road

But arguably globalization could be sourced to the 1st and 2nd centuries BC and attributed to Zhang Qian, a gentleman of the court of Emperor Wu of the Han Dynasty. It was a consequence of his travels that he discovered ancient and unknown civilizations from as far as the Mediterranean coast between 138 BC and 125 BC and then south to India in 115 BC. Whilst his initial mission had a military purpose, it was his observations of 'unusual' products that fuelled his imagination for their commercial value in China and realizing in return huge commercial opportunities for China's great inventions, including silk[5] – hence the term Silk Road (Figure 1.1).

In recognition of Zhang Qian's services in opening up the commercial activities for China, he was awarded the title of Grand Messenger and became one of the top nine officials in the Han government.

The association of the words 'messenger' and 'commerce' can be linked to the Roman god Mercury, as, ironically, can the word 'trickery'. How we 'message' today from a sales perspective is as relevant now as indeed it was then: training agencies help salespeople craft value statements, value propositions and selling proposals.

Following Zhang Qian's reports, China then began to send major trade expeditions overland westwards – up to 11 a year. The Silk Road describes

FIGURE 1.1 Zhang Qian and the emergence of the land-based Silk Roads

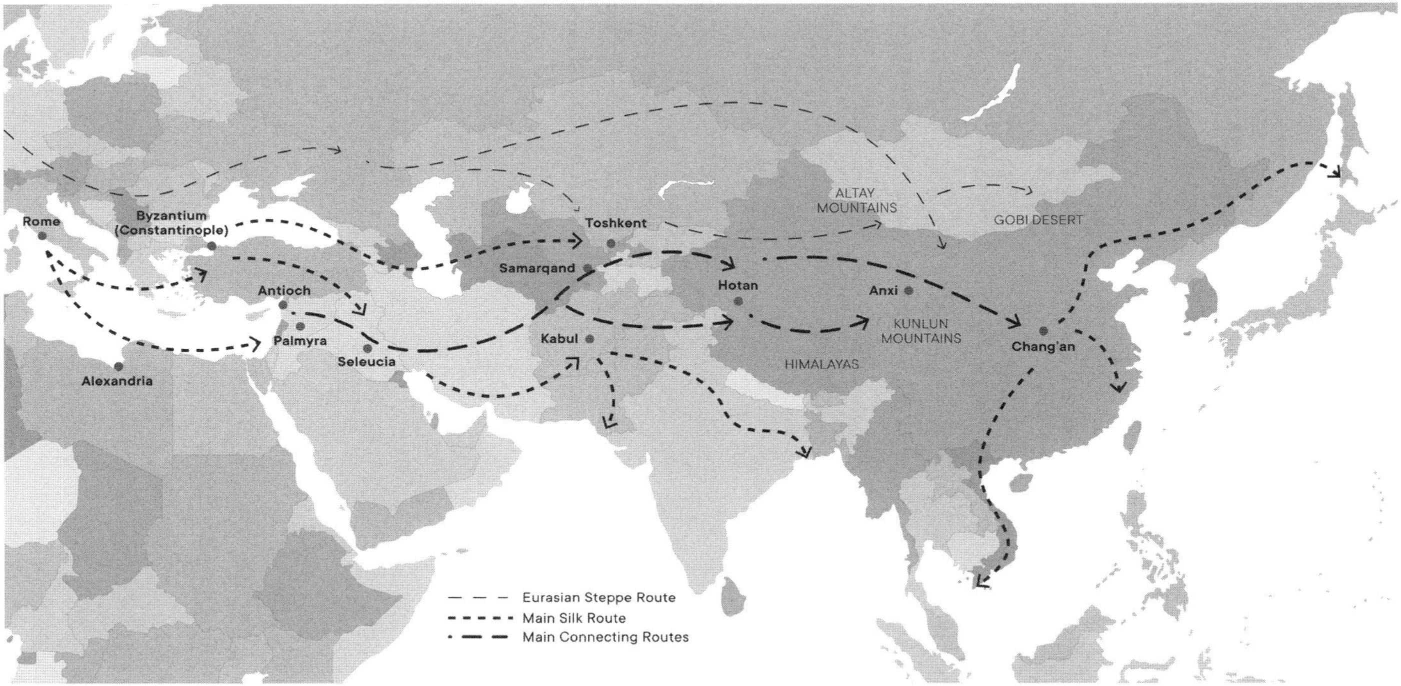

SOURCE Adapted from http://www.east-site.com/images/silk_road_map.gif

the main trading arteries. Routes from China heading west linked with routes from the east heading west. The trade routes from China linked with the earlier developed Royal Persia Road that stretched from Lydia south of Istanbul, and created a gateway to Greece and the Mediterranean, to Persepolis. According to Herodotus, the Persians under the leadership of Darius in the 5th century BC developed this route such that it would take just nine days on horseback to travel its length from the east of the Persian empire to the west, 1,677 miles in all.

Caravansaries, also used by trade delegations, enabled couriers to ride all day with fresh horses to be stabled at regular intervals. In Iran today evidence of these caravansaries that cross the country can be seen, linking what is now Afghanistan, Pakistan, Turkmenistan and Azerbaijan. Such was the demand for silk, particularly by its nobles, that the Roman Empire's gold and silver reserves were severely depleted.

Zhang Qian's initiatives had profound implications for globalization at multiple levels, as with trade comes not only increased economic prosperity but also culture, religion, knowledge and expertise. In China the Han Dynasty was considered its golden era, comparable with the great Greek and Roman Empires.

History repeats itself

History can be seen to be repeating itself now in a modern context. President Xi Jinping of China is building a new modern trade road[6] linking China to Europe – it is estimated that the projected investment in what is referred to as the Belt and Road Initiative will be US$4–8 trillion. A 2019 study produced by global economic consultancy group Cebr predicts that this investment will generate over $7 trillion per annum and raise global GDP 4.2 per cent by 2040.[7] Some regard this initiative cynically as a geopolitical move. In Confucian China, President Jinping could be following the leadership of Emperor Wu 2,100 years earlier, albeit in our current context.

Clearly, without the sponsorship of Emperor Wu, Zhang Qian would not have achieved what he did, and at considerable risk to himself and his family. Twice he was captured. The first time was for 10 years, during which time he met his wife and they had a son. Through his actions he earned their trust and at the same time impressed his captors with his courage as he was seen not to fear death.

Following his capture, he continued his travels to explore foreign lands, and on his return trip he was recaptured by the same Xiongnu tribe. Respected for his commitment and sense of duty he avoided death a second time and managed to escape after two years. Of the 100 people he took with him on his journey, only two returned alive.

What selling attributes did Zhang Qian possess?

As salespeople we can look for examples past and present for inspiration on what makes a great salesperson. Undoubtedly, Zhang Qian was a considerably talented man, able to sell a vision with multiple stakeholders with a set of ethics that was respected even by his enemies. He had the courage to take considerable risk and the curiosity to learn. Later we will look again at the qualities that Zhang Qian possessed and consider these in light of the qualities required in modern-day selling.

But whilst Zhang Qian is credited with the initiation of the Silk Road – the overland connection of East and West – what about the Maritime Silk Route? The lesser known Maritime Silk Route, in a similar fashion to the Royal Persia Road, was partially in existence from the 2nd century BC, linking Indonesia to India and Arabia. It was extended further east to China by Zheng He on a scale that was unprecedented in the early 1400s.

Zheng He: opening up the Maritime Silk Route

Little in Western literature is written about Zheng He, and it was reading a newly published book[8] that prompted a meeting with its author Professor Hum. He was asked to write a book on Zheng He by a group of influential Chinese Singaporean businessmen who felt the leadership qualities of this great man needed to be better explained for modern-day businesspeople.

Zheng He, a Muslim, was captured at an early age and castrated, and as a eunuch entered the service of the Royal Household. His intelligence and bravery marked him out and he became a confidant of the future emperor. He was entrusted by the Emperor Yongle as admiral to lead the world's largest ocean-going fleet in seven epic and peaceful trade voyages to the West (Figure 1.2).

FIGURE 1.2 Zheng He and the emergence of the Maritime Silk Routes

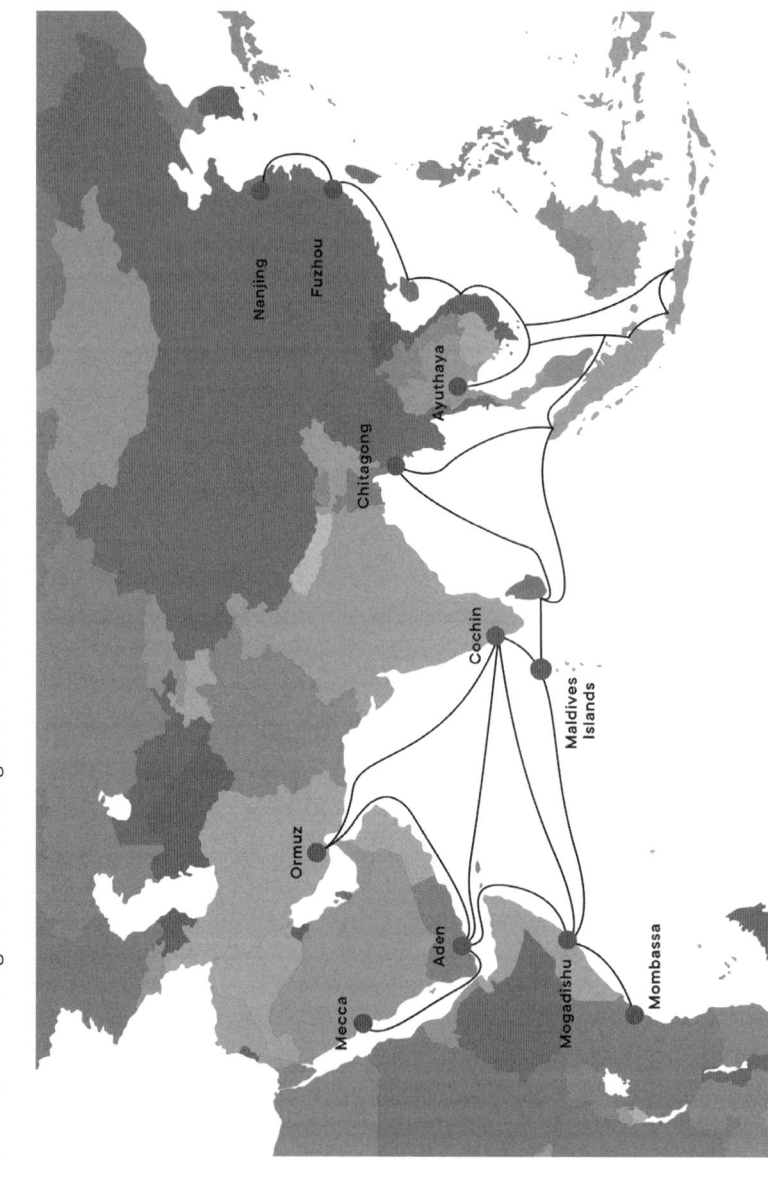

SOURCE Adapted from https://es.wikipedia.org/wiki/Zheng_He#/media/Archivo:Zheng_He.png

What selling attributes did Zheng He possess?

The vision and scale of Zheng He's mission were impressive. He had 300 ships built, some the same size as a football pitch (Figure 1.3). The largest of these trade missions included 30,000 people, all from different ethnic backgrounds. Imagine for a moment the leadership skills, the organization skills and the 'selling' skills required to make these expeditions such a success.

How did he leverage tangible assets (treasures) and intangible assets (knowledge) to create value?

Zheng He's mission was not just to trade but to exchange knowledge. Top doctors and engineers were included in these missions, to exchange knowledge with local communities. Treasures were also included to sell and held in the vast treasure ships. Soldiers were included, not to attack but to protect. In all the seven missions he led, only once were his warships deployed proactively and that was to attack a pirate ship that was in the South China Seas disrupting local trade.

Zheng He set up five major trade posts in key locations, such as Qui Nhon in Vietnam, Champa, Brunei, Malacca in Malaysia and Hormuz in Arabia. Marriages followed with local sultanates in Malaysia that secured long-term relationships. His emotional intelligence clearly was instrumental

FIGURE 1.3 Relative size of Columbus's ship

SOURCE Adapted from https://www.flickr.com/photos/criminalintent/361639903

in gaining trust, not only within the multicultural demographic of his party (all came from different ethnic groups and different religions) but also from the countries that he visited.

Imagine what it must have been like to see 300 ships appear on the horizon as Zheng He's expedition arrived. Anticipating local concerns, envoys were sent in advance to share the purpose of the expedition so that no alarm was made. Gifts were made to the rulers, always of a generous nature. In return He and China would receive knowledge and expertise and be able to trade and develop in a win-win environment.

Significant demonstration of emotional intelligence and generosity

Another example of his diplomatic skills and emotional intelligence can be seen at the National Museum in Colombo, Sri Lanka. It houses a stone obelisk donated by Zheng He. It is inscribed in three of Ceylon's languages and shared the purpose of Zheng He's mission, respecting the different ethnic groups within Sri Lanka. This was donated even after Alagakkonarra, a local warlord, set out to ambush him. Zheng He, forewarned, captured the warlord and, following instructions from the emperor, he spared him. As a result, Alagakkonarra always respected and welcomed Zheng He to Sri Lanka.

This idea of generosity, now not typically associated with selling, has recently been brought to the fore by Professor Adam Grant, whose best-selling book *Give and Take*[9] includes studies on generosity that show, surprisingly, that top-performing salespeople have a particular generosity characteristic called 'otherish givers'. They are genuinely motivated in being generous to others but also with a high level of personal ambition. Selfless givers are totally self-sacrificing and as a consequence tend to be taken advantage of.

In Zheng He's case generosity was not only about following the etiquette of the courts of the time, where gift exchange was a diplomatic formality, but also about the exchange of knowledge and expertise through activities such as sharing almanacs, teaching others China's superior fishing techniques and inviting envoys to come to China. His non-aggressive approach, transparency and the continuity provided by the seven great expeditions over 28 years provided the foundation from which buying and selling of goods could thrive. Zheng He's expeditions laid the foundations of the wealth and cultural success of the great Ming Dynasty.

Again, we can reflect from a sales perspective on the extent to which the important strategies of purpose and approach are relevant today. Which sales approach will be more sustainable or achieve more success? The provocative or push approach advocated by a number of Western-based selling ideologies, or the Zheng He pull approach?

Little research exists on sales and selling

Whilst history has shown the hugely important role trade has played over the years, what documentation sheds light on the practice of selling? If trading played the central role in the economic and cultural development of mankind over thousands of years, one might have expected records to have been written on how trading practices were conducted. However, very little research exists on the evolution of sales practices over time.

Marketing, however, is a different story. There have been various studies on the early origins of branding,[10] such as studies of branded artefacts found in Roman times circa 35 AD. The mass production of textiles, cosmetics and liquor[11] suggests that practices of marketing existed in antiquity, even though it may not have been recognized as such in those times.

The number of academic journals dedicated to publishing peer-reviewed research in the respective 'professions' is an indicator of academic interest in the topic. Over 150 journals are dedicated to marketing;[12] only two currently exist for sales: the *Journal of Sales and Marketing Management* and the *Journal of Personal Selling & Sales Management*.

Why has sales been so poorly served in terms of research?

We need to look to the academic community for the answers. Few in the academic world understand sales and its complexity. Marketing, developed in the early 1900s as an academic discipline, has had a lot more time to develop a body of academic research and also perhaps had a rather distrustful perspective of sales. Even the UK's Chartered Institute of Marketing dropped the word 'sales' from its name in 1968.

The anti-sales bias in academic institutions came to the fore whilst speaking to a prestigious Asian university about co-hosting one of our global sales transformation events. After agreeing the content and speaker line-up, they asked if we should drop the word sales from the event's title as it 'may put off potential delegates'.

Yet in the business world sales has equal or even greater value than marketing.

A recent comment by a retired former international markets MD at a major film company was that:

> I know marketing is important. But of the 100 per cent of my marketing budget, I don't know which half produces the results – it's a black hole. With sales on the other hand we know exactly what results are produced with whom and by whom. Even so it took me a long time to persuade my board that sales should be recognized as important enough to have a seat on its table. In my view if sales do not happen the business does not exist – sales are critical to my business.

Many other CEOs share the same sentiment.

Sales, as defined as the act of buying and selling goods or trading of goods between two parties or bartering goods, actually predates marketing. Yet, the earliest books specifically on the topic of 'how to sell' by salespeople can only be traced to the 1930s. Interestingly, books by 'observers' of salespeople predate those written by salespeople. One of the most amusing titles is *How Tis Done: A thorough ventilation of the numerous schemes conducted by wandering sales canvassers together with the various advertising dodges for the swindling of the public* (1879).[13]

Clearly the modern salesperson has a considerable challenge in developing trust dealing with prejudiced buyers and perhaps many in the academic community who inherently have a distrust of salespeople.

Some good news for the sales profession – but still a long way to go

It's positive news, then, that 'business to business sales' is finally recognized as a profession by the political community in the UK – an official letter allowing the development for a specific degree for sales issued by the Institute for Apprenticeships was received in March 2017. This was followed by the first UK undergraduate apprenticeship BSc Sales degrees for business-to-business salespeople launched in May 2018 by Consalia. It is also positive news that the Association of Professional Sales, a new not-for-profit organization, was incorporated in 2014 to set the standards for professional conduct. Chapter 13, 'Looking to the Future', expands on the implications of these developments.

But globally there is still a very long way to go for sales to be seen as a profession. Few countries outside the USA (now with over 130 universities offering undergraduate sales degrees) and the UK offer specialized sales degrees, and with so many deeply entrenched attitudes about sales politically and in the academic world, it's going to take a while to elevate the brand of sales to that of other worthy professions. The development of these sales degrees will in turn encourage more academic research into sales and enable sales to develop as a profession backed by proper scientific research.

Continued curiosity

The learning outcomes of my doctorate have since been enriched by visiting key places along the land-based Silk Road and the Maritime Silk Route to get a sense of the scale and sophistication of selling activity over the years.

To be inspired by the creativity, ingenuity, subtlety and complexity of the sales process over the last 2,000 years one only has to visit the great temples and trade complexes of places such as the Valley of the Kings in Sicily 500 BC, Persepolis in Persia 515 BC, Baalbek in Lebanon and Palmyra in Syria of the 1st and 2nd centuries AD, and Gyeongju, the capital of the Silla Dynasty 57 BC–AD 935, located at the north eastern arm of the Silk Route in South Korea. It's important to look beyond the scale and beauty of these historic cultural places and recognize that they owe their existence to the simple act of buying and selling.

But whilst one can admire the visionaries who created the global land and maritime trade routes and the sophisticated currency systems that enabled the common units of value to be used across geographic borders, I was curious to know what actually happened at the point of sale between buyers and sellers in this historical context and ask if it informs modern-day sales practice.

This has been particularly challenging given the lack of written documentation available. In the absence of written texts on the subject, I decided to visit some of the ancient but working trading places and observe and document sales practices, taking care to select those that have not been tainted by tourism. The Grand Bazaars of Istanbul, Marrakech and Fez, for example, whilst extraordinary in many ways, are not historically representative of how business was conducted.

A more authentic experience of 'how buying and selling was conducted in historical times' is gained in the more closed, and therefore less touristic and little changed, markets of Syria, Saudi Arabia, etc. Here I was able to make some surprisingly interesting observations about sales approaches, some of which are as relevant today as they were then.

The next chapter starts with a modern-day sales encounter in the world's oldest continuously inhabited city, the now war-damaged Aleppo, to discover more of the techniques of selling alluded to above.

Endnotes

1. Yang B (2011) The rise and fall of cowrie shells: the Asian story, *Journal of World History*, **22** (1)
2. Boomgard, P (2008) *Linking Destinies*, KITLV Press, Leiden, Netherlands
3. Smith, RL (2009) *Premodern Trade in World History*, Taylor & Francis, London
4. Levit, T (1983) The globalization of markets, *Harvard Business Review*, May–June
5. https://en.wikipedia.org/wiki/Zhang_Qian (archived at https://perma.cc/Z2VE-WRBP)
6. https://www.ciob.org/blog/silk-road-silicon-road-how-belt-and-road-initiative-will-transform-global-economy (archived at https://perma.cc/7E7H-8WWS)
7. https://cebr.com/reports/belt-and-road-initiative-to-boost-world-gdp-by-over-7-trillion-per-annum-by-2040/ (archived at https://perma.cc/XX24-7V3Y)
8. Hoon, HS (2011) *Zheng He's Art of Collaboration*, ISEAS Publishing, Singapore
9. Grant, A (2013) *Give and Take: A revolutionary approach to success*, Weidenfeld & Nicolson, London
10. Maran, J and Stockhammer, PW (eds) (2012) *Materiality and Social Practice: Transformative capacities of intercultural encounters*, Oxbow, Oxford
11. Demirdjian, ZS (2005) Rise and fall of marketing in Mesopotamia: a conundrum in the cradle of civilization, in *The Future of Marketing's Past: Proceedings of the 12th Annual Conference on Historical Analysis and Research in Marketing*, ed L Neilson, Association for Analysis and Research in Marketing, Longman, CA
12. https://www.scimagojr.com/journalrank.php?category=1406&type=j&page=4&total_size=158 (archived at https://perma.cc/U89N-9PPE)
13. Harrington, B (1879) *How Tis Done: A thorough ventilation of the numerous schemes conducted by wandering sales canvassers together with the various advertising dodges for the swindling of the public*, Fidelity Publishing Company, Chicago

02

Sales psychology and the pressure of time

'I got you'

ALEPPOEAN MARKET TRADER (2011)

Until the recent war, Aleppo was Syria's largest city and is one of the oldest continuously inhabited cities of the world. It dates back to the 6th century BC. The citadel, built on a hill, towers directly above the souk and has been used as a military guard for almost as long. For over a thousand years it protected an important gateway for the southern leg of the Silk Route – the trading route that linked Asia and the Far East to the Mediterranean and European countries.

Aleppo's covered souk was built in the 11th century and covers 15 square kilometres. It's divided into distinct trading areas, each selling different products, from suit-making to spice selling, textiles, copper and gold. Until the recent war it was the largest covered souk in the world. Unlike other great souks, such as the Grand Bazaar in Istanbul or Morocco's Marrakesh souk, which both cater for tourists, Aleppo's souk caters mainly for the local trade. It is as authentic as it is vast.

It was here that we met Mohammed, six months before the civil war started, in the summer of 2011. Tragically little currently exists of the market and we often wonder what has happened to Mohammed since.

Mohammed, an 'Aleppoean' trader, was found shaving in his shop as we entered. He was brought some mint tea and offered us the same. We accepted his offer and searched around his store of un-priced Syrian textiles.

Our intent was to purchase hammam towels. While talking about the towels, Mohammed showed us a range of other textiles hidden away in a locked cabinet. We were not interested in these, except for looking.

Eventually we noted a range of towels that were expertly hand-woven with tassel fringes. Having asked for his best price, we then opted to see if we could get a better price elsewhere as we were not pressed for time and, frankly, enjoyed the searching. By evening that day and having looked in many other shops, we decided that the choice and price at Mohammed's were the best. We decided to return the next day.

Sensing a more serious opportunity, he welcomed us into his shop – another offer of tea. We explained we liked his towels, recognized their quality, but weren't sure how many we wanted to buy. We enquired to what extent he would negotiate further on a decision if we were to buy more. He offered, 'Well, might there be some other things I could show you as well?'

By this time he knew that my wife was a conservation expert in Islamic textiles and wanted to show us some of his other items. 'Not to buy,' he said, 'just to show.' At this point he went back to his locked cabinet and returned with a number of embroidered bed covers and cushions – all modern but woven with various degrees of skill. One particular textile stood out. This was a beautiful double-bed-sized textile. Its stitching was modern but based on old techniques of tambour embroidery, chain stitching with silk embroidered threads on a silk ground fabric. My wife took a professional interest in this piece and commented on the techniques used – at which point we all closely examined the stitching, commenting on the expertise of the weavers and the time it would have taken them to complete the work. Aleppo, being situated on the Silk Route, has thousands of years' experience in the intricate weaving techniques still practised by hand. Techniques passed down from generation to generation mean that modern pieces are expertly woven to this day.

More tea was offered. Other clients had come into the shop and they also took an interest in the embroidered textiles, now all laid out on the floor of his shop. Mohammed asked my wife how much she would pay for such an item. She replied that she would not be drawn into any discussion on value. She knew and respected the craftsmanship of the textiles and had no intent to buy. He posited, 'How beautiful an item would you see in London and at what price?' He explained that he often sent such items to London. But again, not to be drawn, my wife said there was no way that she would offer a price but would be interested to know what price he had in mind. In fact, some of the other customers were interested as well. They too asked for the price. He said, pointing to some of the textiles on the floor, that these were in the range of £900, but the tambour-stitched embroidered textile was £1,400. My wife responded that there was no way she could afford to purchase the item; furthermore, she would not want to insult him with making an offer that was 'absurdly low'.

At this point we looked at some rather beautiful cushions, similar in style to the bed cover, that would go well on the new sofas we had just bought. We began now the serious process of discussing a deal on the cushions and towels. We pressed very hard to get the best price and, as we did so, Mohammed often returned to the large embroidered piece. He said that it was not often that he had people visit his shop who knew this type of stitching and that he would want to give it to us for a very special price. He pleaded with my wife to just give him a clue as to what she would pay for the textile. My wife resisted being drawn in. She reiterated there was no way that she would want to insult him by offering a price that was very low and more representative of what we might afford, not what it was worth. Still he pleaded, arguing that she didn't have anything to lose by offering a figure. At the very worst all he would do was say no!

My wife and I were now seated opposite each other with some gap between us and he was at the apex of the triangle. He not only directed his questions to her, but also glanced at me to get a sense of where I was on the deal. He could read that I trusted my wife's appreciation of the bed cover. I made it clear it was her decision. From that he knew that all he needed to do was convince her of its value – I would not be an obstacle.

Mohammed said that he would be able to offer an even better price if we bought the towels, the cushions and the tambour-stitched bed cover. He stressed again for us to offer a price. At this point my wife looked across to me and said, 'well, £400.' He then rather theatrically fell prostrate on the floor of the shop and said that she had indeed insulted him with this offer. Getting up, he said that £900 would be a better price, but 'let's meet in the middle?' 'No,' came the answer. '£800?' 'No.' '£700?' 'No.'

It was at this point that my wife's mobile phone rang. Our friends in Aleppo were expecting us for a drink later and wanted to confirm the time. Now we had been in the shop for most of the afternoon and it was getting late. Realizing we were running short of time, we decided to just acquire the towels and the cushions. We went and paid for these. Happy with our purchase and just as we were turning away to leave, Mohammed said, 'OK, you can have it for £500.' My wife rather irritably said no, we could not afford it. Then literally as we were passing through the doorway he said, 'OK, you can have it for £400.' We looked at each other in surprise. The tambour chain-stitched textile that had started out at £1,400 was now in our hands for £400. Furthermore, we knew that it was made of the highest quality – we were genuinely surprised that he had reduced his price so substantially.

My wife and I were rather exhausted with the process but also delighted. We discussed the conversation we'd had. Mohammed said, 'I realized once the mobile had gone that I had lost control of the conversation.' At this point he knew that he had a limited amount of time left and realized he had to act more quickly to see if he could do a deal. This, for him, was a pivotal moment in the sales process.

But then, having paid, and just as we were passing through the door he held open for us, he smilingly whispered in my wife's ear the words, 'I got you!'

The audacity of this statement visibly shocked my wife, who had felt that it was indeed she who had got the good deal. We reflected at length about the words and tone he used and explored what it told us about him and us.

From our perspective we had no intention of buying this particular object at the outset. This undoubtedly hardened our negotiating stance and made us uncompromising on the price we would pay. We got what we wanted at a price that was offered well below what we thought it was worth.

We laughed at the tactics and key strategies Mohammed had used to maximize the sale: his use of humour; the technical appreciation of the objects themselves; the relationship that had been built, recognizing, first, who was the decision-maker and influencer, then second, adapting his approach expertly; the way he even played on guilt; and how he linked the objects together to maximize the value; and finally his patient persistence. Furthermore, we reflected that having paid for the towels and cushion case in advance, we knew we could not leverage this purchase to lower the price even more. Was this a clever negotiating tactic on his part or just luck?

We went on to reflect further. Mohammed had expertly made us very interested in the product by first showing some of the hidden gems that he did not bring out that often. Great to excite curiosity. Through the 'collaborative' technical appreciation and enthusiasm for the product, he then created a 'zone' where both he and my wife were at the same 'level'. This was taken to a higher level, where jointly they explained the differences in craftsmanship to other interested customers by contrasting the poorer quality textiles with those of the highest quality. He knew that he did not have to convince my wife of the quality of the product – she knew its quality.

Once Mohammed had got her interest in a particular object, all he had to do was to find out what was the maximum price he could get for the object and then decide if that price was one that he was prepared to sell for. Hence, he constantly asked her what price she would pay. The moment she gave the figure, he knew the minimum he could get, but he chose to play the game for longer. Every pound he could extract would go to his bottom line. If we had had a deeper emotional desire to make the purchase, we might have paid a higher price, but our motive for purchase was driven more by a technical desire. Hence, he knew he would not get a better price.

He knew he had lost control of the negotiating process when the phone rang. He told us that he had lost the cadence of the conversation and now time was short. He ran the risk of us leaving the shop without a purchase. It was interesting in that he was clearly aware of a sales process in his comments to us about control.

Finally, the words 'I got you!' Said in a jocular way, they showed the excitement that can be had when two parties trade and that all parties can end up winning. Clearly he had the power to decide whether to sell at a particular price. The fact that he made the decision to sell implied that he had made profit on the sale, even at that price.

Contrast this to current methods of selling and buying in a business-to-business and retail environment. How many products are seen without a price label on them? The two-step process of developing interest in a product then determining the value as defined by the customer, not by the seller, would test even the most highly trained of Western developed salespeople. Yet the process that Mohammed went through was both as pleasurable as it was seemingly effortless.

As we know from Chapter 1, the earliest days of trading consisted of bartering as well as exchanging goods for currency. Bartering without a formal currency is not an exact science. Consider the process for a moment. It requires both parties to agree the value of a product or service, where the value of a product or service is based on subjective concepts, ie it is reliant on what someone is prepared to exchange for goods of a different nature. Both parties would need to establish the interest in their respective product and then, in the absence of money, determine what they would be prepared to give for that exchange. The skills required for bartering are thus very similar to those selling skills shown by Mohammed. His skills, learned through generations of family experience and then honed through practice, were as developed as the artisan weavers who created the beautiful hand-woven towels and textiles we spent so much time studying. Thus the value chain of production and sales has its roots in the most ancient of civilizations.

But to what extent are the sales practices of today reflective of the arts and science practised for so many years by these Aleppoean traders? How are the pressures of trading in the modern world influencing our ability to sell effectively?

To reflect on these questions we need to explore the context of the world in which we are selling: to what extent has selling changed over the years, and are there trends that suggest a different approach to selling is required?

03

Changing sources of competitive advantage require a new selling paradigm

Professor Julian Birkinshaw's thought-provoking framework,[1] as represented in Figure 3.1, considers the historical, present and future 'sources of competitive advantage'. He argues that each era requires a different source of competitive advantage and that each era always has a beginning and an end. One organization's competitive advantage in one era may not be so relevant in the next.

It's helpful to consider the role of sales in this context. How has the art or science of selling changed over the years? Are there nuanced differences that will make the difference in sales success according to the different eras in which we seek a competitive advantage? This is important because if we are to master the art of selling or buying, we need to consider its context and anticipate future trends.

I have therefore adapted this framework to consider how salespeople sold in our more recent past, explore how salespeople are currently taught to sell in the present, and suggest what will help them be more successful in the future.

Sources of competitive advantage when selling in the industrial era

Birkinshaw refers to the last 100 years of economic development in three eras. The first is the industrial era (late 19th century to the 1960s), where the efficiency with which units of capital and units of labour were deployed

FIGURE 3.1 The last 100 years of economic development

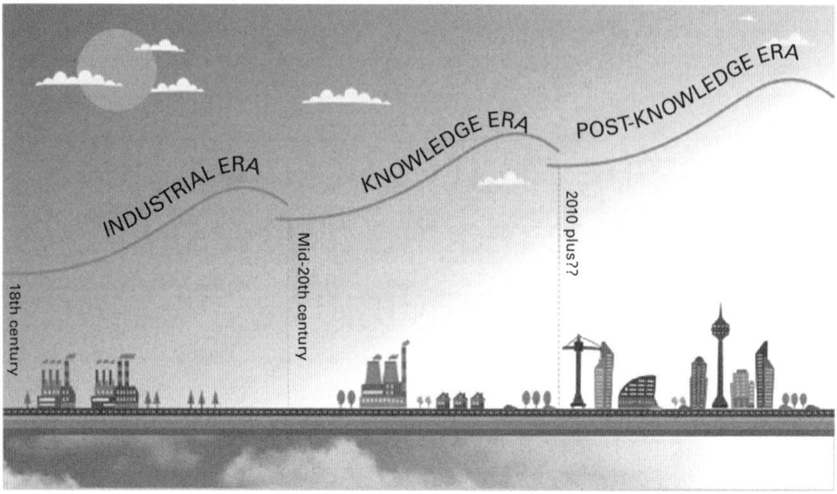

SOURCE Adapted from Birkinshaw (2014)[2]

determined the extent to which organizations were able to compete effectively. A company's ability to achieve a good return on capital was through organization efficiency, often through improved processes. It was their source of competitive advantage. He summarizes a key characteristic of this era as 'bureaucracy'.

In the early era days Britain led the way, its industrial revolution fuelling huge growth of its empire, but in the late 1880s the United States and then postwar Japan dominated. The US led the way in mass-scale manufacturing – think Ford Motor Company – in the late 19th to the early 20th century, followed by Japan, which became more efficient than the Americans by driving cost efficiencies whilst striving for a total commitment to quality – think Toyota.

So what would it have been like to have been in a sales role in the industrial era? In a world in which products were arguably scarce and with 'relatively' little competitive activity, it must have been pretty easy to be in sales. The seller had the advantage of knowing their products, differentiation enabling them to easily articulate the advantages and benefits of their products against others.

This was a seller-controlled era where the source of competitive advantage for the seller would have been a 'features, advantages, benefits' sell supported by product availability and 'fair' pricing. Organizations ensured that their sales teams had controlled sales conversations, adopting a line of leading questions based on extolling the virtues of their product, a presentation that was utterly compelling and a list of objection-handling statements designed to close the order.

Seller-controlled environments though can be and were severely misused. Unscrupulous salespeople took advantage of the uninformed buyer and used highly manipulative and persuasive techniques to close a sale.

The earliest book on the selling methods used in the industrial era was written by Bates Harrington, *How 'Tis Done*[3] (referred to in Chapter 1), and provides great insights into sales techniques used at the time. The irony is that it's written from the perspective of the customer, not the seller – clearly written by someone outraged by the 'scurrilous' sales organizations of the time. It's a well-researched novel, provides ample evidence of unethical sales practices and is designed to inform buyers of what to watch out for! He describes the tricks of atlas sellers, book agents, cloth swindlers, patent medicine sellers, advertising dodges and ready-made love letter sellers. The accounts are both entertaining and informative, and it goes a long way to explain why sales has such a poor reputation.

Could this be why, in 1898, the Gideon Society was formed to arguably counter the unethical malpractice? The Society was created by John H. Nicholson of Janesville, Wisconsin, and Samuel E. Hill of Beloit, Wisconsin – two travelling salespeople who met in a hotel room they shared at the Central House Hotel in Boscobel, Wisconsin, where they discussed the formation of the association. In May 1899, the two met again in Beaver Dam, Wisconsin, where they decided the goal of their association would be to unite travelling salesmen for evangelism.[4]

Indeed, Harrington in his book shares the training manual verbatim of one prominent Chicago-based book publisher who had 95 scripted steps outlining how a bookseller agent must sell and then collect money for the books sold, including a detailed account of how certain objections were to be overcome. 'If you must resort to sarcasm,' the training manual also advises, 'let it be pointed with punctilious politeness. After all, people are to be pitied rather than blamed for lack of breeding.'

Whilst we may laugh at the language used then, how different is this approach from the modern-day sales techniques? This scripted product/supplier-centric approach to selling is still taught by many organizations, wrapping it up with terms such as solution selling or simply sales training.

Sources of competitive advantage when selling in the knowledge era

The industrial era gave way to the knowledge era in the 1960s. The term knowledge worker was first coined by Peter Drucker in his book *The Age of Discontinuity*,[5] written in 1969. Drucker argued that an organization's competitive advantage lies not in humans being viewed as units of labour, as in the industrial era, but in humans' *knowledge and expertise*. It's their expertise and knowledge that provide the competitive edge. Hence Birkinshaw uses the word meritocracy to describe a key trait of the knowledge era.

The internet and computing power in more recent times transformed the knowledge era – in much the same way that the systems and process improvements helped drive efficiency in the industrial era, we can see a similar trend in the knowledge era. The immediacy with which knowledge is gained coupled with the ability to synthesize data creates the competitive advantage. This is enhanced by ever-improving technology, internet and search engines. Organizations are squeezing every bit of efficiency out of knowledge to gain more intelligence and adapting this to the ways procurement professionals buy and sellers sell.

This shift has completely changed the power base – control has now firmly moved from the seller to the buyer. Whereas in the industrial era the seller controlled the sale, from prospecting to qualification to closing, ie most of the steps of the sales cycle, the buyer in the knowledge era has taken control of the sales process. The buyer now decides what problems they want to solve, when they want to solve them, when they want to see a salesperson. They decide which salesperson will be invited to take part in a sales conversation. Though procurement and supply chain management functions have been around for many years, it's since the 1960s that the role of procurement has taken great strides to professionalize.

Furthermore, the buyer will have studied the potential suppliers and have done their own analysis of the competitive advantages of each.

In the industrial era, the seller was often involved at the start of a sales cycle and worked through 100 per cent of the sales cycle. In the knowledge era, the seller enters the sales cycle 57 per cent of the way through,[6] much of the qualification stage having already been concluded by the buyer.

This has resulted in profoundly different sales conversations. Procurement departments, historically on the back foot in the industrial era, have during the knowledge era developed sophisticated negotiating and supplier categorization techniques in order to extract better deals and to optimize the efficiency with which they engage suppliers. They now control the sales cycle.

Coming late into the buying process makes it much more challenging for the salesperson to gain a competitive advantage. Indeed, the professional salesperson of today is also having to overcome a cynical and mistrusting buyer. As we have seen, salespeople have not helped engender trust through their legacy of the selling methods adopted in the past and some perceived practices of what good looks like in the present.

If we assume that knowledge is the driver of competitive advantage, a salesperson should therefore use unique insights, data and intelligence to provoke conversation with customers. The latest sales techniques taught advise salespeople to use information, data or insights to challenge the customer with new ideas (this could help create a need), shape the conversation around the requirements of the customer (this to shape a need), then control the conversation towards an order. Much of the logic of this sales approach is to use insights cleverly to attract attention.

However, if we follow this logic, buyers, now inundated with insight-led sales approaches from competing salespeople, find it much more difficult to differentiate sales arguments from one supplier to another. Hence buyers resort to taking control of the buying cycle and involving salespeople later in the sales process when they may require further clarification of products and services in order to make the final decision. In the knowledge economy of today, it is becoming more and more difficult for sellers to attract people's attention.

It's not all bad news, though, for sellers. The advent of technology also offers considerable advantages for sales leaders and the salespeople who report to them. For many years the sales function has lagged other departments such as finance, manufacturing, marketing and HR in having sophisticated systems to make its operations more efficient. It's relatively recently with the advent of Salesforce, SAP CRM, Microsoft Azure, etc, that sales processes can more efficiently be adopted using state-of-the-art technology. In addition, technology solutions such as LinkedIn and search engines make it easier for salespeople to identify influencers and make contact with them. But what evidence is there to show whether sales, with the considerable advantages of technology, has improved its productivity in the knowledge era?

A 2016 research study published in the *International Journal of Sales Transformation*[7] explores the investments 150 organizations in Europe have been making in CRM and sales training. The research tracked certain performance ratios at a seven-year interval to assess trends.

FIGURE 3.2 CRM and sales training spend

SOURCE *International Journal of Sales Transformation* (January 2016)[8]

Figure 3.2 shows a steady increase in investment over the years – CRM spend rising from just over US$2 billion to US$3.8 billion and sales training from US$1.8 billion to US$2 billion over the same period.

One would expect that – with the steady increase in investment in both the 'hard' systems of CRM and the 'soft' skills training – sales productivity would increase. The research study also explored the conversion rates of the number of leads generated from marketing to closed business.

Surprisingly the research found that over the same period of time, the marketing-generated leads to closed business ratio reduced from 2006/07 to 2013/14, and the lead to order ratio reduced from 3.5 per cent to 2 per cent.

In considering Figure 3.3, it's important to understand what is being measured. It's not the conversion ratios from a first meeting with a salesperson to a closed order that is measured. It's the conversion ratio from a lead generated to an order.

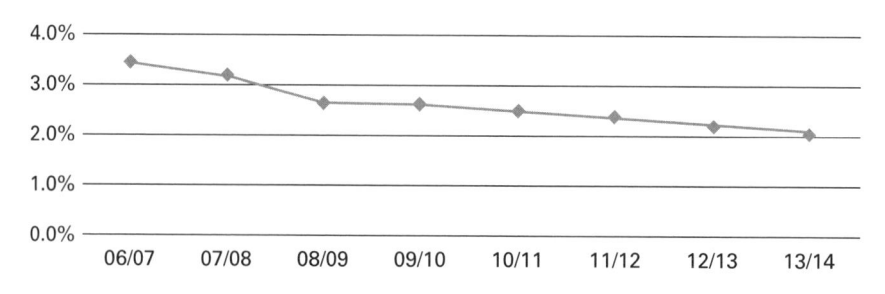

FIGURE 3.3 Pipeline conversion

SOURCE Adapted from https://www.journalofsalestransformation.com/fixing-the-revenue-process-bit-by-bit/

FIGURE 3.4 Marginal gains

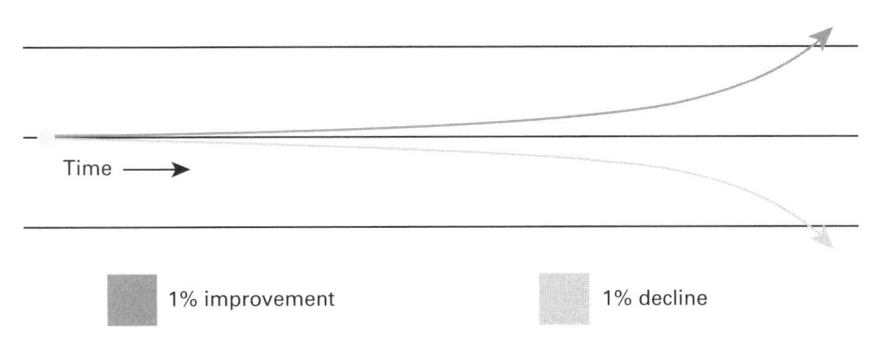

1% improvement   1% decline

This is perhaps counterintuitive. The conclusions could at face value suggest that the considerable investments organizations are making in CRM, digital marketing and sales training are having no impact at all and are therefore a waste of money. How can we, therefore, explain the diminishing returns on pipeline conversion? Perhaps buyers having more control of the buying cycle are making it more difficult for sellers to convert leads to orders.

However, the research also showed that there was a significant upside in performance for those organizations that made marginal gains in developing improved CRM systems and in initiatives in developing selling skills (Figure 3.4).

Just a 1 per cent improvement could result in significant improvements (shown in Figure 3.5) in sales productivity in a range of critical areas.

FIGURE 3.5 Marginal gain – productivity improvements

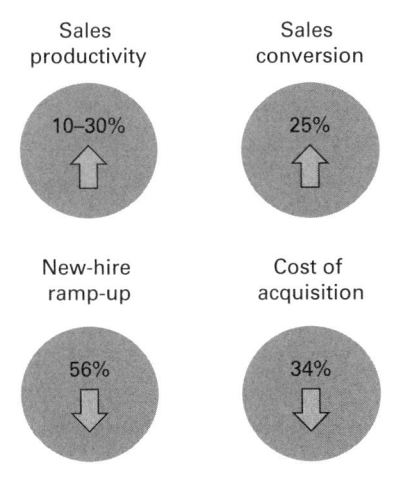

Sales productivity: 10–30% ⇧

Sales conversion: 25% ⇧

New-hire ramp-up: 56% ⇩

Cost of acquisition: 34% ⇩

What the research showed was that those organizations that implemented CRM efficiently saw a significant improvement in sales productivity and sales conversion ratios. In addition, training and development of the salesforce coupled with CRM enhanced the speed at which new hires generated revenue sales and the cost of winning new clients reduced.

Overall, though, the research demonstrates that many organizations fail to implement CRM effectively or fail to train their salesforce effectively, hence diminishing returns of effectiveness. In spite of technology solutions now being able to help salesforces improve their effectiveness, many sales operations fail in their execution of systems to realize these benefits. What is clear is that sales departments have to work harder to make the incremental changes required to make sales operations operationally more effective.

Sellers will need to consider other angles to seek competitive advantage.

Sources of competitive advantage when selling in the post-knowledge era

So what might become the source of competitive advantage for buyers and sellers in the future? Birkinshaw labels the next era as the post-knowledge era, which is dominated by two characteristics – one he terms *adhocracy*, the other *emocracy*.

He argues that in order for organizations to compete they need to lose the bureaucratic structures of the past that hinder the ability to be agile. The future competitive advantage will be in an organization's ability to respond quickly to market pressures, new competition, new innovations and the digital economy. Agility becomes the new norm in the adhocracy era. We can see this in the emergence of new internet-based retail businesses challenging the status quo of bricks and mortar retailers.

Organizations such as boohoo, founded in 2006, and Asos (1998), for example, have in a short space of time taken market share from Marks & Spencer (1889) and Top Shop (1964). Thomas Cook travel agency, founded in 1841, had lost market share (before its collapse in September 2019) to online travel organizations such as Iglu (1998).

The technology-enabled transformation fuelled by the internet is affecting all types of organizations, including traditional manufacturing companies such as SKF, a global manufacturer of ball bearings, which is now learning to sell web-based maintenance programs that can predict when bearings need to be serviced, enabling their customers to plan downtime. Software companies such as SAP, Adobe and Microsoft are moving from on-premises licences to utility-based cloud models, allowing their customers the ability to pay by use, simplify updates and provide better storage security.

Babylon, the London-based unicorn healthcare technology business, provides a glimpse of the future. It's amazing to learn how its artificial intelligence system was able to pass the final exam taken by medical doctors.[9] With its artificial intelligence solutions it is challenging even the established professional domain of doctors and GP surgeries.

As new entrants with new business models threaten traditional markets, the business imperative for us all is to reinvent, and reinvent quickly, a defensive strategy or to establish new markets as an opportunistic strategy. This is not just an organizational imperative but a personal imperative as well.

What if we don't adapt – Nokia

Just months before the launch of the iPhone in 2007 I was conducting a research programme with telephone operators and mobile phone distributors. This comment from a senior marketing manager of a major telephone operator in Germany has stuck with me for many years.

> We [telephone operators] have 13–15 per cent market share; they [Nokia] have 40 or 45 per cent market share. It doesn't mean they have three times as much wisdom or knowledge than we have. They let you feel that they don't worry much about you since they think it is the right way to do it.

Such was the market dominance of Nokia at the time that it dictated the terms by which it did business with its partners. It was seen by many at the time as being quite arrogant.[10]

So when the smartphone market opened up, the operators globally switched from Nokia to other suppliers. From a global market share of 50 per cent in Q4 2007, it dropped to less than 5 per cent by Q2 of 2013.[11]

Few case studies so dramatically illustrate the impact of new technologies, the requirement for strategic agility and the developing of what I refer to as relational capital (and explore more in the final chapter) as the demise of Nokia to Apple iPhone and Samsung. Where companies have mistreated customers, it does not take long, when given an alternative source, for those customers to walk or run.

So what's the new norm?

Cross-functional teams are now working together in temporal structures in order to expedite change more quickly. Cross-functional teams are coming together to make strategic decisions on how their organizations need to adapt to the marketplace. The bureaucratic processes of the past have to be replaced with much faster decision-making processes. We only have to see how governments are simplifying loan processes, approvals for testing new vaccines, etc, commitment to major projects (without the bureaucracy of purchase order (PO) processes), to witness the speed at which decisions are being made.

This trend is supported by the CEB (now Challenger Inc), whose research showed that the average number of decision-makers making buying decisions on a single business-to-business (B2B) procurement rose from 5.4[12] in 2015 to 6.8 in 2017.[13] So it is more difficult for the seller to target the final decision-maker and influence the different stakeholders, many of whom will not be known to the seller. The idea of the economic buyer, the final decision-maker, is a concept of the past. Now it's a much more consensus-driven decision-making process.

So what does this mean for buyers and sellers in a world that changes so fast?

Procurement processes change

Not that long ago the average length of time to procure a $20,000,000 managed services solution was a year, perhaps longer. Organizations cannot now afford to wait a year. Procurement cycles have drastically reduced, with similar-sized deals now being done in a three-month window. From both the seller's and the buyer's perspective, there is significant risk attached to a shortened sales cycle as well as significant opportunities. Where time is putting pressure on both the buyer and the seller to produce results more quickly, trust between a buyer and seller becomes critical. Buying and selling organizations will have to work more collaboratively, particularly in strategic purchasing decisions, if a more creative outcome is required in a time-scarce environment.

This point was endorsed by one of the UK's leading procurement experts, who provided some insights into how procurement are themselves transforming to deliver more value-adding services. Instead of just focusing on total cost of ownership, procurement teams are also looking at total value of ownership. He referred to a consulting project he was working on with a large Spanish fashion 'etailer'. See the case study below.

> The fashion 'etail' market is enormously competitive; with low margins and high volume, the efficiency of the supply chain is critical.
>
> A group of procurement managers working for the etailer were meeting to discuss ways that they could make further efficiencies.
>
> The time it takes from design to manufacture was at the time 20 days for a new product launch. Furthermore, an analysis of the supply chain showed that the injection moulding machines required for each new product design were expensive and added a lot of cost to production.
>
> The buyers argued that they were doing all they could to source competitive quotes from tenders so that they were getting the best prices and helping generate a better return on investment (ROI) for the company.
>
> The CEO dropped in on the meeting, and said, 'What I care about most is getting our products to market quicker, as this potentially adds much more value.' He then set a challenge: 'I would like you to find a way to reduce the 20 days to 4 days' – at which point he left the meeting.
>
> After a little head scratching, the question was asked: why do we always source quotes from multiple providers? This is the bottleneck; it takes time and manpower to go through this process each time. Why don't we source from one provider – the best we have in terms of quality – and guarantee them a level of commitment and maybe a five- to seven-year contract, but in return demand that they produce and tool the injection machines to meet our four-day target?
>
> Did they try to negotiate a lower demand-driven price? No, they did not. Once they changed their mindset and moved away from a traditional procurement, price-led approach, they unlocked the potential to drive a huge amount of value internally by working with one supplier in a smarter way.
>
> This case demonstrates that for those businesses in a fast-moving market (most are) and where agility is their competitive advantage, they will have to work with fewer suppliers, ones they can trust, and work together closely to drive a much higher value of ownership.

This is a great story and shows that procurement can, though not always, work with salespeople strategically. However, let's consider whether the same deal could have been conceived in a different way.

- What if the idea for a single source of injection moulding machines *came first* from the supplier?
- Would the CEO have taken a call from a salesperson if they approached him with the idea that they could reduce the time to market from 20 days to 4 days by working more closely together?

The head of procurement said yes, most probably.

Rather than the post-knowledge era being a buyer-controlled era, we are now entering what we consider is a co-creation era, where buyer and seller work extremely closely to develop new solutions to challenging problems. This is particularly crucial in the time-scarce world in which we now live.

Trust therefore becomes the competitive advantage for sellers. Organizations are naturally going to partner with suppliers that they feel *really* understand their business. This is not about one party, ie the buyer or seller, controlling another; it's about working together to create mutual benefit in a climate of trust. Trust is foundational, but relying on trusted relationships alone is simply not enough, as we will explore later in this book.

This view supports Birkinshaw's term *emocracy*, the second characteristic of the post-knowledge era. He posits that humans are essentially social beings. As robotics, artificial intelligence and the digital economy become drivers of efficiency in the future, we as humans will be driven more by our social values. It's the *experience* of working with organizations, their values and their purpose, that will drive buying decisions. Birkinshaw suggests that it's an organization's ability to appeal to the emotional context of the buyer that will result in greater success and be the source of competitive advantage in this post-knowledge era. This idea is also supported by Simon Sinek, with his golden circles theory.[14] Most organizations, he suggests, focus on the 'what' and the 'how'. He argues that what inspires people to buy is the 'why'. It's the authenticity and relevance of purpose that are so attractive to customers.

However, in a business-to-business selling environment, our ability to develop the kinds of relationships that customers seek is limited by our capacity in time and also, apparently, the size of our brain.

Professor Robin Dunbar, Head of Oxford University's Institute of Social and Cultural Anthropology,[15] has found through his studies of apes and primates that size of brain matters when it comes to how many relationships one can have. The number of relationships for humankind approximates to 150, a figure now known as Dunbar's number (Figure 3.6). These are the relationships on which we build trust and develop reciprocity. The 150 is not homogeneous, meaning that there are different levels of relationship we develop. The 150 includes family, friends, business colleagues and customers, etc. The inner circle comprises five or so people. This is the inner core where the relationships are closest. The surrounding circles contain 15, 50 and then 150 people. The further from the inner circle, the more distant the relationship. Each scale in relationship to each other is a factor of three.

FIGURE 3.6 Dunbar's number

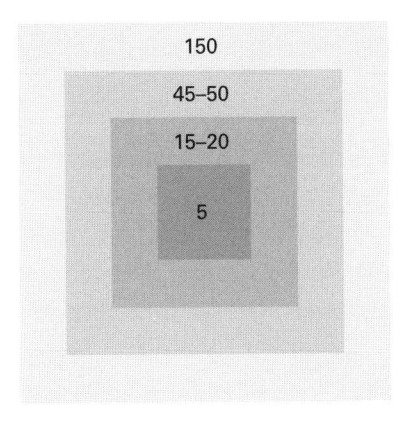

150
45–50
15–20
5

Dunbar argues that even with the advent of Facebook and Twitter, etc, we still revert to this model. In spite of the ease with which we can communicate globally, with mobile telephony and internet-enabled technologies, we still revert to the same size relational communities as we did in times gone by. As Dunbar points out, medieval villages often contained around 150 inhabitants, as this was the maximum number that could be contained in a relational community.

So if relationships are *foundational*, as suggested earlier, as we move into the post-knowledge era, the people with whom we work need to be carefully chosen. This has implications as to the number of accounts that salespeople can cover and the number of key accounts that key accounts managers can manage.

The way sales organizations are currently structured could in part explain why the quality of relationships is poor. Sales teams may not have the capacity, time wise, to develop the kinds of relationships customers seek. This provides opportunities for salespeople who come across accounts that have been poorly served relationally by incumbent suppliers.

Concluding comments

Sales has been around a long time – it predates marketing and many other professions. While the term globalization was coined in the 1970s, traders have been selling globally for thousands of years.

Humankind has a lot to thank sales for. Sales has unquestionably fuelled economic growth, which has then led to global cultural centres around the world, academic learning environments and many other benefits.

Through the work of Birkinshaw we have examined how the context for selling has changed more recently, in particular the more recent 100 years, and explored the idea of competitive advantage. We have seen the shift from the seller-controlled industrial era to the buyer-controlled knowledge era, and now a co-creation era, where sellers and buyers are required to work in a more collaborative manner. Now we must adapt our sales approach accordingly to one based on agility and *emocracy*.

Customers are often cited as the most important asset of any business and, therefore, a supplier's sales strategy is a source of competitive advantage (Cheverton, 2006;[16] Hanan, 1999;[17] Storbacker, 2006;[18] Wilson *et al*, 2002[19]).

Given all this history and experience, one would have thought that the art and science of selling would mean that today we as salespeople are much better at selling than we were in the past. As we have seen, companies spend billions on customer relationship management systems designed to make selling more efficient and on sales training to make salespeople more effective.

The findings, though – from my doctoral[20] research process (2004–2009) and research that continues to this day – are that an alarmingly small percentage of salespeople sell effectively. Why? Why, after thousands of years of practice in the art of buying and selling, and more recently with the benefits technology can potentially bring, are the experiences of buyers still so negative towards sales?

Endnotes

1. https://www.youtube.com/watch?v=GVP0tb6FzCs (archived at https://perma.cc/UU8R-36JR)
2. Birkinshaw, J (2014) *The Changing Sources of Competitive Advantage*, London Business School Global Leadership Summit, 29 August
3. Harrington, B (1879) *How 'Tis Done: A thorough ventilation of the numerous schemes conducted by wandering sales canvassers together with the various advertising dodges for the swindling of the public*, Fidelity Publishing Company, Chicago
4. https://en.wikipedia.org/wiki/The_Gideons_International (archived at https://perma.cc/7RBD-K4XM)
5. Drucker, PF (1969) *The Age of Discontinuity: Guidelines to our changing society*, Harper & Row, New York
6. Adamson, B and Dixon, M (2011) *Challenger Sale*, Penguin, London
7. https://www.journalofsalestransformation.com/fixing-the-revenue-process-bit-by-bit/ January 2016 (archived at https://perma.cc/DUQ7-VBDN)

8 https://www.journalofsalestransformation.com/fixing-the-revenue-process-bit-by-bit/ (archived at January 2016 https://perma.cc/4SZN-86AW)
9 https://vimeo.com/296338633 (archived at https://perma.cc/WNN4-Z3BC)
10 https://medium.com/multiplier-magazine/why-did-nokia-fail-81110d981787 (archived at https://perma.cc/W39P-S8FG)
11 https://www.statista.com/statistics/263438/market-share-held-by-nokia-smartphones-since-2007/ (archived at https://perma.cc/4N2D-DJDS)
12 https://hbr.org/2015/03/making-the-consensus-sale (archived at https://perma.cc/29Y2-T7W7)
13 https://hbr.org/2017/03/the-new-sales-imperative (archived at https://perma.cc/4P6A-Y2Y8)
14 https://www.ted.com/talks/simon_sinek_how_great_leaders_inspire_action?language=en (archived at https://perma.cc/QF2E-44NL)
15 Dunbar, R (2015) *How Many Friends Does One Person Need?* Faber & Faber, London
16 Cheverton, P (2006) *Global Account Management*, Cambridge University Press, Cambridge
17 Hanan, M (1999) *Consultative Selling*, Amacom, New York
18 Storbacker, K (2006) *Driving Growth with Customer Asset Management*, WS Bookwell Oy, Helsinki
19 Wilson, K, Speare, N and Reese, SJ (2002) *Successful Global Account Management: Key strategies and tools for managing global customers*, Kogan Page, London
20 Squire, P (2009) *How Can a 'Client-Centric Values' Approach to Selling Lead to the 'Co-Creation' of a New Global Selling Mindset?*, DProf Project Report, Middlesex University

04

A new paradigm of selling based on values

The research journey

This chapter explains the research process that led to the development of a new framework based on the values that customers look for in salespeople. It explores the 'lens' through which academics and popular writers have approached their published theories of sales effectiveness. This chapter introduces the concept of 'professional' bias and questions whether the theories of selling in the past are fit for purpose in the current context of the world in which we operate.

The spark that ignited the research – '95 per cent of salespeople are a complete waste of time'

One of our technology clients was keen to get some feedback on how effectively their customers felt they were being sold to. This was the first time they had asked the question.

The then chief information officer (CIO) of IMS Health was the first to be interviewed. The interview was structured around three topics – I wanted to first understand the challenges a CIO faces when operating within a global company; given these challenges, what qualities they look for in a salesperson; and finally, what expectations they have of salespeople. The final question was: 'What percentage of salespeople meet your expectations?' To which he answered, '90 per cent of salespeople are, in my view, a complete waste of time. In fact, I would say 95 per cent are a complete waste of time.'

The second interview was with Chris Burke, then chief technology officer of one of the world's largest mobile phone operators. After his interview he said that, in his view, only 10 per cent of salespeople 'get it'. Two out of these three initial interviewees were very critical of the performance of salespeople.

The third interview was with the main board director of a major bank. He did use a percentage but expressed a view that salespeople need to be much more focused on selling a solution to a particular problem and felt that most salespeople were more interested in their products than in the problems of the bank.

By the end of 2003, a further 10 customers had been interviewed. Of the ten, eight said either that they had a very low opinion of salespeople, or that less than 10 per cent of sales people met their expectations.

Whilst this sample was still small, those I had interviewed were senior-level executives from a range of different industries, including banking, telecoms, retail and pharmaceutical. Like the first three, these executives had significant experience in dealing with salespeople. Most salespeople under-perform according to customer expectations. Now we had more data to work with and felt we could bring together a focus group to review the data and suggest reasons for poor performance.

There were three clear takeaways:

- These senior executives were collectively responsible for hundreds of millions of dollars of spend.
- Most of the big consulting groups, large IT companies and niche consulting agencies that sold to these senior-level executives were not selling in ways that these executives expected – in spite of training they would have received.
- There was a real opportunity for those in the 10 per cent who 'do get it' to differentiate themselves in the way in which they sell.

A number of our clients were keen to take part in a broader research project: a global telecoms business headquartered in Germany, a manufacturer headquartered in Sweden, and a professional services business based in the UK. Their involvement enabled the research to be scaled significantly.

The research demographics

By the time the doctorate research was completed, a total of 79 customers had been interviewed, face-to-face, about their perceptions of salespeople.

The demographics of the interviews are shown in Figures 4.1 and 4.2.

FIGURE 4.1 Research demographic, by sector

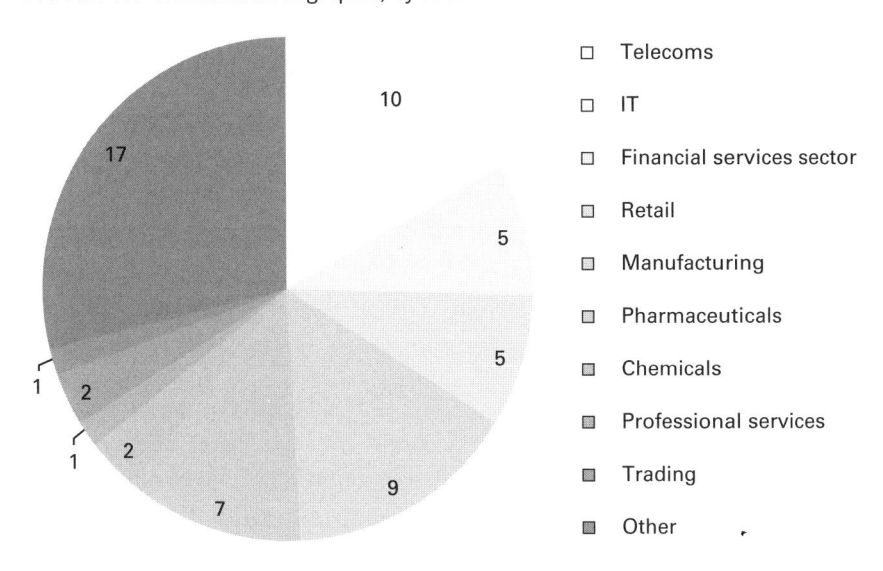

- Telecoms: 10
- IT: 17
- Financial services sector: 5
- Retail: 5
- Manufacturing: 9
- Pharmaceuticals: 7
- Chemicals: 2
- Professional services: 1
- Trading: 2
- Other: 1

FIGURE 4.2 Research demographic, by role

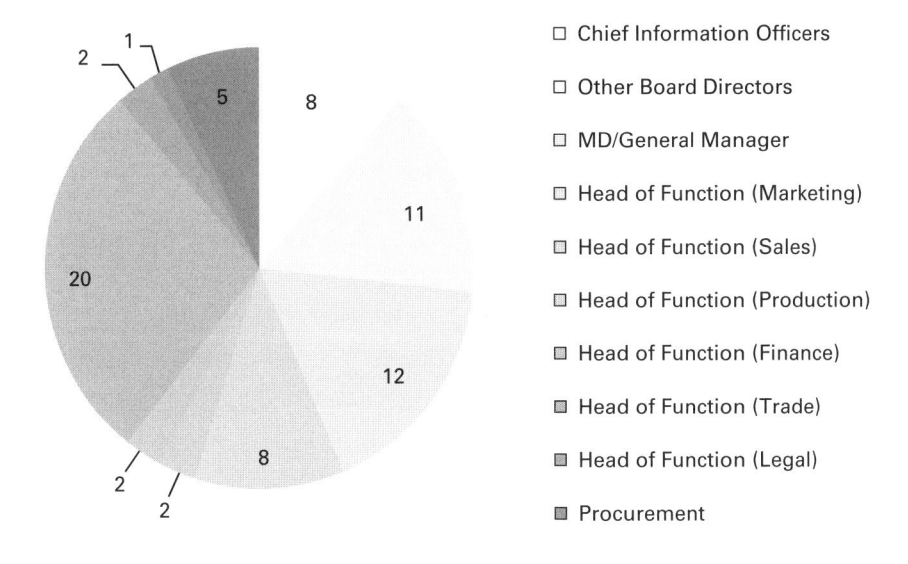

- Chief Information Officers: 1
- Other Board Directors: 2
- MD/General Manager: 8
- Head of Function (Marketing): 11
- Head of Function (Sales): 12
- Head of Function (Production): 8
- Head of Function (Finance): 2
- Head of Function (Trade): 2
- Head of Function (Legal): 20
- Procurement: 5

The interviews were conducted with seasoned executives who represented different functions and industries and who were in different locations around the world. Twenty-one per cent of the interviews were UK-based; the rest were based outside of the UK. Face-to-face interviews were conducted from Seattle, USA, to Kuala Lumpur in Thailand.

There was no discernible cultural bias from country to country – customers continued to express low opinions of salespeople, frustrated that most salespeople did not listen enough, did not present solutions aligned to their requirements, were manipulative, and lacked trust.

So how did we start to make sense of the data to define the attributes required to make it into the category of top-performing salespeople?

First attempts at solving the problem – how to make it into the winner's circle

With the support of Professor George Yip, a global expert on global account management, we brought together account sales executives and procurement experts into a forum to review the research data and use their collective experience to articulate the key attributes required to be in what we refer to as the 10 per cent winner's circle – the winner's circle being those salespeople whom customers deemed exceptional.

During the forum a list of competencies was developed. These were grouped into those that were 'company-facing' and those that were 'customer-facing', as shown in Figure 4.3. Though not specifically mentioned in the customer interviews, we added 'resiliency', 'constraints' and 'processes', as these were issues raised by the participants as having an effect on the ability of account managers/salespeople to sell effectively.

FIGURE 4.3 Competencies, attributes and processes

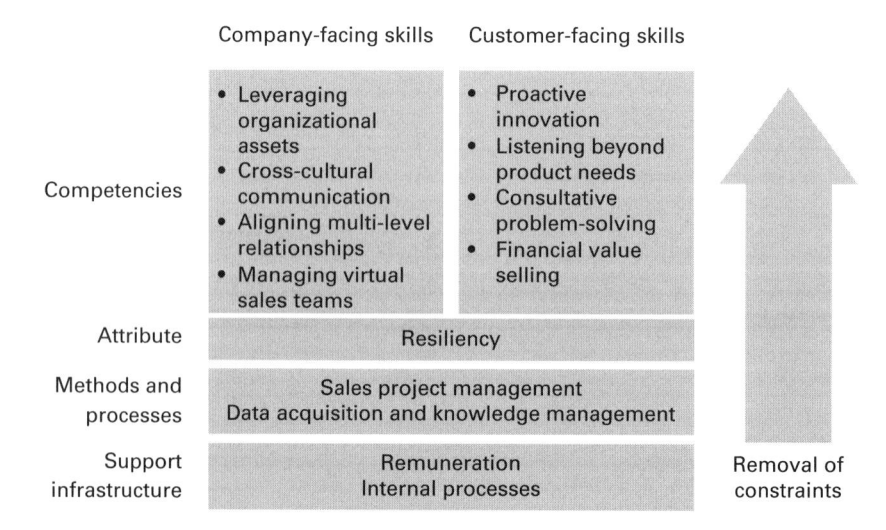

	Company-facing skills	Customer-facing skills	
Competencies	• Leveraging organizational assets • Cross-cultural communication • Aligning multi-level relationships • Managing virtual sales teams	• Proactive innovation • Listening beyond product needs • Consultative problem-solving • Financial value selling	
Attribute	Resiliency		
Methods and processes	Sales project management Data acquisition and knowledge management		
Support infrastructure	Remuneration Internal processes		Removal of constraints

Resiliency, the account managers argued, was important, because the biggest challenge they faced was trying to energize their company and its resources to bring value to their customers. They considered they 'spent more time trying to sell internally than selling to their customers'.

Sales methods and processes also affect sales productivity. Here, we refer to project management processes, proposal writing templates, risk analysis processes, and sales support tools, plus those one would expect in a CRM application. In addition, the types of remuneration and targeting processes ('support infrastructures') have a significant influence on how salespeople spend their time. The role of managers was to remove the constraints to allow salespeople to sell effectively.

The main reasons, we concluded, as to why so many salespeople were 'getting it wrong' were because they did not have the requisite *competencies* or because the *processes* that supported them were at fault. However, though we did not realize it then, our conclusions were mistaken.

Yet the platform still burnt

We continue to conduct voice-of-the-customer interviews to track customer perceptions of sales practice, using the same structured interview process as we did when we started in 2002. We still receive similar feedback. Eighty per cent of the interviewees say that less than 10 per cent meet their expectations.

Why, when organizations invest so much in sales training, are customer perceptions of salespeople so low? Why do salespeople, after the training, still not seem to get the basics right? After all, it's not exactly rocket science to listen carefully, to ask questions, to tailor presentations, etc – behaviours that customers look for but don't witness in the majority of cases.

Why, after the significant investments companies have made in complex customer relationship management systems with a view to improving their sales process, are customers' perceptions of salespeople still so low?

We began to challenge our thinking – the competency approach designed to effect the 'right behaviours' seemed not to be working.

The $22 billion-plus problem

The troubling thought for sales organizations is this: how effective is sales training? As the ripples of a stone dropped into an ocean lose their impact quickly, so too, our research would suggest, do current approaches to sales training. Current practice in terms of content and delivery approach is not sustainable – at what cost and why?

A 2017 article in *Harvard Business Review*[1] showed that US organizations spend annually $1,475 per salesperson on sales training – more than on any other function of a business. In the USA alone this is a $22 billion problem.

As the UK and most other countries globally lack data on spend on sales training per salesperson, we have assumed a similar process to calculate spend per salesperson. We estimate that the UK market for sales training is therefore $3.3 billion, based on 2,254,714 'salespeople' working in the B2B market.

What enabled a breakthrough

We began, with colleagues and customers, to challenge the deeply held assumption that sales performance was primarily linked to sales competence and sales methodology, but we were not sure what alternative perspective would help. We seriously challenged our own bias in how we were assessing our research data. To what extent was our thinking influenced by assumptions being made on what good looked like? To what extent was this restricting our ability to find new insights into the way we think about sales?

Covey refers to this as 'autobiographical listening'.[2] This is where we listen with the intent to respond rather than the intent to listen. We ask questions with the intent to prove our hypothesis is right. Covey's concept of autobiographical listening is hugely important whilst considering the ethical dimension in research being undertaken.

The customers, buyers and researchers involved in reviewing data with us were forming conclusions based on their own deeply held beliefs of what good looks like. We realized we had not properly considered what was influencing our bias; we questioned whether the conclusions we were reaching were more subjective than objective. Furthermore, we realized this bias was happening unconsciously.

This was to trigger a paradigm shift in our research approach and eventually enable a breakthrough. We started to explore in more detail the bias that currently exists in assessing the levers that drive sales performance in two key domains:

- One was to explore what the current academic trends were in terms of exploring sales effectiveness through the evaluation of academic and peer-reviewed papers.

- The other was to assess more 'popular' books and approaches taught by the leading sales training consultancies, including our own.

Sales academic research

I have already commented on academic interest in sales and lamented the fact that compared, say, with marketing, there are fewer peer-reviewed journals to review. Nevertheless, it's interesting to discover what academics are interested in in terms of sales research on selling effectiveness and where their sources of data come from.

What follows is an overview of some of the premises sales academics use when conducting research.

Two models for understanding salespeople's performance have been used quite extensively since the late 1970s. These are defined as adaptive selling and customer-orientated selling. The adaptive model emerged from research conducted by Weitz in 1978.[3] He emphasizes what he refers to as 'adaptive nature' by suggesting that salespeople collect information on customers, develop a sales strategy to sell to the customer, communicate messages based on the strategy, evaluate a customer's reaction, and then react accordingly. Salespeople adapt their approach based on what they discover in the sales process.

Adaptive selling (ADAPTS) suggests that salespeople become more effective if:

1 They recognize that different sales approaches are needed for different sales customers.
2 They have the confidence in their ability to use a different approach during an interaction.
3 They collect information to facilitate adaptation.

Spiro and Weitz (1990)[4] recognized some years later that, given the difficulty in researching unique adaptive capability of personal selling, little empirical research has been conducted on this aspect of sales behaviour. They explored the degree to which salespeople are seen to be practising the ADAPTS approach and assessed whether performance can be linked to this approach. They concluded that the ADAPTS scale 'can be useful for managerial activities and general research, however, additional research is required to investigate further the validity of the scale' (p67).

The concept of customer-orientated selling was developed by Saxe and Weitz (1982).[5]

They defined customer-orientated selling as:

1 The desire to help customers make satisfactory purchase decisions.
2 Helping customers assess their needs.
3 Offering products that will satisfy those needs.
4 Describing the products accurately.
5 Avoiding deceptive or manipulative behaviour.
6 Avoiding the use of high pressure.

Sales orientation-customer orientation (SOCO) is used as a measurement system for customer orientation and contrasts this with the more pushy sales orientation. Salespeople who are customer-orientated develop actions and strategies designed to develop long-term customer relationships. They would not take decisions which, whilst beneficial in the short term, would adversely affect the customer in the long term. Salespeople who are highly customer-orientated have high concern for others and themselves, whilst salespeople with low customer orientation have low concern for others and high concern for themselves.

It is interesting to note that the construct for the models referred to above has been developed through interviews with salespeople, not with customers. If the object of a salesperson's approach is to sell to a customer, does it not make sense to research what customers perceive to be good and poor practice?

Academics challenging academics

Schwepker (2003)[6] has been helpful in observing how the SOCO model has been used for research by different academics. He developed a number of hypotheses for future consideration of SOCO research approaches, these hypotheses being based on his review of 37 different studies of SOCO research papers.

1 The more ethical the firm's climate, the greater the customer orientation of the salesperson.
2 The more ethical the firm's ethical climate, the less the negative impact of outcome-based control on customer-orientated selling.
3 The higher salespeople's moral values, the greater their customer orientation.
4 When the organization and individual salespeople both value customer needs, customer-orientated selling will be associated negatively with role conflict.
5 There is a positive orientation between customer orientation and customer trust.

Of particular note was Schwepker's observation (2003: 21)[7] of the importance of values in the sales process, particularly as they relate to the values of customers and the organizations they are selling to.

His research did not define the values required of salespeople, and it is not entirely clear whether he is referring to the values of customers or the values of the organization that the salesperson is working for. It is, though, interesting that he has raised the issue of values and suggests that this is taken into consideration for further research.

Further investigation into values led to Swenson and Herche (1994),[8] who conducted empirical research into the extent to which social values affect a salesperson's performance. They were keen to explore the effect certain values have on performance. Their values constructs were based on Feather's (1975),[9] Maslow's (1954)[10] and Rokeach's (1973)[11] work on values.

The list of values (LOV) they investigated is:

- sense of accomplishment;
- self-respect;
- self-fulfilment;
- being well respected;
- fun and enjoyment;
- excitement;
- warm relationship with others;
- sense of belonging;
- security.

Their research was based on studying 271 salespeople. Their conclusions were that whilst the 'accomplishment' dimension reported higher levels of performance than did salespeople who expressed other values, there was a requirement to conduct further research into the role values play in the sales process. They linked their research to the ADAPT and SOCO models and suggested this extended the thinking of customer-orientated selling.

We concluded the following about the principal research methods and studies used by many academic sales researchers to date:

- Methods are based on research conducted with salespeople, not with customers. The salesperson's perspective, ie bias, limits our understanding of what is required for sales effectiveness as it is measured through a restricted lens. Does it not make sense to research how buyers want salespeople to sell to them and then test if that approach works?

- Little academic research has been conducted on the topic of values as it relates to the sales process.[12] We began to realize this topic was where the breakthrough could be achieved.
- Those who have researched values have based their research on values important to salespeople and not to customers. As above, this is a restricted lens.
- They suggested that values could play a key role in successful sales conversations.

It's been interesting to bring the 'academic' perspective of sales into the sales communities with which we work. It is fair to say that as many academics have a mistrust of salespeople as do salespeople of academics. The term 'too academic' has been used by salespeople of academics referring often to the fact that 'in order to understand selling you need to have a quota' (sales target) or have had a quota. How many academics have worked in sales? Perhaps, though, there is a misguided bias on both sides. For sure, academics can learn from sales and vice versa. More on this topic is covered in the concluding chapter.

Peer-reviewed journals are mainly shared between academics – a shame, as certainly we can benefit from their research conclusions. Most salespeople do not have access to the academic journals as this requires access to academic libraries. Plus, many journals are not written in an easily digestible way for salespeople.

Salespeople do have access to books and now podcasts.

Popular books on selling

It's interesting to do a short review of some of the best-selling books on sales over the last 50 years in order to better understand what underpins their suggested approach and to assess if they collectively demonstrate any particular bias. (I do apologize to readers if I have missed referring to their favourite books!)

SPIN Selling

SPIN Selling[13] was written by Neil Rackham[14] in 1988 to help anticipate and navigate tough sales situations. The method was the result of research culled from over 35,000 sales calls. This model takes the approach that customers will be motivated to buy something only if they identify there's a need. And because there are times when prospects are not even aware there's a problem, the opening qualifications questions asked by salespeople are key.

- Situation questions.
- Problem questions.
- Implication questions.
- Need-payoff questions.

Situation questions: These form the starting point for your conversation. By asking situation-type questions, you can develop an understanding of context. This is about understanding the wider context before zooming into the details. The key to succeeding with situation questions is to do research in advance of the conversation.

Problem questions: If you can get a customer to acknowledge there's a problem that needs to be fixed, they're far more likely to listen to your solution. So ask questions that will uncover problems that your product can address. Problem questions achieve just that, by probing to discover what's causing your prospect pain. If you are selling tractors, ask about maintenance costs, breakdowns and so on. If you are selling life insurance, ask about how many dependants the person has. A trap here is to dive straight into presenting the benefits of what you are selling. You may know the problem, but they do not! Going straight to the sales pitch will just get you objections.

Implication questions: The purpose of these questions is to make the customer eager for a solution to the problem they've just identified. The goal is to get them to see and feel the problem. By asking questions that draw out the implications of the problem, they get to feel the pain that will drive them towards your product. For example, the person selling tractors might ask about implications of un ploughed fields. The life insurance salesperson could carefully ask what would happen to the children if the prospect died or became very ill.

Need-payoff questions: These *encourage a prospect to consider how valuable a solution to the problem* they've identified would be. The secret to getting results with need-payoff questions is to ensure the buyer specifies the benefits themselves. Encourage them to visualize and imagine what would be different with that problem gone. That way, your customer will be able to place a value on what you have to offer. Need-payoff questions need to evoke positive emotions. It feels good to know that a pressing problem can finally be solved.

Whilst elements of SPIN are still relevant, the context of the world in which we live has moved on. Its methodology is now 40 years old and was developed before the internet-fuelled knowledge era took off. There is really no excuse for turning up to meetings without the latest news on each customer – to ask 'situation' questions could be a death knell to any new or existing customer relationship. Customers expect salespeople to have done their research.

Solution Selling

Solution Selling,[15] like SPIN, discusses the importance of salespeople discovering the 'pain' – in other terms, the critical needs – customers have. Most buyers, Bosworth says, are not in the market for a supplier's products. The challenge for salespeople is, therefore, to create a need.

He describes three levels of what he calls the buying process – latent pain, pain, and then vision. The goal of salespeople is to transform what might be a latent pain into pain that the customer recognizes they have, then provide a vision as to what the salesperson can do to solve the pain. He develops a method to explore each of the stages of the buying process. His approach is based on 'situational fluency'. He proposes that salespeople need to adapt their behaviour to suit the customer's situation. Much guidance is provided on how to handle objections and recognizing different types of objections. Bosworth suggests techniques to lead the buyer whilst staying strategically aligned.

Outsell Your Competition

Robin Fielder (2002: 1)[16] recognizes that 'traditionally, sales training focuses on the steps the seller takes in making the sale, but people buy using *their* buying pattern not our sales pattern'.

He defines the different stages of the buying process as:

- recognize the gap;
- ask internally;
- criteria for ordering;
- evaluate competing options;
- resolve final concerns;
- negotiate;
- implement.

He summarizes five key insights into selling solutions as:

- Be a specialist.
- Reduce risk.
- Believe in your solution.
- Use questions, not reasons, as your main persuasive tools.
- Understand the power of positioning.

While Fielder discusses the importance of trust and transparency within the context of his book, this occupies a few pages. His recommendations for selling are to follow a set process. He quotes only 10 per cent of salespeople being top performers, though does not explain where his statistic comes from.

TABLE 4.1 Traditional and customer-centric selling

Traditional	Customer-centric
Make presentations	Converse situationally
Offer opinions	Ask relevant questions
Focus on relationship	Focus on solutions
Gravitate towards users	Target businesspeople
Rely on product	Relate product usage
Need to be managed	Manage their managers
Attempt to sell by: • convincing/persuading; • handling objections; • overcoming resistance.	Empower buyers to: • achieve goals; • solve problems; • satisfy needs.

Customer-Centric Selling

In 2004, Bosworth and Holland outlined their customer-centric methodology in their book *Customer Centric Selling*.[17] They contrast 'traditional' selling with 'customer-centric' selling, as shown in Table 4.1.

As with Fielder, these authors suggest that 'perhaps 10 per cent of sales professionals' sell in a client-centric way. Again, it is unclear how they have arrived at this figure, as they do not present evidence of research. They suggest codifying the art of selling, and suggest that it should define:

- when the buying cycles begin;
- the steps in making a recommendation;
- the steps necessary to have the buyers understand their requirements;
- the steps needed for buyers to understand how your offering addresses their goals and problems;
- an estimated decision date documented to confirm the buyer's agreement.

Whilst they discuss the notion of having intelligent conversations with customers, they question the importance of relationships in decision-making in a similar way to that espoused by the 'challenger', another sales methodology that we review later.

Consultative Selling

Hanan (1999: xix)[18] argues that it 'is the ability to free price from cost and competition by relating price to an investment' that produces success. He says that to be successful means 'selling new profit dollars, not enhanced performance benefits or interactive systems, but the new profits that can add value to the bottom line'. He suggests strategies for consultative selling. He observes that 'vending' has hit the wall and that the future is about selling value (p19). His book focuses on how to articulate the economic value of your product or service.

A section of his book is entitled 'knowing current customer values'. He defines consultative selling as 'a sale is a transfer of values: a customer's resources – time, talent and money are transferred for the contribution to customer profits made by a supplier's products or services'. It is clear that Hanan's notion of the word 'values' is aligned to the monetary sense and not from the perspective of ethics or moral standards. Nonetheless, he highlights a very important aspect of selling – how to nail the financial benefits.

He compares the differences between consultative selling and vendor selling, as shown in Table 4.2.

Bag the Elephant: How to win and keep big customers

Steve Kaplan[19] (2005: 12) provides insights into selling to large companies. He refers to large companies as 'elephants'. Kaplan discusses important and strategic success factors for selling to large accounts.

TABLE 4.2 Consultative selling and vendor selling

Consultative selling	Vendor selling
The seller supplies profit as their product.	The seller supplies product.
The seller offers a return on the customer's investment.	The seller charges a price.
The seller uses a profit improvement proposal.	The seller uses an order form.
The seller quantifies the benefits from their customer's investment.	The seller attempts to justify their cost.
The seller attaches their investment to the customer's return.	The seller attaches their price to their product.
The seller helps their customer compete against their customer's competitors.	The seller competes against their own competitors.
The customer closes.	The seller tries to close.
The seller sells to a business manager.	The seller sells to a purchasing manager.
The seller features their customer's improved performance.	The seller features their product's performance.
The seller's product is improved customer profits.	The seller's product is equipment, a service, a process, or a system.
The seller sells to a dedicated industry and to dedicated customers within it.	The seller sells to a dedicated territory.

The factors include:

- one and done (you only get one chance to win the account);
- priority one (make the customer feel special);
- whatever it takes (be flexible);
- long-term vision (do not aim for short-term results);
- breath of fresh air (have fun);
- partner (think of your customer as a partner).

He describes different types of salesperson as: the Sage (a salesperson who is cautious, highly knowledgeable, trusting); Pals (a salesperson who builds relationships, is friendly); or Pit Bulls (a salesperson who is focused on the bottom line, profit-driven, competitive).

He suggests that salespeople need to be like chameleons, adapting their approach to different types of 'customer'. This supports the ADAPTS model. Kaplan's book refers to his personal sales experience and draws upon his success. His suggestions are not supported by any academic referencing or research.

Buyer Approved Selling

It is rare to find a book based on a customer's perspective on salespeople, so it was pleasing to discover this one.

Schell (2003)[20] conducted interviews with 228 buyers. When asked to define the essence of effective selling, their response was effective communication, building trust and respecting time. His research methodology follows the sales process of prospecting, preparing, meeting, proposing, closing and maintaining.

His evidence (shown in Table 4.3) supported our research that salespeople fail to meet expectations in most instances.

TABLE 4.3 Buyer's response to sales process

Stage of the sales process	Buyer's response
Prospecting	The majority of buyers said that most reps did not seem to have done any research prior to their sales meetings.
Preparing	Almost half the buyers said that reps rarely handle objections proactively and positively. The majority of buyers said that most reps did not ask good questions on sales calls. The vast majority of buyers said that most rep teams were clearly unprepared for meetings.
Meeting	The majority of buyers said that only about one in two reps arrived with a prepared meeting structure, and less than half took the time to be sure that they had answered complex questions clearly. Forty-six per cent of the buyers said that the majority of reps neglect to summarize the key points of a meeting.
Proposal	Forty-five per cent of buyers said only about one in two reps provide quality proposals.

Challenger Sale

Challenger Sale[21] has been the go-to book of the last 10 years. It's very well researched and concludes that 'time-tested' sales techniques no longer work the way they claim to work given the context of the world in which we live has changed so dramatically. Through their data analysis of top-performing salespeople, the authors identified five rep types.

1. **The hard worker:** persistent, does not give up, self-motivated.
2. **The relationship builder:** builds empathy, develops a high degree of trust.
3. **The lone wolf:** assertive, assured, difficult to manage, but often produces good results.
4. **The reactive problem-solver:** a customer service rep in sales rep clothing, responsive and detail-focused.
5. **The challenger:** offers unique perspectives tailored to their customer's situation; excellent communicators; are assertive and look to control the conversations.

Their findings were that the challenger profile was the one that the very top sales performers exhibited and suggested controversially the classic relationship builder is losing ground. Moreover, studies of the sales team types suggested that they were mainly formed of relationship builders.

They provided a framework, though, of how salespeople can sell in a challenger way. This based on:

- Teach.
- Tailor.
- Take control.

Teach the customer something new and valuable about how to compete in their market. This includes not only new perspectives on your products and services but also new perspectives on how they can compete in the marketplace. CEB research[22] shows that this is the exact behaviour that wins customers for the long term.

The salesperson must *tailor* the message being taught – to the different types of customers and to different individuals within an organization. To do this the salesperson must have good knowledge of both the organization and the individuals.

Take control is about the salesperson's ability to assert and maintain control over the sale. Assertive does not mean aggressive. Assertiveness takes two forms:

1. Asserting control over the discussion of pricing, and money more generally. It's about not giving in to a request for a 10 per cent discount but bringing the conversation back to the overall solution – pushing for agreement on value rather than on price.
2. The ability to challenge the customer's thinking and influence the customer's decision-making cycle – to reach a decision more quickly.

Golden Circle Secrets

In our research on books that explored the values for selling, we came across the lesser-known *Golden Circle Secrets*.[23] Ben and Dale Midgley (2005) argue the importance of values because the way in which a company sells reflects everything about a company. They conclude that 'words' to live by are integrity, determination, competence, loyalty, cooperation, leadership, consistency, persistence and love. They advocate not using tricks to get the sale, as customers can see through these. They recognize that customers do not like to be sold to and do not like to be controlled. They suggest that the process for building good relationships can be taught effectively, but argue that people who naturally show care and concern in other areas of their lives will understand the process intuitively. They argue that the only way to hit budgeted sales is to make the customer experience authentic. As some of their interviewees conclude, few customers are fooled, dazzled or even pleased by the approach of the tired sales principles developed long ago. They are particularly concerned about the adoption of neuro-linguistic programming (NLP) in the sales process. They suggest that the idea of mirroring does not focus on being genuinely concerned. They argue that trust should not be manipulated or created as the 'impression' of trust. Trust must be earned over time.

Values Sell

Thompson and Soper (2007)[24] also promote the idea that adding 'values-driven' or 'socially responsible' to business goals adds a new paradigm to the success equation. Its focus is mainly to do with being socially responsible. This is an interesting topic in its own right but provides little insight into research on other values required for selling.

Values Based Selling: The art of building high trust client relationships

Bachrach (1998: xxxiv)[25] recognizes that in the financial services sector, the 'public trust us less than ever'. He says that the 'two most critical elements in creating profitable client relationships are *emotional involvement* and *trust*' (p26). He suggests a framework called values conversation that is based on a 'staircase'. The staircase seems to be based on Maslow's hierarchy of needs – the first stair being security, the last stair being satisfaction (life has purpose). He proposes arguably manipulative questioning techniques to help determine the stair the customer is on and provides other suggestions such as 'three strikes and you are out' (p58) if the customer is uncooperative.

While again the title of the book, *Values Based Selling*, suggests an interesting angle, its focus is on business-to-consumer selling.

Back to the central question: why do so few salespeople sell in a way customers want?

We started to consider the role that logic and reason play in how we decide how we act. If Raz,[26] an academic expert on reason (1999: 19), is correct in that 'activity is related to the proper functioning of the processes which govern our mental lives, our beliefs', the act of doing something or not doing something reflects our values and beliefs.

The critical role of lived values in our research approach was also highlighted by Professor Jean McNiff, one of the world's leading authorities on action research living theory: it's not competence or logic that determines what we do or how we behave; it's our values and belief systems that determine how we act and also how we interpret data.[27]

It may be logical, for example, to adopt a certain selling methodology, but its implementation is down to the values and belief systems of salespeople to enact it.

Take one small example: most salespeople would agree with the importance of writing a summary of a sales call, yet, according to Schell's research,[28] 46 per cent of buyers said salespeople neglect to do so. Whilst writing a summary of a salescall requires skill, the reason it is done or not done reflects their belief in the value of such an activity.

If they aspire to the belief that writing summaries is good practice, they will act on it if their belief is sufficiently strong to promote action.

Raz's (1999)[29] concept of social practices is relevant – he refers to them as 'sustaining practices'. This is the essence of what we refer to as lived values – lived values are sustaining practices – they are absorbed by assimilation, by habits that are formed.

This is interesting in the context of developing salespeople. It's important to adopt sustaining learning practices that improve their selling effectiveness.

Perhaps this explains why current sales training efforts fail to succeed. The sales profession has focused on sales methods and techniques and, in doing so, perhaps overlooked the pedagogical approach, ie the methods of training required for best practices to be absorbed into the cultural values of the organization. This is another theme that we pick up later on in Chapter 13.

Paradigm shift in research approach

The importance of values and their link to sustaining practices was to trigger a paradigm shift in our research approach and enable the breakthrough we were looking for through a new way of thinking.

It prompted a deep enquiry into the construct of values, their importance in the sales process and enabled us to reflect on all the interview transcripts through a very different lens.

Rather than reviewing customer interviews with a competency-based mindset, we now explored the interview transcripts with a values-based mindset.

The logic was pretty simple: customers are critical of many of the behaviours they see in salespeople, and they also describe how they want salespeople to sell to them. Behaviours of salespeople are influenced by competencies as well as values.

Having the 'right' values would influence the right behaviours. For example, a salesperson who truly held a value that was customer-focused would naturally be inclined to listen carefully to what a customer was saying, would not want to manipulate the conversation, and would ask the right questions, conduct the right research, etc.

We also recognized that if we started to define a set of values and belief system that customers wanted, and that salespeople needed to have, we would most likely be having to address in parallel, and in varying degrees depending on each salesperson, a transformation – *a selling transformation* – one where only the change of core values and beliefs would result in sustainable change.

The link between behaviours, competence and values/mindsets in the context of transformation is well explained by Professor Fred Korthagen.[30] We now use his 'onion' model for many of the sales transformation projects we work on as it helps to have discussions on the levers required to affect sales transformation.

Korthagen argues that only a *total* alignment of our core, our identity, our mission, our beliefs, our competencies and our behaviours with the environment will result in transformational change (see Figure 4.4). Understanding this is particularly important for those organizations that require transformational change. Often change programmes focus on the what and the how of change, ie at a process, method and competence level. They fail to have all buy into the purpose of the change and align values and beliefs around this purpose.

We have adapted Korthagen's model slightly for simplification to describe the interconnection between our core purpose, values (and beliefs), competencies and behaviours, and to show the role of systems and processes in supporting that transformation.

FIGURE 4.4 Onion model (adapted)

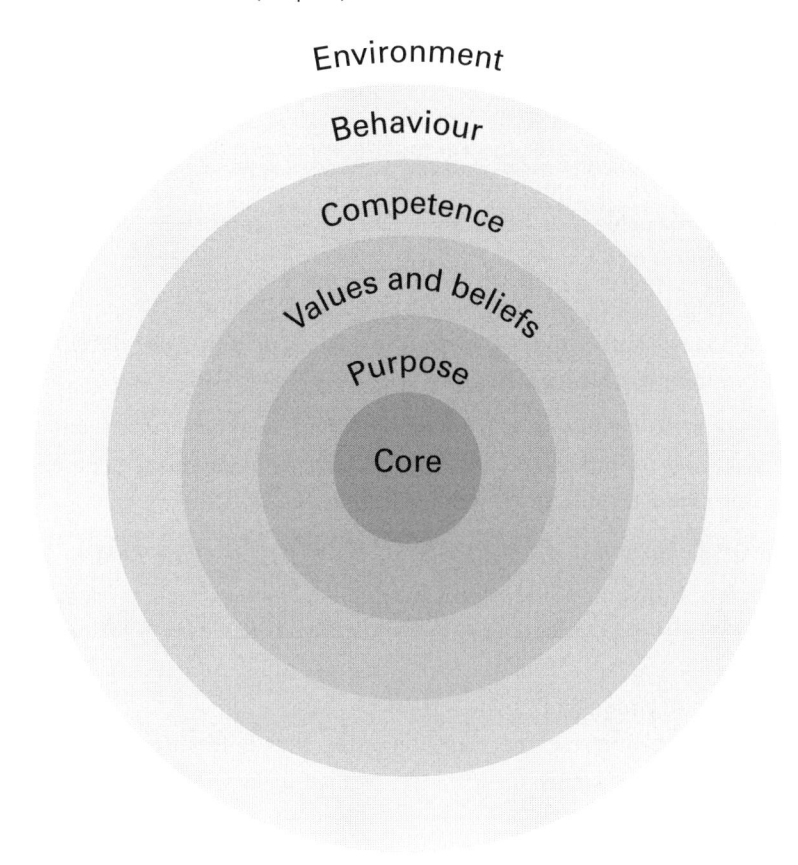

Environment
Behaviour
Competence
Values and beliefs
Purpose
Core

SOURCE Adapted from https://korthagen.nl/en/wp-content/uploads/2018/07/Levels-in-reflection.pdf

- **The core** relates to a person's essence – some may refer to this as one's soul. This remains unchanged over time.
- **Purpose** relates to one's reason for existence and can be applied at a personal and an organizational level.
- **Values and beliefs** are influenced by what we are taught when we are young and through the results of our own experiences. They are acquired through life and can change. They influence how we think, act and react to the world around us. We can feel deeply distressed when our values are compromised. Alternatively, where values are aligned, deep trust is created. Values are a predictor of behaviour – understanding our values helps make sense of how we can behave in certain situations. Beliefs are similar to values and they do not necessarily need to be supported by facts. For example, religious beliefs

are not based on scientific fact yet they can be a very important determinant of how we choose to behave.

- **Competencies** describe what you are able to do in the world. This is the area most addressed by organizations' development strategies – wanting to ensure the workforce has the right competence to conduct their task. Having the right competence to conduct tasks is key, but it's not a predictor of behaviour. Someone who is highly competent may not carry out their job well.
- **Behaviour** relates to the verbal and non-verbal communication that takes place. Many sales training methodologies approach sales development and training at this level.
- **Environment** relates to the market context in which an organization operates. It is influenced by factors such as regulation, competition, supply chain, economic growth or decline.

Most of the sales training delivered by the better-known global brands – whether it's Huthwaite's SPIN, Challenger, Miller Heiman, Sandler, Richardson, Mercuri – focuses on process technique or learned behaviours. Effectively, they are addressing the outer layer of Korthagen's onion. They are well documented, researched and compelling.

At this stage our research was suggesting that unless the underpinning values and belief systems are in place, behaviour-based methodologies are compromised.

As we live our careers in sales, we pick up practices that we hold to be true and these in turn become our beliefs in how sales should be conducted. A belief could be as simple as salespeople should wear a suit for all sales meetings (some organizations insist this is the case), or it could be the notion that paying sales commission is the best way for increasing sales performance. Others may argue that sales commission does not encourage client-centric behaviour and that other forms of reward are more effective. Belief systems are often developed on the back of a particular selling programme attended or taught or something the sales director holds to be true.

Taking a values perspective becomes an interesting framework when two people are meeting for the first time. Both are trying to understand what makes the other one tick – by looking for clues in the spoken and unspoken word. Both will be observing behaviour; both will be looking under the surface at competence as well as values. Both parties will be wanting to predict how the other will act and react as the sales or buying cycle progresses. If all we focus on is behaviour, we miss values.

Clearly, as so many buyers have a low opinion of salespeople, we could only surmise that the underpinning competencies or values were misaligned. Perhaps in the case of salespeople, such is the pressure to close a deal that they may use behavioural sales techniques that, quite frankly, turn the customer off. Remember that the hurdle is set high for the consummate sales professional as customers have been burnt with poor sales experiences in the past.

We started to consider if, during sales conversations, customers, whilst observing behaviour, look for values, as in most cases the account executives had the right competence to do the job. Just one or two interviewees mentioned the word competence. If so, was it possible to discern which values were deemed positive and which were negative?

Furthermore, we hypothesized, if the values were engrained, ie lived, would competencies evolve naturally and be sustained?

Other questions followed:

- Could it be that companies had never seriously considered the role of values in the sales process?
- Could the disconnect between buyer and seller be a values misalignment rather than a behavioural issue?
- To what extent were companies seeking to align their values framework with those of their customers?
- How could it be proved that living the values customers want to see in salespeople would lead to improved sales performance?

Thus, the doctoral research objectives were to codify the values that customers look for in salespeople:

- Could a new values-based framework emerge that would enable sales practitioners to develop closer, deeper and more profitable relationships with their key customers?
- Could the values-based framework improve sales performance?

Creating a new vernacular: values for selling

Many salespeople are asked during and after research – what are your values? Their quick response is often 'honesty, integrity, performance-orientated, results-focused'. The awkwardness and the hesitation of their response belie the fact that they have not really thought in detail about what they are. When questioned further on what evidence they can provide to demonstrate these are lived values, they are often lost for words or struggle to give thoughtful examples.

As the journey began in considering the values that customers sought of salespeople, it became clear it is not an easy process. Values evolve over time – for many in a totally unconscious way. Like many of the salespeople we work with and have interviewed, we recognize that it's difficult to articulate our values, as it's rare to be asked to describe what they are and what evidence there is to support them.

The process of self-reflection and being critically honest in defining values is an important step in determining the 'authentic' persona and additionally would hold in check potential bias and allow, in our case, a more innovative approach to data analysis.

As said before and to stress again, *by understanding your values, you can better predict how you will act in any given situation*: by understanding your values, the customers can also predict how you will act on their behalf.

Customers will choose to work with people whose values are aligned to theirs. This idea of prediction is important – no one likes surprises, customers in particular. As a reminder, customers have experienced so much overselling and underperforming by poor salespeople that the hurdle for the sales professional is set very high. It takes a long time to build trust and a short while to lose it.

Customers continuously assess salespeople's values systems throughout the buying process. They do not necessarily do this consciously; as Gladwell (2005)[31] argues in his book *Blink*, our minds work instinctively as a result of acquired knowledge and experience. We know without thinking.

No one is born with a set of values. Values are developed as a consequence of the social environment in which we are brought up. Values developed over time come into play and unnoticeably influence how we act and behave. At work our values are influenced by the values of our managers and the organizations for which we work.

Values and belief systems can be challenged and changed. For example, pivotal events happen that are life-changing and change our world view and how we choose to live our lives. A spiritual experience, a bereavement, a breakdown, a pandemic, an accident can have a dramatic effect on the way we choose to live our lives and conduct ourselves.

We became confident that if we could first define the values that customers look for in salespeople, we could test those values in action with groups of salespeople. We could evaluate the results of a new approach over time. Furthermore, if we could test the new approach with a control group of salespeople, we could evaluate their performance against that of others to see what impact this could have on sales performance. Little did we appreciate at the time quite what effect it would have.

To conclude

It's important to recognize that the profession of sales has been in some sort of crisis for years. We have shared our proprietary research findings that it's relatively few salespeople (less than 10 per cent) who make it to that winner's circle. Books have also cited similar statistics to ours. The 10 per cent problem has been around for some time.

The data suggests that attempts by organizations to improve sales effectiveness are not working that well. The current practices of behavioural training methods are not making that much of a difference. In addition, improved CRM processes are not making a difference in terms of how salespeople engage with customers. The current competency bias and the focus on sales methodology are not on their own the answer.

Why should we care? Well, as we know, it's a billion-dollar problem. We have explored the statistics from the UK and the USA and considered the evidence of Harvard professors.[32] We estimate that in the UK this is also a billion-dollar problem. Current ROI performance of sales training is underwhelming.

We questioned whether behaviour-led training, practised in different forms since the 1960s, provides sufficient return.

The lens through which we are seeing the problem and wanting to solve the problem is missing an essential perspective. We need to ask what are the underpinning values that create a negative or positive selling experience and what impact these have on sales performance.

Endnotes

1 Cespedes, FV and Lee, Y (2017) Your sales training is probably lackluster. Here's how to fix it, *Harvard Business Review*, https://hbr.org/2017/06/your-sales-training-is-probably-lackluster-heres-how-to-fix-it (archived at https://perma.cc/DE5S-WZVW)

2 Covey, S (1989) *The 7 Habits of Highly Effective People*, Free Press, New York
3 Weitz, BA (1978) The relationship between salesperson performance and understanding of customer decision making, *Journal of Marketing Research*, **15** (November), pp 501–16
4 Spiro, RL and Weitz, BA (1990) Adaptive selling: conceptualization, measurement and nomological validity, *Journal of Marketing Research*, February, pp 61–69
5 Saxe, R and Weitz, BA (1982) The SOCO scale: a measure of the customer orientation of salespeople, *Journal of Marketing Research*, 19 August, pp 345–51
6 Schwepker, CH (2003) Customer-orientated selling: a review, extension, and directions for future research, *Journal of Personal Selling & Sales Management*, 22 March
7 Schwepker, CH (2003) Customer-orientated selling: a review, extension, and directions for future research, *Journal of Personal Selling & Sales Management*, 22 March
8 Swenson, MJ and Herche, J (1994) Social values and salesperson performance: An empirical evaluation, *Journal of the Academy of Marketing Science*, **22** (3), pp 283–89
9 Feather, NT (1975) *Values in Education and Society*, Free Press, New York
10 Maslow, AH (1954) *Motivation and Personality*, Harper, New York
11 Rokeach, M (1973) *The Nature of Human Values*, Free Press, New York
12 Swenson, MJ and Herche, J (1994) Social values and salesperson performance: An empirical evaluation, *Journal of the Academy of Marketing Science*, **22** (3), pp 283–89
13 Rackham, N (1988) *SPIN Selling*, McGraw-Hill, New York
14 https://en.wikipedia.org/wiki/Neil_Rackham (archived at https://perma.cc/JGZ5-V58U)
15 Bosworth, M (1995) *Solution Selling: Creating buyers in difficult selling markets*, McGraw-Hill, New York
16 Fielder, R (2002) *Outsell Your Competition*, McGraw-Hill, Maidenhead
17 Bosworth, MT and Holland, JR (2004) *Customer Centric Selling*, McGraw-Hill, New York
18 Hanan, M (1999) *Consultative Selling*, Amacom, New York
19 Kaplan, S (2005) *Bag the Elephant: How to win and keep big customers*, Austin Bard Press, Austin, TX
20 Schell, M (2003) *Buyer Approved Selling*, Approved Publications Inc, Vancouver
21 Dixon, M and Adamson, B (2011) *Challenger Sale*, Penguin, New York
22 Dixon, M and Adamson, B (2011) *Challenger Sale*, Penguin, New York
23 Midgley, B and Midgley, D (2005) *Golden Circle Secrets*, John Wiley & Sons, Hoboken, NJ
24 Thompson, NA and Soper, AE (2007) *Values Sell*, Berrett-Koehler Publishers, Inc, San Francisco, CA

25 Bachrach, B (1998) *Values Based Selling: The art of building high trust client relationships*, Aim High Publishing, San Diego, CA
26 Raz, J (1999) *Engaging Reason on the Theory of Value and Action*, Oxford University Press, Oxford
27 https://www.jeanmcniff.com/items.asp?id=11 (archived at https://www.jeanmcniff.com/items.asp?id=11)
28 Schell, M (2003) *Buyer Approved Selling*, Approved Publications Inc, Vancouver
29 Raz, J (1999) *Engaging Reason on the Theory of Value and Action*, Oxford University Press, Oxford
30 https://korthagen.nl/en/wp-content/uploads/2018/07/Levels-in-reflection.pdf (archived at https://perma.cc/SKT4-YL5V)
31 Gladwell, M (2005) *Blink: The power of thinking without thinking*, Penguin Culture, New York
32 Cespedes, FV and Lee, Y (2017) Your sales training is probably lackluster: here's how to fix it, *Harvard Business Review*, 12 June

05

Values creating a positive or negative selling experience

This chapter sets out to explain how the values that create a positive or negative mindset were defined. We provide excerpts of interviews that illustrate how we came to our conclusions. We also explore the link between trust and values.

We support our hypothesis with two sets of interviews – one between HP and Starbucks, and one with a professional services company (DCL) and a retailer – that define the link between underpinning values that create either a negative selling experience or a positive selling experience.

Before we share our findings – it's helpful to clarify some of the terminology we use. Howard Gardner, the American development psychologist and Harvard professor, globally known for his theories for multiple intelligences, is author of *Five Minds for the Future*, in which he argues that the words 'minds' and 'values' can be used interchangeably.[1] The same logic is applied in *Selling Transformed*. For values please read mindset and vice versa.

Table 5.1 is an abbreviated description of the negative values.

These were defined following a detailed review of the interview transcripts of the 79 interviews where we linked observed behaviour to the values that influence that behaviour.

What follows is a narrative explaining the values.

Manipulation

Having been 'over-sold to and under-delivered to' many times, customers are very wary of sales techniques. They can sense when a salesperson is listening inauthentically to their needs. Any sales qualification approach that is manipulating the answer to a given result tells a customer where the salesperson's true priorities are.

TABLE 5.1 Negative values/mindsets

Negative values/mindsets	Drives behaviour that can be seen as being:
Manipulative	Pushy, insincere, pressurizing, dishonest, glib, annoying
Supplier-centricity	Reactive, lacking foresight, disinterest, lacking accountability, unstrategic, unknowledgeable
Complacency	Egotistical, self-satisfied, inattentive, unconcerned, lazy, unoriginal
Overt arrogance	Motivated by self-interest, arrogant, individualistic, opinionated, controlling

Many procurement experts are themselves trained in the techniques that salespeople use, so they often spot and predict how salespeople will behave. Most salespeople are taught techniques of asking questions in order to obtain information that can enable them to qualify the opportunity, control the conversation, handle the objection, close the sale. What many don't realize is that the nature of the questions they ask of customers gives the customer more information about the salesperson than the salesperson gains about the customer.

What the salesperson thinks is a good question is seen by the customer as a templated technique. It's often so leading in nature that it's clear it's asked for the benefit of the salesperson rather than the benefit of the customer.

Supplier-centricity

This is driven both by the self-centred nature of the salesperson and by the influence exerted on them by the organization for which they work. The self-centred salesperson filters data that they want to hear – remember the bias that we referred to earlier. The self-centred salesperson will shortcut the sales process to try to get a sale; they do not spend sufficient time finding relevant solutions for customers.

Often salespeople are not helped by the organizations for which they work – much sales training conducted by clients is better described as product sales training and puts scant focus on authentically solving customer problems. Even marketing doesn't help – what has been called solution selling is better described as product bundling.[2]

Complacency

As customers judge salespeople by their actions, they will also judge salespeople by their inaction. Arguably inaction is a stronger driver of dissatisfaction. Inaction promotes doubt, uncertainty and, in the extreme, outrage!

Complacency is observed when there is a perceived lack of investment (of time) in a customer. For example: if it's a key account where senior executive sponsors only get involved when a deal is due to be closed, or where the only creative solutions to problems are those prompted by the customer, or when there is a dearth of new thinking and assumptions that the status quo should be maintained.

This is a particular problem for larger organizations with dominant brands. Or where a particular product is in such great demand that the salesperson is better described as an order taker and spends too little time understanding the precise requirements of the customer and too little time understanding how they can be a better resource.

Overt arrogance

Films such as *Wall Street* (1987) and *The Wolf of Wall Street* (2013) have as their principal characters the super-confident, fast-talking salesperson, the one with the 'gift of the gab' – characteristics often considered key for a 'natural salesperson' by all but professional buyers. Too much confidence, assumed knowledge, quick responses are a big 'no'. There is such a fine line between being confident and being arrogant.

In some cases suppliers see the organizations for which salespeople work as being arrogant and 'tar' salespeople 'with the same brush'.

Scientific research carried out by Joseph A Vandello, Nadav P Goldschmied and David A R Richards of the University of South Florida in 2007[3] interestingly shows people consistently favour the underdog to win and conclude that those viewed as disadvantaged arouse people's sense of fairness and justice. This puts those in a market-leading position at a disadvantage. Salespeople may assume that because they are market leader the customer will welcome them with open arms; the reality may be different.

Below are extracts from some of the interviews that 'led' us to defining the four negative selling values.

Don't make statements about yours being the best product or best of breed because nobody has the best product and best of breed; it depends on what the business requires... I'm not the person who can be pestered into doing things. Why? Because the selling becomes intense. The selling becomes something that's almost becoming hormonal, becomes in their genes that they're trying to push something to you. When somebody promises you everything in the world, you are probably going to get about 10 per cent of that everything. And this is when you begin to worry about delivery.
(Chief Information Officer, communications group, Singapore)

They are really not paying attention and listening. They haven't taken the time to get to know your business and you really don't sense they are part of your team. They are there for meeting a quota. In a very short timeline. They are really only interested in talking to you if there is a short-term opportunity. You can just sense the pressure in their approach.
(Chief Marketing Officer, coffeehouse chain, USA)

They never really get engaged. They take very fleeting, superficial moments of time from a variety of people's diaries and then retire resigned back to their own desk or cubby hole back in their own company. It's outrageous! Salespeople should be spending all their time for their customers. Their cell phone should be on all the time. And if a customer is calling, they should leave an internal meeting because there is nothing internally that could be more important than what a customer has to talk to you about. Those very simple things aren't done – or are done by so few salespeople. It's outrageous... I just don't think they get it. I don't think they actually understand. There is stuff up on their walls in their sales office saying the customer is always right, engage the customer, all this kind of stuff. And yet if you ask them to dump their diary for a week, I bet you dollars for donuts 50 per cent of their time it's absolutely nothing to do with the customer.
(Chief Technology Officer, telecommunications company, UK)

Too many relationships were not respected, eg sly conversations round the back trying to find out information from other ways. Very frustrating, doesn't lend itself to trust. You end up not sharing things with that supplier. You become very defensive.
(Chief Procurement Officer, telecommunications company, UK)

Arrogance. I've met a lot of suppliers over the last six years who were and still are very successful. It's pure arrogance. In terms of how they treat the

customer. In terms of body language in the way they discuss business with you. They just express arrogance.
(Chief Sales Officer, multinational conglomerate, Germany)

Very often a vendor will come in with what we call a boiler-plate approach. The boiler plate being they have just dragged off a presentation they have done previously, topped it and tailed it, changed the names, changed the company, changed a few of the themes and then presented to you what *they* think you want to hear as opposed to what you've *told* them you want to hear.
(Chief Information Officer, healthcare company, UK)

They don't know enough about their business. They don't know our market situation. They don't know our aims for the market. So that's why they can't solve our problems. They just sell.
(Head of Manufacturing, dairy company, Finland)

We have 13–15 per cent market share; they have 40 or 45 per cent market share. It doesn't mean they have three times as much wisdom or knowledge as we have.
(Marketing Manager, telecommunications company, Germany)

So there have been examples of where a vendor has gone and spoken to me to get my views on a new product. Then they have gone to another part of the business to get another view, which in some respects is a logical approach. But if the objective of that is to try to divide people within the organizations and thereby through that to then win through the decisions that you want to achieve, then that's not the right approach.
(Marketing Manager, telecommunications company, UK)

I was speaking to the team in my office and various other people and saying how would you want to be treated and hard sell came out quite a bit. We just don't want to be put in a room and sold double glazing... You know, we want to feel special, the emotional side of it; no one likes to sit there and just get sick and tired of a hard-nosed salesperson pestering you or giving you a hard time all the time. It's not the way to develop a relationship with us.
(Chief Procurement Officer, telecommunications company, UK)

Customers can tell when you're trying to sell the same old thing but dressed it up. We know, usually, when that's happening to us. So, you can't fool the customer.
(New Ventures Head, coffeehouse chain, USA)

We connected these quotes with Korthagen's model (Figure 4.4 in Chapter 4) to consider the underpinning values that influence or lead to a particular type of behaviour.

Why do salespeople use such words as 'best product' and 'best of breed'? Think about the word 'pestering'. Think about the comment on 'over-promise and under-deliver'. What are the values that drive this type of behaviour? This behaviour links to the values of supplier-centricity and manipulation.

Why don't salespeople 'pay attention and listen', or invest sufficiently in getting to know their customer? This is really basic sales best practice and salespeople are not doing it. The reference to 'meeting a quota' suggests that the KPIs are seen as driving negative behaviour – this links to the complacency and supplier-centricity values.

Why were the words 'fleeting and superficial' used, words that suggested a poor focus on defining customer needs and a lack of attention? What prompted the buyer to say, 'Those very simple things aren't done'? Why aren't the simple things done? The customer thinks it's not rocket science and is clearly frustrated at the often-seen behaviour. These behaviours link to the supplier-centricity and manipulation values.

Why did the customer refer to 'sly', suggesting that any hint of underhand behaviour results in key information being withheld from that supplier? This links to the manipulation value.

Why, when presenting proposals, is there this quick fix, lack of 'tailored' content? This behaviour is so overt to most customers that it's no wonder that credibility is instantly destroyed. Why should a customer trust a salesperson who 'tops and tails' presentations? Such basic mistakes are being made by so many. Salespeople cringe when they hear this yet admit that they do it. Why? These behaviours link to the complacency value.

Why use the phrase 'they just sell'? Again, this shows how sensitive customers are to being sold to. This links to the manipulation value.

Why did the customer explain they just 'express arrogance'? This comment is particularly seen of salespeople who represent market-dominant organizations. Often, and sometimes unconsciously, salespeople use a language that is seen as arrogant. This can be linked to the overt arrogance value.

Why do customers express the comment, 'We don't want to be sold to'? Ironically perhaps those people who try to sell too hard are disliked and mistrusted. Customers do not like being sold to. They feel manipulated and not listened to.

Why would someone say 'you can't fool the customer'? This comment is similar to the 'boiler plate' comments made earlier. It's very difficult to fool the customer. Customers are extremely sensitive to being manipulated. It takes so long to build trust and a very short time to destroy it. We link this to the manipulation value.

The negative impact these values can have – at a personal level in the case of an account manager, and for the organization for which they work – is quite shockingly illustrated below. Not only do the negative values damage reputational value, but commercial value as well, in this case a multi-million-dollar account.

Please note the names of the individuals and company have been changed.

> DLC, a firm of auditors, were unexpectedly asked to take part in retendering for a contract for their service and wanted us to conduct an independent audit of their account relationships.
>
> DLC in their field was the largest in Europe. Six years prior we had worked with their key account team to win the Robertson's contract. Robertson's, a large retailer, became their largest contract in Europe and over the six years they had contributed a much larger than expected £200 million to Robertson's bottom line.
>
> It was a surprise to all that this retendering process was suddenly instigated. Angela, DLC's CEO, immediately asked Robertson's if they could undertake research on the understanding that a summary of the research findings would be shared with the other bidders.
>
> Over a one-month period 16 different stakeholders were interviewed. What surprised us was the frustration about the DLC Key Account Director, Paul – feelings that had been totally unseen and unnoticed in spite of the annual review meetings and regular monthly operational meetings that had taken place.
>
> Early in the first interview it was suggested by the CFO, quite candidly, that Paul should be replaced as the relationship person in spite of the fact they recognized he possessed such an in-depth knowledge of their business. He also went on to say, 'I would expect other people at Robertson's, if they're being as open as I am, to say the same thing, to be quite honest.'
>
> The relationship had become quite toxic. The CFO was not sure how much this was to do with Paul's approach or the pressure Paul was under by DLC to sell additional work. He was particularly concerned with the strategy that Paul had adopted of widening his wide and unofficial relationship base at Robertson's.
>
> Though Paul seemed to say the right things, there was a sense at Robertson's that DLC were intent on feathering their own nest. The speed at which trust was destroyed was fast.

His final comments of Paul were:

I think a lot of the problems that Paul faced are to some extent of his own making, and Paul may have been able to smooth those over if he'd behaved perhaps in a different way. But I think, going forwards, I just think there's a new breath of fresh air, different stance, different approach.

It was clear from the outset that Paul had to step down from this account. This had a big impact, as Paul was so entrenched in that account and very highly respected inside DLC. Over the four years the outstanding revenue growth from that account had made Paul the 'go to' person for all matters relating to strategic account management. Paul clearly knew that something was up and, when hearing the news of the meetings, agreed he had to leave the account. All along he had said we need to do what's best for DLC and the client.

It was clear that DLC had assumed that as they were contributing so much to Robertson's bottom line, they were meeting or exceeding Robertson's expectations. But Robertson's thought otherwise – DLC was criticized for not being quick enough to respond: 'Sometimes you could ask them something and you'd get a response that day. Other times you'd have to ask them things and chase and chase and chase.'

Another interviewee commented that DLC were quite secretive, that they played their cards deliberately very close to their chest – all they seemed to care about was how much revenue they could generate for themselves as their fees were performance-linked.

DLC certainly were not proactive in helping Robertson's improve systems and processes – a core value-add that Robertson's were looking for.

Unsurprisingly, DLC lost the prime contractor role, though the speed at which they had responded to the tender and desire to find the root cause of the problem impressed Robertson's and left the door open for one or two secondary contracts.

At a loss review, the key learnings for DLC were summarized as follows:

- This case demonstrated how the negative values of complacency, manipulation, supplier-centricity and overt arrogance can pervade an account, such that it goes unnoticed and suddenly it becomes urgent. It was, as Angela herself said, 'a boil that burst; we had to make a change.'
- Familiarity breeds complacency.
- What you see is not what you get. There is fragility in relying on the assumed. Customers see this as arrogance and not listening; this is where suppliers are seen as overtly supplier-centric.

- Trust is slow to build and fast to destroy. It was interesting to note that the seeds of distrust were sown early on (manipulation) but manifested five years later, by which time it was too late to act.
- The seeds of mistrust started with a few individuals then spread through the organization, through formal and informal conversation. It feeds on itself like a virus; it spreads to such an extent that a cultural perception is developed, not only about individuals but also about the organizations for which they work. Paul tainted the brand image of DLC and DLC tainted the brand image of Paul.

Table 5.2 provides an abbreviated description of the positive values. As with the negative values, these were defined following a detailed review of the transcripts of the 79 interviews, where we linked observed behaviour to the values that influence that behaviour.

We summarized four key positive differentiating mindsets that customers look for from salespeople that, if lived, would put the salesperson in the winner's circle – ie the top 10 per cent.

Authenticity

It captures many of the words that customers referred to, such as being transparent and acting with integrity, being honest and ethical. It also means of 'undisputed origin' and, from that, being original. Originality of thought and ideas helps salespeople stand out. The combination of being 'original'

TABLE 5.2 Positive values/mindsets

Positive values/mindset	Drives behaviour that can be seen as being:
Authenticity	Honest, credible, unpretentious, sincere, ethical, trustworthy, dependable
Client-centricity	Interested, investigative, knowledgeable, dedicated, passionate, accountable, attentive
Proactive creativity	Strategic, forward-thinking, innovative, creative, reflective, above and beyond
Tactful audacity	Daring, bold, challenging, aware of limits, diplomatic, unconventional, enthusiastic

with transparency, being unpretentious and sincere, creates a climate of trust, important in the origin of new ideas. With this mindset, salespeople will be themselves and avoid what is sometimes perceived as a scripted sales approach – as in method acting. Buyers will observe unauthentic behaviour very quickly when a seller is using a sales method and will immediately see the salesperson as having the negative mindset of manipulation. Remember, buyers themselves will be trained on the current sales techniques of the day and spot this behaviour a mile away.

Client-centricity

It's not just about the customer – it's their entire ecosystem, including partners, suppliers, customers, competitors. Client-centricity requires curiosity, interest, passion to do the right thing for the client, going the extra mile to find out more, going the extra mile to leverage more value for the customer, demonstrating non-autobiographical listening skills. It's consistently searching for new knowledge of the customer's business and looking for ways to add value to their business.

Proactive creativity

Proactive creativity requires a more strategic thinker, being one step ahead, coming up with ideas that the customer has not thought about before, believing that through collaboration new ideas can be formed – using subject-matter experts where they see they lack key knowledge from both inside and outside their organization. These could be big ideas or little ideas or even crazy ideas – as long as these ideas are grounded in the first two values described above. Lead with the relationship – once trust is built, it's easy and more believable (from the customer perspective) and the salesperson will not be seen as complacent.

Tactful audacity

This is the art of knowing how far to go without going too far. It's very difficult to do if parties are not known to each other – an unsolicited approach from a salesperson may well trigger a great idea, but the customer may then go and talk about it with their preferred incumbent. After all, they already have a relationship with them.

The word 'tact' is important, as we know many customers see salespeople, particularly those who represent major brands, as assuming a cloak of arrogance. No one wants to be controlled. So 'tact' is key – emotional intelligence coupled with the courage, ie audacity, to be bold and courageous in presenting news ideas or in the negotiating process in the right way will lead to salespeople being in the 10 per cent. No one likes to be challenged inappropriately.

These are extracts from some of the interviews that 'led' us to defining the four positive selling values:

> If you don't know about banking and you tell bankers how to be bankers, that's a problem. But if you know the industry and you can add to our business and tell us what we need to know, we will love you for that.
> (Head of Innovation, bank, UK)
>
> I'm yet to find a supplier who says, 'Can I come and work in your production department for four days so I can get to know your business?' If you really want to understand the frustrations of our business, come along and do it. Spend a night shift with our guys. It would be a wake-up call. You can't train that – you have to experience it. There are very few people who do that.
> (Operations Director, manufacturer, UK)
>
> The salesperson should be aware of all the market trends; the salesperson should be aware of what is happening in the market, should be aware of the usage of the product, should be aware of the problems that he is facing… Should be a person who knows the problems that we are facing, should know our supply chain properly, should help and assist in decreasing our operational costs – because it's to their advantage.
> (Head of Marketing, manufacturer, Dubai)
>
> I'd say the most important quality is knowledge of our business and really being engaged in that, so being a business professional, asking the questions that aren't a leading question about what are you going to buy from me today, but trying to understand what our challenges are, what our objectives are in the enterprise.
> (Chief Information Officer, coffeehouse chain, USA)
>
> There's no reason why you shouldn't add your input and advice on things unrelated to that particular line of business if you're good at what you're doing.
> (Head of Innovation, bank, UK)

> We're looking at awareness not just from the perspective of awareness of each other's businesses but awareness of the entire ecosystem.
> (Head of Incubation, hospitality company, USA)
>
> They have to be charismatic enough to get in the door, which is actually quite hard. And then intellectually powerful enough to be able to challenge us in a way that we haven't thought of.
> (General Manager, bank, UK)
>
> But nor would I expect any account manager or any person to sort of sit back and let us do the work. I would expect them to challenge us. I would expect them to keep us on our toes all the time. We don't always know the answers. We need suppliers to generate ideas for us, to come to us and say, 'Look, what about this, what about this promotion, why don't we try this with this product? If we did this, could we generate more sales?'
> (Global Head of Procurement, telecommunications company, UK)
>
> I want a marriage where you express you are faithful. That you will be together until you don't live any more. Where it is predictable what you do – transparent what you do. Where what you say today also counts tomorrow and in three months.
> (Chief Information Officer, telecommunications company, Denmark)
>
> In terms of how we like to be approached, I think we'd rather people be up front – hidden agendas don't work well.
> (Global Head of Procurement, telecommunications company, UK)

As before, Korthagen's model (see Figure 4.4 in Chapter 4) is used to consider the underpinning values that influence or lead to a particular type of behaviour.

What values is the customer looking for in their comments 'if you know the industry' and 'can add to our business' – client-centricity and proactive creativity.

What values is the customer looking for when they suggest that if you want to really understand their business, come and do a night shift with their operations team – very few people do. A similar value is sought when references are made to 'market knowledge' and 'knowledge of the supply chain'. It's clear that customers have a very high expectation of the knowledge salespeople have of their business; a knowledge of the customer's business ecosystem is very helpful – client-centricity.

What values is the customer looking for when saying 'don't ask the leading questions'? The problem with sales approaches that try to control the conversation, or through pain-related questioning techniques, is often they are transparent to buyers. Salespeople are taught that the key to uncovering needs is to ask the right questions; however, our natural bias, as we have explored briefly before, influences the words used when asking. This bias becomes quite clear to customers, and in fact, these leading – and in their view, manipulative – questions, at least to the well educated, tell the customer more about you than them. The overall message here is be authentically client-centric.

What values is a customer looking for when they say there is no reason why you should not add your input and where they use words like 'we would expect them to challenge us'? Proactive creativity and tactful audacity.

What mindset would a salesperson have to be considered 'charismatic' (and not arrogant) and intellectual? It's clear that however we define the mindset that drives the behaviour, it will need to capture the emotional intelligence required to tread the line between a brazen idea (arrogance) and creative thought – hence proactive creativity and tactful audacity.

What values is a customer looking for when using 'marriage' as a metaphor? Why avoid 'hidden agendas'? These words suggest integrity and transparency. Another key word used was 'predictability'. Earlier in the book we made reference to the connection between values and predictability: when a customer understands your values, and vice versa, the relationship becomes more trusting, more predictable – authenticity and client-centricity.

Starbucks

The following case study illustrates the impact the positive values can have in driving collaborative transformation and new business opportunities. The case study explores the thought process at Starbucks that led them to issuing a request for proposal (RFP) for building an internet solution at their stores and that of Compaq (later acquired by Hewlett-Packard (HP) in August 2002) which won the deal.[4]

Two years later the team at HP and Starbucks were involved in interviews about how the partnership came about. This provided some great insights into how salespeople could operationalize the positive values/mindsets into their sales practice.

By 2002 Starbucks was well on the way to creating one of the world's most recognized global brands. From opening its first store in Seattle in 1995, it then had over 1,000 outlets in the USA, a global franchise network and was responsible for buying 1 per cent of the world's coffee beans. Turnover was approaching $3.3 billion.[5]

With many Starbucks outlets being in prime locations, it is not hard to work out that you need to sell a lot of coffee to break even. Critical to Starbucks' success is encouraging customers into its outlets, securing higher levels of consumer spend, and ensuring processes are in place to encourage smooth service and short queues.

But where is the differentiation? Why should customers come into a Starbucks? After all, a coffee is a coffee – though, arguably, some make a better-tasting coffee than others.

Starbucks' intent was not to be a coffee shop but a destination, replicating what was already being achieved in Europe, where the café lifestyle was ingrained into local culture. Howard Schultz, its CEO, wanted Starbucks to be the 'third place'.[6] First place was home, second place was work and third place was Starbucks. The concept was to create an environment where people would want to meet.

This had significant implications for Starbucks' strategy. It meant not focusing on quick in-and-out service, but creating a place where people could relax – a place that felt like someone's living room, a place where friends could meet. The logic seems fine until you consider the cost of creating this type of environment. The challenge was how to improve revenue per square foot by increasing customer flow and encouraging people to spend more. It's not enough to just sell coffee, tea, cakes and sandwiches – what more can we do?

Starbucks' top marketing team met to consider potential initiatives to fuel the next stage of the company's growth. It was clear that they had to attract large numbers of profitable customers – individuals who had higher-than-average disposable income. But how could Starbucks develop new income streams that did not impact its traditional core products?

At about the same time there were some interesting developments on the technology front. Compaq had announced the launch of its first iPAQ, the PDA (personal digital assistant), and Hewlett-Packard and Dell were fast following suit. The telecommunications companies (telcos) were also getting excited about the future of mobile computing, paying huge fees for wireless operating licences. The advent of the PDA and wireless computing meant that business could be done by anyone anywhere – the much aspired-to mobile office of the future was fast becoming a reality. Internet cafés were springing up, but unlike Starbucks, their business model was based on a different concept – they wanted to drive consumers whose primary interest was getting onto the internet.

Starbucks recognized the opportunity to introduce wireless technology into all of its outlets. By providing internet access, it would attract the upwardly mobile professional and encourage a higher frequency of off-peak purchases. Businesspeople could have a coffee, check emails, go onto the internet, have another coffee and meet clients. Knowing that all outlets were wireless-enabled gave them a place where they could work in relative comfort.

Solutions to drive growth – but at what price?

So, a great idea, but at what price? Starbucks realized that the 'cool image' of technology would resonate with their customers, as their research indicated that 90 per cent of their customers were online, and 40 per cent had a laptop, a PDA or other mobile device. They started to look at what it would cost to have Starbucks outlets wireless-enabled and estimated that the investment would be a significant $100 million when all the costs were taken into account. The hardware and services complexity was in installing the hubs, creating new internet portals and servicing the solutions. There was the additional collaboration complexity of having to work with both a telco and a hardware vendor.

Meeting ROI objectives meant selling huge volumes of coffee. The risk was high. On one hand, Starbucks wanted to style itself as innovative, cool, high quality and relaxing, but on the other hand, it had to make money. They were wary of the risks involved – but they were convinced there was a way to make this work. They firmly believed that other parties would be willing to share the risk – particularly those already in the wireless sector.

How Starbucks created its value proposition

The marketing team started to look at why a vendor might be prepared to install this equipment – at their investment cost. They knew that technology companies were investing millions in new wireless-based technologies. Time to market was critical – not only to generate sales but to capture the target market group of mobile professionals. Starbucks soon recognized that this was exactly the type of market that it already serviced. They knew from their studies of consumer demographics that there was a close alignment between their consumers and the customers these mobile phone and IT companies wanted to secure.

The Starbucks team recognized that they had priceless insights into this hugely important consumer category, insights that the IT vendors at the time did not possess. What value could these companies place on partnering with Starbucks?

This argument on its own may have been sufficient as a value proposition. However, Starbucks' market research department came up with more information that further strengthened the value proposition and gave them higher levels of confidence in approaching potential partners. Starbucks already knew how many people visited their outlets – 15 million every week. By the time we interviewed the team the figure had increased to 20 million. What was more staggering, 55 per cent of these customers visited Starbucks five times a week. Starbucks asked: 'What value would wireless and IT companies place in having their brand and technology in front of 7 million of their target customer group five times a week?' It was clearly a powerful proposition.

Starbucks would offer one telecommunications company and one IT company the opportunity to install their technology throughout the 1,200 US outlets, allowing them access to Starbucks' customers.

Discussions with potential partners started in January 2001. After developing the value proposition, the marketing team drew up a list of potential partners and, given the strategic nature of the proposition, they knew that the respective CEOs would most likely have to be involved.

If we just stop and reflect on what mindsets we can see being exhibited by the 'customer', we can certainly see proactive creativity and tactful audacity.

Innovation in Compaq's response

Compaq's regional director was charged with developing the strategy and recommending whether Compaq should invest $100 million in the deal and on what terms. At the time, they had 3 per cent of Starbucks' IT spend. Incumbent competitors were IBM, Dell, Sun Solaris and EMC.

Clearly there was an opportunity to grow the 'share of wallet'; however, whilst Starbucks was a well-recognized global brand, their total IT spend was quite low compared with that of other companies. Even so, the team recognized the value of having access to Starbucks' huge consumer base. In addition, consultation with Compaq colleagues in its personal systems group indicated that the company was keen to develop innovations in the music industry. The account team began to evaluate how a partnership model could work and to define a value proposition that they could take first to Michael Capellas, CEO of Compaq.

Working with some of the emerging technology gurus, Compaq realized that if they were going to get the full value of the relationship, they would need to see what internet innovations were already emerging. For example, downloading music from the internet was one such area to help make the most of Starbucks' potential. The account team also realized that by becoming a type of 'channel', Starbucks could sell Compaq's iPAQ through its outlets.

Gaining confidence

At the time, Compaq's iPAQ and wireless technology products put it at least six months ahead of the competition. The team believed that Starbucks would want to partner with Compaq as it had the strongest technology solutions in this area at this point in time.

With some confidence, Mark (the then regional account manager) and his team's counter recommendations were as follows:

- Scale down investment required to wireless-enable the outlets.
- Compaq would become the preferred vendor for Starbucks' desktops and servers.[7] To broaden their services business into Starbucks, Compaq and Starbucks would work together to explore other technology innovations.
- Compaq and Starbucks would work together on environmental and social community projects.
- They would create joint publicity and marketing arrangements, such as Starbucks becoming a vendor.

On 21 August 2002, Starbucks announced the expansion of a high-speed wireless internet service to about 1,200 Starbucks locations in North America and Europe. The Compaq team – now the Hewlett-Packard team – had won the deal![8] But did the deal work? What value was created for both parties?

HP developed a 'sell with' and 'sell to' strategy for Starbucks. They realized that they had to implement these strategies with separate teams. A new account executive was brought in to manage the account from a 'sell to' perspective, while another headed the marketing incubation team as greenhouse manager for 'sell with' ideas.

Significantly, HP found out that the Starbucks IT department was 'fairly negative' towards the alliance – they did not want Compaq and HP technology 'shoved down their throats'.

They felt that HP were not 'relationship orientated'. Dealing with the politics was one of the most difficult challenges for the account executive, but after two years HP had secured all of Starbucks' desktop and laptop business. They had also won consulting revenues, sold HP software, and won some business, for the first time ever, in the retail stores, where IBM had dominated before, and sold managed services.

In total, HP had moved their share in the account from 3 per cent to 55 per cent over two years. In addition, they had gained a huge amount of visibility for their new wireless capability.

The value created was not one-way. As a result of the wireless technology secured for minimal investment, Starbucks now had a wireless environment with minimal investment. In addition, they saw customers visit their stores more frequently and stay for longer and, importantly, in off-peak hours.

Internal research indicates that T-Mobile HotSpot subscribers visit Starbucks more often than they visit other coffee shops – an average of eight times per month – and spend more time in the outlets – the average connection lasts approximately one hour. Nearly 90 per cent of T-Mobile HotSpot accesses are during off-peak store hours, which are after 9am.[9]

Let's now consider the underpinning values that led both parties to this deal

Proactive creativity is required to differentiate one coffee house from another. Starbucks came up with the idea of the third place and with this idea was able to create differentiation around what is a commodity product, ie coffee. The company was passionate about ensuring the concept was supported by the correct branding of the stores' environment, packaging, furniture and lighting. Even the head office reflected the same branding as the stores. Theirs was a systemic approach. Consistency and meticulous attention to detail are important in packaging a concept. Starbucks' sales growth has reflected the success of its differentiation strategy.

Creative logic is required to find ways of keeping customers in the store for longer. Starbucks' concept is the opposite of the fast-food concept of quick service. Sustained growth requires constant innovation, market data and a deep knowledge of the customer base.

Client-centricity is a central value to Starbucks. They have to understand their consumer target market in order to create a compelling value proposition. Their coffee is not the cheapest. They recognized the importance of understanding the customer, not only in terms of how many times they bought coffee but also in terms of what lifestyle their customers have. This knowledge of the customer enabled Starbucks to understand that their consumers were also users of technology, were mobile, and would value easy access to the internet. They also recognized the threat posed by the new numbers of internet cafés opening up. It's interesting to see how, in the context of the world in which they operate, their third place concept is adapting.[10]

The audacious idea of approaching IT vendors came from Starbucks recognizing the power of its brand. **Creativity** was used by Starbucks to develop the idea of creating a wireless environment in the store. **Audacity** was used to suggest that IT vendors invest $100 million over five years in implementing the idea in Starbucks' stores. They used their knowledge of marketing-led thought processes to sell the value that potential partners had to create. They made sure they spent time strengthening the business case.

This case shows that the architects of the deal were not frightened to ask the most senior people to get involved. The fact that Starbucks CEO Howard Schultz and Compaq/HP CEO Michael Capellas were personally engaged in the deal was an important factor in enabling the deal to be finalized. Peer-to-peer selling works well. Again, be bold. Be audacious. It takes two like-minded companies to forge this type of deal.

A key learning from this case study is that most of the creativity and audacity was driven by the 'customer', ie Starbucks. Certainly the initiative was! What if the same values were applied from the 'sellers'?

Proactive creativity can also be seen from the Hewlett-Packard account team. In order to create value out of the deal and make the numbers work, they developed a 'sell through' and 'sell to' concept. They not only wanted to supply the wireless environment but also saw the potential in Starbucks selling personal digital assistants. HP was now mirroring the Starbucks creative culture. This was unusual for HP and reflects excitement over the new relationship.

Whilst the marketing team were delighted with the deal, the Starbucks internal IT team were less than happy. Perhaps Starbucks should have engaged with their internal IT department. This reinforces the importance of relationships – stability, **respecting** internal decision-making processes, **transparency**, working to the right values and being **authentic**. For a deal of this magnitude, the essence of **collaboration** is important as well as **sustained innovation**.

In creating the greenhouse team, Hewlett-Packard provided a conduit for innovation that led in later years to the co-development of other initiatives, such as music downloading as well as green and sustainability initiatives.

Hewlett-Packard saw value in the deal in both tangible and intangible terms. This is important. The account manager of HP worked with HP's internal executives who were in a position of authority and who were able to quantify the intangible business value. For example, having access to the

7 million customers who visited a Starbucks each day has a PR and advertising value that is difficult to quantify precisely, but one appreciated by the then executive vice president of HP's mobile division.

The idea of Starbucks creating their strategy around the concept of the third place and how they have used this to reflect on how they work with their suppliers led to the development of third perspective thinking. This is a framework that encourages salespeople to think of all aspects of the value chain as it relates to sales. It enables a salesperson to think not only of their immediate customer but also of their customer's customer. It also enables a salesperson to consider both the tangible and intangible aspects of their offer. The framework encourages the sales team to think in a creative way about value creation. Its use by salespeople is intended to demonstrate what we later defined as **proactive creativity** and, once the business case is shaped, **tactful audacity** in the way the ideas can then be put to the client.

Whilst Starbucks' case was a very rich source of data, it stimulated a lot of thinking about the values and mindsets required of salespeople to make it into that winner's circle of 10 per cent: what additional evidence is there to determine the positive, underpinning values that drive what is seen as ethical behaviour and great sales behaviour?

Emerging conclusions from our research at this stage

Living the first two values/mindsets of authenticity and client-centricity is the baseline for building a trusting relationship. It earns the salesperson the right to move the relationship to an altogether higher and more strategic level. But to earn the right to be in that winner's circle, they will want to see proactive creativity and tactful audacity.

At least this was our theory at the time. We had at this point in the research journey perspectives from many customers; we also had insights provided through very carefully analysing, in the Robertson's case, a specific deal that went wrong, and in the Starbucks case a deal that created wins for both parties.

But what excited us was we were now talking a new language (one based on lived values and mindsets) and had taken the research on a topic of values for salespeople to a deeper level – a topic that has never been seriously researched before.

In addition:

- When we looked back on our literature review, we also concluded there were potentially significant gaps in their approach – so many of the popular books written on how to sell were convincingly written by salespeople based on their personal and therefore potentially biased perspectives and not through the perspective of the customer. This was also the case with many of the academic research papers on selling. We felt that a better research logic was to work back from the customer needs and then find the solutions to what they need. Ironically, this is the advice given by most authors on the topic.
- Most sales training vendors addressed the solution to improving sales performance from a particular patented method, behavioural or process perspective. SPIN, solution selling, challenger and others, for example, suggest that by following a certain methodology, success is guaranteed – at least that is what is implied.

What we were beginning to question was: which is more important – mindset or method? We even questioned: do you require method at all if the mindsets are in place? Yes – one needs to have a language to hang your CRM sales process on, but we asked: does it really matter what type of method of selling is adopted if the right mindset is in place and lived? Surely a salesperson who genuinely lived the values of, say, customer-centricity would listen more carefully, ask the right questions, conduct the right research, etc, etc. Surely a salesperson who lived the values of proactive creativity and tactful audacity would bring insights to customers and challenge customer thinking not by following a method by rote but because they genuinely believed in it.

The new logic we were developing was ground-breaking in its theory: the research in its scope was both reliable and accurate but was as yet unproven. What we did not know at this stage was would this new theory work – is it possible to change salespeople's mindsets? Would the right behaviours flow if they did change? Could we avoid a highly regulated methodology and allow a free spirit to emerge in a new customer-centric sales approach? How would salespeople buy into this new approach?

So far we have defined the characteristics of each mindset at a high level. In the next chapter we will cover these in more detail, link the mindsets framework to trust, and finally share the results of an amazing two years during which we tested these in action with a control group of a major IT giant, with surprising results.

Endnotes

1. Gardner, H (2009) *Five Minds for the Future*, Harvard Business Review Press, Boston
2. Tuli, KR, Kohli, AJ and Bharadwaj, SG (2007) Rethinking customer solutions: from product bundles to relational processes, *Journal of Marketing*, 71, July, pp 1–17
3. Sage Publications (2007) Why do people support underdogs and find them so appealing?, *ScienceDaily*, 20 December
4. https://www.macworld.com/article/1006504/starbucks.html (archived at https://perma.cc/KM5N-6GEJ)
5. https://www.sec.gov/Archives/edgar/data/829224/000089102002002061/v86608e10vk.htm (archived at https://perma.cc/SY5H-GJYD)
6. https://www.starbucks.com/responsibility/learn-more/policies/third-place (archived at https://perma.cc/HLL5-NC7A)
7. https://www.cbsnews.com/news/another-way-to-get-wired-at-starbucks/ (archived at https://perma.cc/CRL7-M56H)
8. https://www.cbronline.com/uncategorised/compaq_to_join_starbucks_and_microsoft/ (archived at https://perma.cc/7AEL-JBN6)
9. https://www.t-mobile.com/news/starbucks-builds-continued-success-with-t-mobile-hotspot-the-wi (archived at https://perma.cc/27J4-LTVN)
10. https://www.businessinsider.com/starbucks-reimagine-third-place-2019-3?r=US&IR=T (archived at https://perma.cc/6BF8-MWN2)

06

Values that are an antecedent to trust

This chapter sets out to explore at what point in the sales cycle or the customers' buying cycle the values are important. We explore both the relationship between trust and positive values, the difference between being trusted and entrusted, and question how quickly trust can be developed. We consider an academic perspective on the topic, particularly on relationships with key accounts.

We illustrate the relative importance of values during the sales cycle (Figure 6.1).

Pre-call planning: making that first contact

For prospects

Making that first contact is often one of the hardest tasks in sales – how to get noticed from the many sales representatives trying to gain time in a buyer's diary. No one will give a 'rep' the time of day if they haven't taken the time to do at least some research on their business – *client-centricity*.

If it's a cold contact, one can develop '*authentic*' non-sales conversations with people, even if through LinkedIn – but there has to be some authentic *reason* for starting that conversation. It takes time to develop those online conversations – our research suggests that at least five LinkedIn messages are needed. At some point *tactful audacity* could be used to get an appointment.

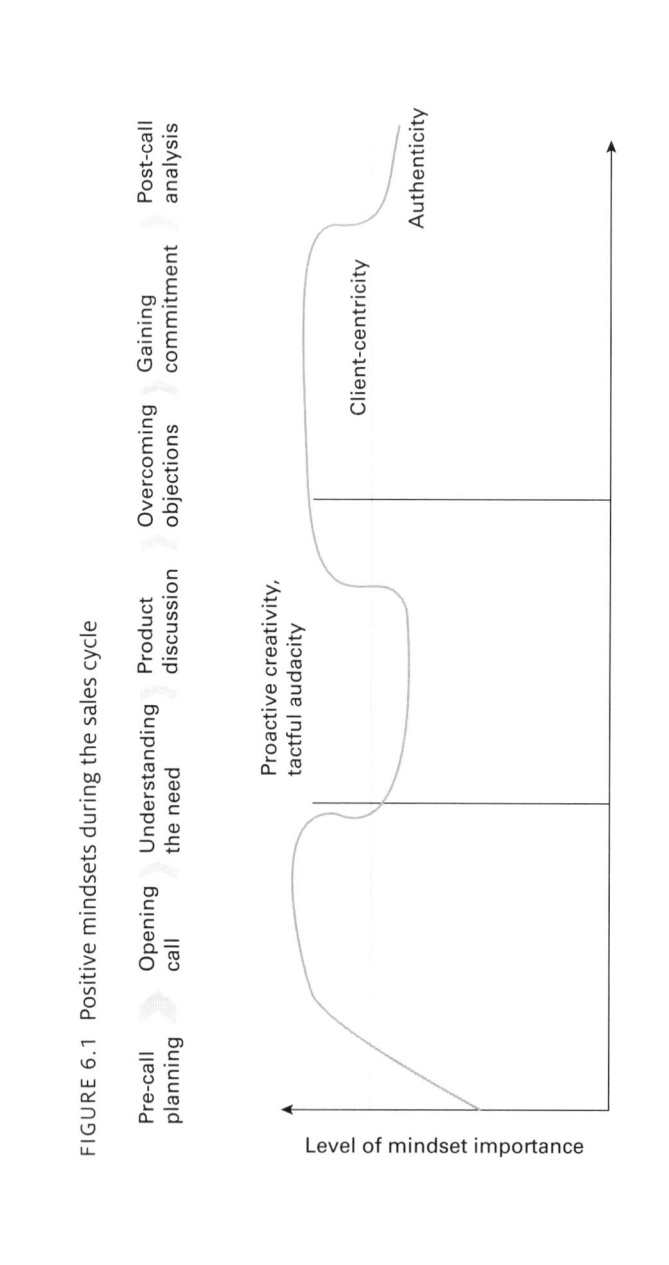

FIGURE 6.1 Positive mindsets during the sales cycle

Pre-call planning → Opening call → Understanding the need → Product discussion → Overcoming objections → Gaining commitment → Post-call analysis

Proactive creativity, tactful audacity

Client-centricity

Authenticity

Level of mindset importance

One such approach demonstrating *tactful audacity* and *proactive activity* was shared by our US partner the Summit Group. A woman selling paper cups noticed in the trade press that a major fast food brand was launching a new 'gas station franchise'. She started a conversation with the head of the 'gas division' with the statement, 'I see you are opening a franchise in gas stations and there is something that I think you may not have yet considered.' Few would not be intrigued to know what the something might have been. Potentially this unsolicited call could be seen as rather arrogant – but the use of the word 'may' and the tone of the conversation worked in her favour. In this case the 'not yet considered' was to do with the paper cup sizes. Indeed, they had not, at that point, considered what the cup size had to be in order to compete with the 'cola' bottles on sale already at the gas station.

She went on to become one of their suppliers, not necessarily because other suppliers could not supply this particular cup, but because she was seen to be creative in her approach and not frightened to question the customer.

For existing customers

Avoid complacency – with a 'client-centricity' mindset conduct research before the call. The world is changing so much that there really is no excuse not to seek news on the customer, and it can be done quickly. Plan your objectives for the meeting, and send and discuss agendas in advance, as collaboration is key to being client-centric.

Opening the call

Having a *client-centric* mindset means you will search for any clues as to the state of mind or approach that a customer wants to take. A keen sense of observation will enable you to sense the emotional context of your customer in order to decide how to open the call. *Tactful audacity* may help shape the conversation at the start.

Understanding the need – what does the customer *really* care about?

Leading with a *client-centricity* mindset will: influence the salesperson's qualification questions; adopt a non-autobiographical listening approach;

prompt original research into the client's business; drive curiosity and passion to fully understand the customer's requirements. It also involves summarizing and reframing the customer's requirements with the customer to ensure their needs are totally clear before solutions or products are discussed. The *proactive creativity* mindset will be searching for the unexplained and unconnected, but as long as this is grounded with a genuine intent to do the best for the client, this will not cause offence or give the client the idea you are trying to manipulate the conversation.

At a rather simple level there are arguably three types of sales conversations that lead to a sale:

- **Supplying a need:** a customer has identified a requirement, specified what this is and selected the suppliers that could potentially fulfil this requirement. The customer selects your solution. Many 'requests for proposals' fall into this category.
- **Shaping a need:** a customer has identified a requirement, they are not too sure what the specification is to fulfil that requirement, and they selected you as the supplier that best shaped the need *and* provided the most relevant solution.
- **Creating a need:** a customer does not recognize they have a need. They had not thought, therefore, of the specification of the solution to that need. The salesperson has triggered the idea/need through careful questioning and then made suggestions based on the client requirements. The customer is happy that the salesperson has proactively helped define a problem that they did not know about.

Of these types of sales conversations, it's clear that a combination of all the mindsets enables a salesperson to conduct the three types of sales conversation. The third type requires the most skill and is where those in the winner's circle, ie those who live the values of *proactive creativity* and *tactful audacity*, will have a distinct competitive advantage over others.

Product discussion/presentation of solution

This phase of the sales cycle connects the needs of the customer with solutions in a new and creative way. The *proactive creativity* and *tactful audacity* mindsets lead this part of the sales cycle. This is particularly important if the commercial strategy is to shift the customer's perspective in some way or to change their mind. Customers may have asked for x, but you believe that y is the better solution (for these reasons). The argument you put forward, and the logic for the shift you are suggesting the customer makes, requires courage.

Handling objections

Again, *proactive creativity* and *tactful audacity* are the dominant mindsets if objections are raised, but *client-centricity* also plays an important role here – with a genuine intent to listen to the customer's concerns. As we have said earlier, many salespeople fall into the trap of listening with the intent to respond, rather than listening with the intent to understand. These mindsets are particularly important in the negotiating phase, where objections may be raised or demands made, such as, 'you are too expensive'.

Gaining commitment

Making it clear you really want their business, asking for the order and seeking a commitment require, for some, a degree of courage. Those with a *tactful audacity* mindset will find it easy and natural to do. When we have assessed sales teams on their perceptions of the mindsets, we have often found that tactful audacity is their weakest spot. Yet it is one of the most desired of salespeople, by customers, but only if the customer sees the other positive mindsets at play. There is a fine line between tactful audacity and overt arrogance.

Post-call review

Remember Schell's research,[1] in which 46 per cent of buyers said salespeople neglect to write a summary of a sales call. What would make a salesperson have the discipline to write a summary of a sales call? It would be that they felt it important enough to do so. This would be driven by a mindset of client-centricity but also, potentially, of proactive creativity and tactful audacity.

But what about the buying cycle?

Of course the 'sales cycle' many times does not start with the salesperson. It starts with the buyer. The buying cycle starts well before buyers talk to a salesperson (Figure 6.2). They will go through an awareness stage where they will be determining the problem they need to solve; this will involve them discussing the problem with colleagues. Once defined, the buyers will move into a consideration phase. This could involve desk research, or talking with other organizations that may have the same problems. (Remember, the research suggests that the time when customers talk to salespeople is anywhere between 57 and 90 per cent[2] of the way through the time it takes to make a buying decision, depending on the complexity of the purchasing decision being made!)

Even in the consideration stage, the buyers may not as yet have contacted potential suppliers. Then finally, as they move further into the consideration phase, a salesperson working for a supplier may get a call or an invitation to follow up on a lead. So as a salesperson this is when the sales cycle starts. Consider therefore the mindsets and values required as the salesperson enters the buying cycle at this late stage.

It's going to be tough for a salesperson to influence or question a buyer who has already spent much time defining the problem and talking to potential suppliers. The first challenge is to build trust and, if we consider the values, authenticity and client-centricity will be very important.

There will be little chance for the seller to change the scope or challenge the buyer if trust is not developed. Time is not on the side of the seller unless the buyer is compelled to make a quick decision. Buyers know how to play the 'time card' well. They know the pressure on sales teams to meet quarterly targets; they know that this intensifies at year end. They deliberately wait

FIGURE 6.2 When buyers engage with salespeople

Question: At what point during the buying process do you want to talk to a salesperson?

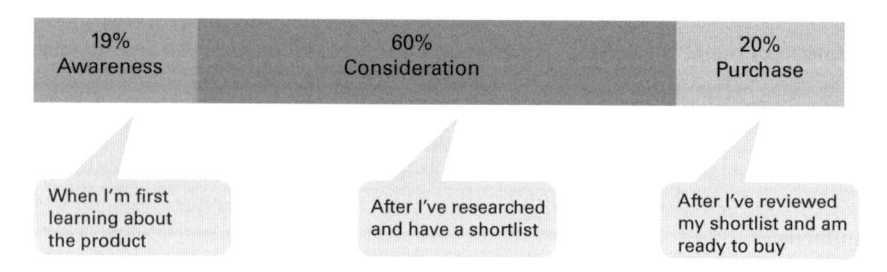

19% Awareness	60% Consideration	20% Purchase
When I'm first learning about the product	After I've researched and have a shortlist	After I've reviewed my shortlist and am ready to buy

until these critical periods to make their final decisions. As in the example presented in Chapter 2, the Aleppoean trader Mohammed knew that the moment the phone went off, control had passed from seller to buyer. But it's not impossible to gain control of 'time' if trust is developed early and the salesperson demonstrates that the route the customer has taken is perhaps wrong (tactful audacity) or that the route the customer has taken is right and that the salesperson's solution is the one best placed to solve that need (proactive creativity and tactful audacity).

Given the shortened timeline, the four mindsets are critical – all need to be consciously in play as salespeople are in pursuit of a deal/sale. Authenticity and client-centricity values are critical during the early part of relationship building and required of the salesperson before they then earn the right to challenge or question customers.

The connection between values and trust

Clearly there is connection between a people's values and the trust created between them. If values are misaligned, there will be suspicion on both sides of the table.

The academic research conducted on the topic as it related to sales is worth exploring and, in particular, research that focused on developing key accounts or the more complex type of sale.

Frequently researchers cite the lack of empirical and practitioner-based research on the topic (Kohli and Jaworski, 1990;[3] Homburg et al, 2002;[4] Kempeners and Van der Hart, 1999;[5] Millman and Wilson, 1995;[6] Tuli et al, 2007;[7] Wengler et al, 2006[8]). Research into key account programmes has generally fallen into organizational and relational streams. 'Organizational' relates to how to select accounts, how to structure an account team, and how to develop internal processes to support teams. The values research, though, took us more into the trust side and what relational qualities are required to make the supplier–customer relationships effective.

Given that key accounts in particular are of strategic importance and therefore receive special focus, one would expect to see much improved relationships and profits. To what extent do key account programmes improve client–supplier relationships? In 1997, Napolitano's exhaustive survey[9] of the effectiveness of the key account manager (KAM) suggested that the majority of key account programmes are ineffective.

More recently, research on key account relationships (Ivens and Pardo, 2008: 470[10]) and ordinary supplier–buyer 'dyads' regarding differences in suppliers' relational behaviours and customers' perceptions of relational qualities suggests that:

> while as compared to ordinary relationships – suppliers put in significantly more effort in 'value-creating behaviours' in key account relationships, they do not modify their 'value-claiming behaviours'… on the customer side, suppliers' increased value-creating activities lead to increased commitment. However, customers are neither more satisfied nor do they trust their suppliers more when they receive key account status.

This research also supports the earlier study by Schwepker,[11] which concludes that formal KAM programmes add no intrinsic value to the relationship.

The notion of 'trust' is central to key account programmes (Raimondo, 2000[12]) and one that should be explored in more depth because values alignment between buyer and seller is important as a means of developing trust.

Abratt and Kelly (2002[13]) concluded that 'suppliers and their key account customers have similar perceptions of the key account success factors in the customer–supplier partnership'. If both parties have similar perceptions, why is there a disconnect between what suppliers deliver and what customers expect? For example, while trust is considered a key success factor for both supplier and customer, Abratt and Kelly suggest that what constitutes trust is different between suppliers and customers. Customers view trust as not breaking a contract; suppliers view trust as the sharing of information. This difference in perception suggests that customers desire a transactional relationship, ie 'manage by contract', while suppliers are looking for a more strategic relationship, ie based on transparency and sharing information.

Raimondo (2000: 2)[14] conducted an interesting review of measurement of trust. She argues that while trust is a crucial factor in moving relationships from 'discrete market transactions to continuous exchange relationships' (sales practitioners note how academics talk about selling), there is, as yet, 'no complete agreement about its definition, nor about its measurement'. The paper recognizes the important role of 'trust' in value creation in key accounts. Raimondo (2000) explained that different researchers have defined trust constructs in different ways:

- Castaldo (1994[15]) defines trust as the 'predictability of the behaviour of the subject – or the organization – in whom trust is placed, which comes from learning based on experience; the second one is the certainty that the person concerned could not behave opportunistically and that his actions would be aimed to achieve joint benefits' (p2).

- Zaheer et al (1998[16]) define trust as being the expectation that an actor can be relied on to fulfil obligations, behave in a predicable way and will act fairly when the opportunity for opportunism is present (p30).
- Geyskens et al (1996[17]) define trust as being the extent that the channel member believes the partner to be honest and benevolent (p29).

Through her analysis of research approaches, Raimondo (2000: 1) argues that without a universal framework for defining what constitutes trust, there is a lack of 'completely satisfying and widely agreed models and methods of organization, suitable for the evaluation of trust in market (read sales) relationships and its process of generation and growth over time'. For example, Andaleeb (1992[18]), Busacca and Castaldo (1996[19]), Doney and Cannon (1997[20]), Fletcher and Peters (1997[21]) and Ganesan (1994[22]) all suggest that motives and ability are components of trust. Others (Crosby et al, 1990;[23] Moorman et al, 1993;[24] Morgan and Hunt, 1994;[25] Selnes, 1998;[26] Swan and Nolan, 1985;[27] Swan et al, 1985[28]) feel that ability and motives are an antecedent for trust – meaning that trust happens as a result of these attributes.

Categories of trust

Andaleeb[29] created an interesting construct of trust where he linked ability and motives to different levels of trust. A motive is a contemplated end, the desire for which influences or tends to influence a person's actions (Oxford English Dictionary[30]).

The highest form of trust – 'bonded' trust – is created by someone who has a positive motive and high ability. If the motive is negative but ability is high, this creates 'unstable' trust. If the motive is high but the ability is low, this is hopeful trust. If motive is low and ability is low, a climate of mistrust is created.

A supplier looking to sell customer experience software was asking a series of questions to define the ROI benefit of a solution. Are the motives for the questions driven by the supplier-centricity mindset, because they have been told to ask ROI questions of me because they are under pressure to close the sale? Or is it that they are trying to help me by being client-centric? The answer is that I simply do not know – we are more at the unstable trust level.

The idea of different levels of trust makes intuitive sense. Later in this chapter we explore the relationship between Consalia's positive and negative mindsets and the construct of progressive trust.

Maister et al (2002: x), authors of the seminal book *The Trusted Advisor*,[31] write:

> with ever increasing frequency, clients conduct a microscopic examination of their providers' bills, challenging expenses, questioning how projects were staffed, and how much time various tasks required... There was a time when clients trusted professionals automatically, based solely upon their honourable calling.

They argue that unless you earn your client's trust, you will fail to get access to clients more often and fail to persuade the client to make introductions to others in their organization. This, therefore, reduces the chance to cross-sell solutions to customers.

Their construct of trust is based on the equation:

$$T = \frac{(C + R + I)}{S}$$

where T = Trustworthiness, C = Credibility, R = Reliability, I = Intimacy, S = Self-orientation.

They suggest that the client–advisor relationship evolves, as shown in Figure 6.3.

Like Andaleeb, Maister et al recognize the importance of ability, ie subject-matter expertise, and, like Andaleeb, they also suggest that there are different levels of trust in a relationship. Let's consider the analogy of going to a surgeon (subject-matter expert) to have a serious operation. Do I require a personal relationship in order to elevate them to trusted advisor status? Probably not. If I had to have a heart operation, I would not care whether I liked this person; the only thing I would care about is whether they are capable of doing the

FIGURE 6.3 Depth of personal relationship

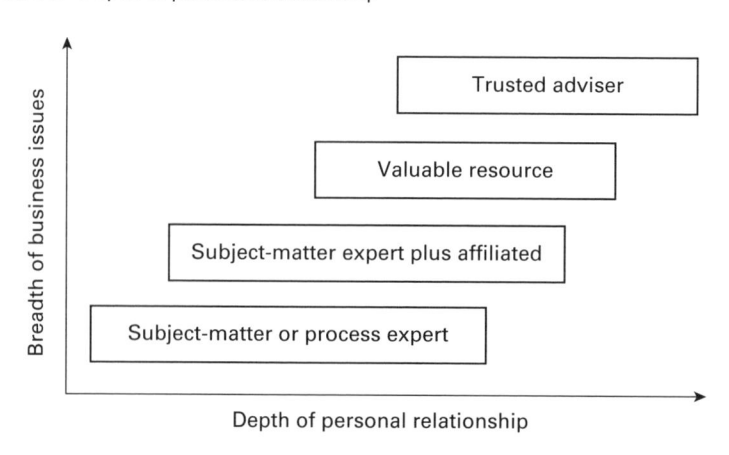

operation to the highest standard. However, given the choice of selecting from two surgeons who are equally as capable, we would probably choose the surgeon with whom we had a better personal relationship.

Where there is choice, relationships are a differentiator

In sales, it is rare to find a market where there is no choice. Therefore, we can conclude, as do Maister and others, that relationships are critical when a buyer has choice, ie most of the time! So to what extent do values influence trust and therefore the basis on which good relationships are formed?

How do the values impact trust?

There is a direct link between trust and mindsets. Figure 6.4 explains how trust can be strengthened when the customer recognizes the salesperson is living the positive values and weakened when living the negative values. It's possible that over time customer perception changes.

For example, at the point of sale, there is often a honeymoon period where both parties are excited to work with each other and where high levels of trust exist. However, over time, if expectations are not being met or the salesperson becomes complacent, their perception can change and change quickly. We have seen this with the Robertson's case, where the chief financial officer said that trust quickly diminished when they were convinced the motives of the account manager were negative.

Is there a difference between being 'trusted' and being 'entrusted'? For example, is it possible for someone to trust another totally but not entrust them with certain information or certain tasks? Clearly this is an important question for those wanting to create strategic buyer–seller relationships.

What 'ability' earns the right for someone to be entrusted? If ability can be defined as the quality in a person that makes an action possible, it goes beyond the knowledge and skills that someone may possess to how that person *thinks* and connects, be it data, intelligence and/or relationships. This ability is particularly relevant in our VUCA[32] world, where the world is changing so fast that people cannot be expected to necessarily have the knowledge, but can be expected to have the capacity to know where to get the knowledge if so required and the mental capacity to connect the dots. This is a rarely seen capability according to customers we have interviewed.

The customer will perceive you as a trusted supplier, not yet a trusted advisor, if the main values they observe are authenticity and client-centricity.

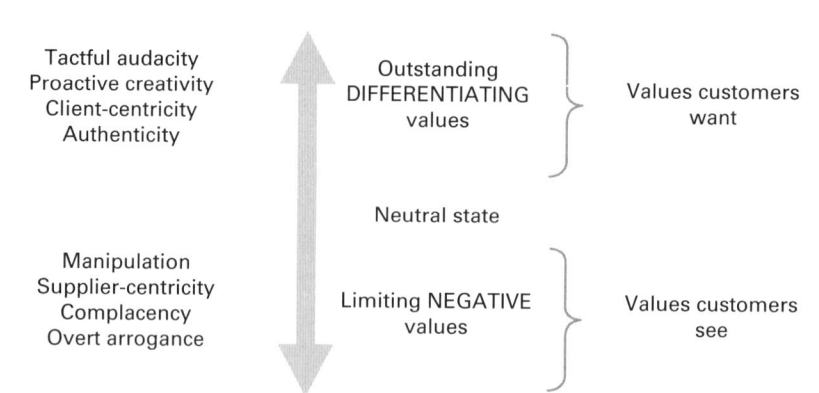

FIGURE 6.4 Consalia's hierarchy of values – progressive trust in 'brand'

Tactful audacity / Proactive creativity / Client-centricity / Authenticity	↑ Outstanding DIFFERENTIATING values	Values customers want
	Neutral state	
Manipulation / Supplier-centricity / Complacency / Overt arrogance	↓ Limiting NEGATIVE values	Values customers see

Arriving at the winner's circle is when the customer perceives the salesperson living the values of proactive creativity and tactful audacity. Similarly to Andaleeb, we suggest there are degrees of trust and mistrust (Figure 6.4).

We can link the mindsets to progressive levels of trust, where earning the right to be entrusted requires all four mindsets.

We often ask groups of sales directors what would they prefer – a team of salespeople with the right mindsets but not necessarily with the right skills, or a team with the right skills but the wrong mindset? One hundred per cent of the time they say they would prefer those with the right mindset. Often, though, we find when they talk about mindset they use words such as tenacity, perseverance, the desire to win, etc – but if these are the only ones that matter, they are mistaken. They often lead to behaviours that are seen by customers as living the negative mindsets.

Different types of assessment can be taken to define selling mindsets. The most legitimate are ones where *customers* assess the salesperson/team on lived values. These perceptions are then contrasted with their self-assessment of lived values and their manager's perception of the salesperson's lived values – a 360-degree perspective.

We have, though, had a lot of fun with the simple questionnaire in Table 6.1, in particular when the results are shared amongst peers. It's not a bad starting point. So if you are interested, log on to www.consalia.com/mindset-survey, enter your name and email address, and you will receive an automated chart showing you your perception of the balance of your positive and negative selling values. Be honest in your answers.

TABLE 6.1 Consalia Mindset Survey

Name:
Date:
Instructions:

Please answer the following 20 questions as honestly as possible. The survey should take less than 10 minutes to complete. Each question has two statements; make sure to read both carefully before answering. When answering a question, you must provide a numeric value for both statements on a scale of 1–7, where 1 = 'never true' and 7 = 'always true'. The sum of the two statements must not exceed 7 – an example has been provided.

		Score
Example	I believe in developing long-term relationships with customers.	5
	I believe that customers often take their suppliers for granted and therefore always put our interests in a deal first.	2
Q1	I believe in developing long-term relationships with customers.	
	I believe that customers often take their suppliers for granted and I therefore always put our interests in a deal first.	
Q2	To be in sales is to be manipulative.	
	I never make my customers feel pressured to buy.	
Q3	I enjoy thinking 'outside the box'.	
	I often think that I know my customers better than they (the customers) do.	
Q4	I keep up to date with our own products and services.	
	We tend not to invest in insights that are not geared to our own products and services.	
Q5	I deliberately set out to make people feel uncomfortable.	
	I know the limits for how far to push a suggestion with a customer and I do not overstep these.	
Q6	Customers approach me and ask for new ideas.	
	I have always managed to reach my goals with the minimum of effort.	
Q7	I am productive in progressing the project/transaction and take personal responsibility for identifying and solving problems.	
	I have so many accounts to manage that it's impossible for me to be proactive in thinking about what is in the best interest of my customer.	
Q8	People are essentially motivated by self-interest and, in order to win, you need to be better at letting others have their way.	
	All data I present is factual and never manipulated to prove a particular point.	

(continued)

TABLE 6.1 (Continued)

Q9	Once I hit my sales targets, I tend to push future deals into the next quarter/year.
	I spend time reflecting on my customer's issues and what my organization could offer that would add value to the areas they care about.
Q10	I ensure that creativity and innovation are included in the deal-making or transaction process.
	While it may benefit the customer, it's sometimes so hard to get things done internally that it's not worth the effort.
Q11	I never withhold information from the customer or try to cover the truth, even if it is to my own or my company's advantage.
	It's not that I lie but I may not share the full story in order to best position my company's services and products.
Q12	People will exploit any sign of weakness; to counter that I deliberately come across as extremely self-confident.
	I am bold and daring in presentation of ideas and solutions.
Q13	To promote efficiency, we tend to produce standard presentations – customization makes the sale process inefficient.
	I listen carefully to what the customer is saying and ensure they feel they have been understood.
Q14	I have creative ideas which go beyond the customer's brief and can be for any area that would benefit them.
	One can waste a lot of time working on new ideas for customers that will never come off.
Q15	I have a disregard for conventional/traditional thoughts and approaches.
	I know I talk too much and don't listen to customers – but then, as long as it's to their advantage, does it matter?
Q16	I use whatever means to reach my sale targets.
	I am never pretentious.
Q17	I don't care if I hurt someone's feelings; it's all part of the job of being in sales.
	I carefully plan and prepare each audacious approach to a customer – to ensure maximum value and impact and minimum offence.
Q18	As a salesperson I have to be arrogant to get things done.
	Customers consider me forward and audacious and not afraid to stick my neck out.

(continued)

TABLE 6.1 (Continued)

Q19	I am passionate about my role and about helping customers to improve their business or personal situation.
	I do not see the point in carrying out research on our customers before every call or meeting I have with them – often I just don't have time.
Q20	I enjoy being in control of sales conversations in order to I get what I need.
	My customers always find me to be honest, dependable and trustworthy.

Hewlett-Packard case study – evidence linking values to sales performance

The first published evidence that linked the positive values to sales performance was in 2008.[33] The article described was achieved by HP's large deal pursuit teams developing sales strategies on live deals, exploring ways to operationalize the mindsets in a programme called Winning Value Propositions WVP©. This programme involved key members of HP's account teams, solution architects, pricing experts, legal and sometimes marketing executives. Sometimes the customer was involved in the process.

HP's win rates in their Western Europe region at that time had improved by 250 per cent to 67 per cent. By 2009 this had further improved to 77 per cent.[34] This compared to 33 per cent in the Central Europe region (Table 6.2).

Finally, the impact of the increased sales performance on market share was assessed. Figure 6.5 shows that over a three-year period, HP increased their market share in the managed outsourcing business from 0.1 per cent to 7.2 per cent.

Furthermore, a number of the deals won by HP have been published: one with the consumer goods giant Unilever, where a memorandum to do the deal was signed in 2007[35] and closed the following year,[36] and another with Anglo American.[37]

The journey for HP had not been easy. Breaking the cultural mindset that existed inside HP was as difficult as changing the cultural mindset with customers. In situations where customers see these deals as purely transactional and where procurement departments are trying to have all vendors compete at the same level so they can compare apples with apples, salespeople have to be particularly compelling, creative and audacious to change the transactional mindset to a values-based mindset. This also applies internally to leveraging

TABLE 6.2 WVP win rates comparison

	WVP	Value	Non WVP	Value
No of deals	13		12	
Lost	3	$342	8	$3,836
Won	10	$4,883	4	$394
Conversion	77%		33%	

across the different silos of an organization, where the same resistance can exist. We found it was important to consciously use the mindsets when seeking to break some of the entrenched silos that existed inside the organization.
So what did we learn about the application of the mindsets?

1 Their application is potentially non-sequential. While there may be logic in starting at building trust at the baseline level – and in that case 'authenticity' and 'client-centricity' is where we would start – in some cases, and where we felt there was nothing to lose, we used tactful audacity as a means of getting noticed.

2 The process of asking the sales teams to just think of the mindsets as they went through the sales cycle was, for many, a liberating and creative process. Essentially, we were recognizing the capability of salespeople to use these mindsets to create their own, and therefore authentic, version of how these mindsets apply to each sales conversation they have. They were developing their own theory of practice, albeit with guiding principles and some frameworks to help their thought processes.

3 The sales mindsets can be seen as guiding principles.

4 We realized that the sales mindsets are a sales operating system that supports sales applications. The applications could be a company's sales processes, or sales methods such as SPIN or challenger, or our own frameworks and specifically designed tools (Figure 6.6).

5 There is a logic to when the positive mindsets come into play during the sales and buying cycle – but at all times in the sales cycle we would advocate that any decision taken, question asked or action taken consider all four. How do 'these' fit with the mindsets? Are we demonstrating the positive mindsets as much as we should? Could we improve?

FIGURE 6.5 Impact on market share

HP's TPI EMEA market share grew from 0.1% to 7.2% over 3 years

and the WVP-based deals grew from 0% to 95% of the total

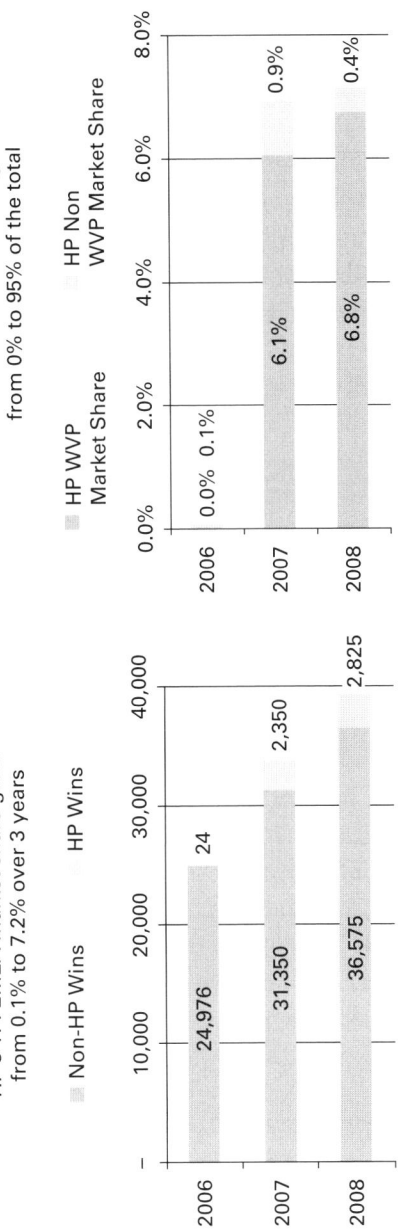

SOURCE Consalia 2009

Values for selling: as guiding principles

We are not born with values. They are developed and nurtured over time. Families, education, religions, culture all play their part in shaping the values we end up living. It is within the capacity of all to choose the values we live as they relate to how we sell – provided we have what Carol Dweck[38] defines as a growth mindset, one that accepts failure as a prerequisite for learning and developing oneself, having an approach to learning driven by curiosity.

Organizations are so preoccupied with the questions 'what do we sell?' and 'how do we sell?' and 'how much do we sell?' that they rarely ask the question 'why do we sell?' What is our purpose for selling? Is it for financial gain? Is it for recognition? Is it to help customers solve problems? What is our motive for selling?

Many salespeople fell into the sales profession accidently; very few seem to have made a conscious decision to pursue a career in sales. Yet many end up in sales for different motives.

In the early days the attraction/motive might have been the chance to earn good money, have a car, be out of the office, have an expense account – the job in a way is incidental. The what you sell and why you sell is perhaps secondary; you may not care too much, just feel grateful that someone out there will give you a job. But customers, as we have seen, will sense the passion a salesperson has for their role, the belief in the product and the desire to help them solve their problems. Success in sales long term – and with it career and financial progression – will entirely be driven by the perception that others have of one's values and to what extent these are aligned with theirs.

So if the outcomes of the research are perceived as being conclusive, how best do we develop a values-based approach? How do we use the values as guiding principles in the way we conduct ourselves in our sales career?

The next four chapters set out some of the tools and techniques that can be used to adopt the values. If we talk about adapting and changing values and belief systems, we are talking about a transformation, as once new values are acquired, a new philosophy of selling and practice of sales develop, making the process both sustainable and irreversible.

It makes sense, therefore, that we first look at arguably the most important of all the principles, the foundation, the value of authenticity.

FIGURE 6.6 Values: the operating system

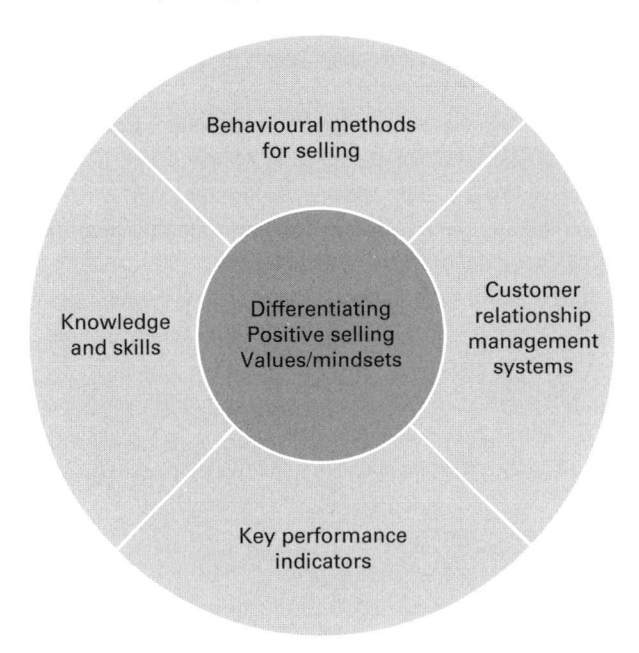

- Behavioural methods for selling
- Customer relationship management systems
- Key performance indicators
- Knowledge and skills
- Differentiating Positive selling Values/mindsets

Endnotes

1. Schell, M (2003) *Buyer Approved Selling*, Approved Publications Inc, Vancouver
2. https://go.forrester.com/blogs/13-01-23-accelerating_revenue_in_a_changed_economy/ (archived at https://perma.cc/4VGX-H9X2)
3. Kohli, AJ and Jaworski, BJ (1990) Market orientation: the construct, research propositions, and managerial implications, *Journal of Marketing*, 54 (April), pp 1–18
4. Homburg, C, Workman, JP and Jensen, O (2002) A configurational perspective on key account management, *Journal of Marketing*, 66 (2), pp 38–61
5. Kempeners, M and Van der Hart, HW (1999) Designing account management organisations, *Journal of Business and Industrial Marketing*, 14 (4), pp 310–55
6. Millman, T and Wilson, K (1995) From key account selling to key account management, *Journal of Marketing Practice: Applied Marketing Science*, 1 (1), pp 9–21
7. Tuli, KR, Kohli, AJ and Bharadwaj, SG (2007) Rethinking customer solutions: from produce bundles to relational processes, *Journal of Marketing*, 71 (July), pp 1–17

8. Wengler, S, Ehret, M and Saab, S (2006) Implementation of key account management: who, why and how? An exploratory study on the current implementation of key account management programs, *Industrial Marketing Management*, **35**, pp 103–12
9. Napolitano, L (1997) Customer-supplier partnering: a strategy whose time has come, *Journal of Personal Selling and Sales Management*, **17**, pp 1–8
10. Ivens, BS and Pardo, C (2008) Are key account relationships different? Empirical results on supplier strategies and customer reactions, *Journal of Business and Industrial Marketing*, **23** (5), pp 301–10
11. Schwepker, CH (2003) Customer-orientated selling: A review, extension, and directions for future research, *Journal of Personal Selling and Sales Management*, 22 March
12. Raimondo, MA (2000) *The Measurement of Trust in Marketing Studies: A review of models and methodologies*, IMP Conference Papers, Bath University, Bath
13. Abratt, R and Kelly, PM (2002) Customer-supplier partnerships. Perceptions of a successful key account management program, *Industrial Marketing Management*, **31**, pp 467–76
14. Raimondo, MA (2000) *The Measurement of Trust in Marketing Studies: A review of models and methodologies*, IMP Conference Papers, Bath University, Bath
15. Castaldo, S (1994) *La fiducia nelle relazioni di mercato. Il caso dell'innovazione di prodotto, Tesi di Dottorato*, Università Bocconi, Milano
16. Zaheer, A, McEvily, B and Perronne, V (1998) Does trust matter? Exploring the effects of interorganizational and interpersonal trust on performance, *Organization Science*, **9** (2) (Mar–Apr), pp 141–59
17. Geyskens, I, Steenkamp, J-BEM, Scheer, LK and Kumar, N (1996) The effects of trust and interdependence on relationship commitment: a trans-Atlantic study, *International Journal of Research in Marketing*, **13**, pp 303–17
18. Andaleeb, SS (1992) The trust concept: research issues for channel distribution, *Research in Marketing*, **11**, pp 1–34
19. Busacca, B and Castaldo, S (1996) *Il poténziale competitivo della fedeltà alla marca e all'insegna commerciale. Una metodologia di misurazione congiunta*, Egea, Milano
20. Doney, PM and Cannon, JP (1997) An examination of the nature of trust in buyer-seller relationships, *Journal of Marketing*, **71** (April), pp 35–51
21. Fletcher, KP and Peters, LD (1997) Trust and direct marketing environments: a consumer perspective, *Journal of Marketing Management*, **13**, pp 523–39
22. Ganesan, S (1994) Determinants of long-term orientation in buyer-seller relationships, *Journal of Marketing*, **58** (2), April, pp 1–19
23. Crosby, LA, Evans, KR and Cowles, D (1990) Relationship quality in services selling: an interpersonal influence perspective, *Journal of Marketing*, **54** (3), July, pp 68–81

24 Moorman, C, Deshpande, R and Zaltman, G (1993) Factors affecting trust in market research relationships, *Journal of Marketing*, **57** (1), January, pp 81–101

25 Morgan, RM and Hunt, SD (1994) The commitment-trust theory of relationship marketing, *Journal of Marketing*, **58** (3), July, pp 24–38

26 Selnes, F (1998) Antecedents and consequences of trust and satisfaction in buyer-seller relationships, *European Journal of Marketing*, **32**, pp 305–22

27 Swan, JE and Nolan, JJ (1985) Gaining customer trust: a conceptual guide for the salesperson, *Journal of Personal Selling and Sales Management*, November, pp 39–48

28 Swan, JE, Trawick, IF and Silva, DW (1985) How industrial salespeople gain customer trust, *Industrial Marketing Management*, **14**, pp 203–11

29 Andaleeb, SS (1992) The trust concept: research issues for channel distribution, *Research in Marketing*, **11**, pp 1–34

30 https://www.oed.com/search?searchType=dictionary&q=motive&_searchBtn=Search (archived at https://perma.cc/8W2Q-FGTN)

31 Maister, D, Green, C and Galford, R (2002) *The Trusted Advisor*, Simon & Schuster, London

32 https://hbr.org/2014/01/what-vuca-really-means-for-you (archived at https://perma.cc/UHG3-TAAB)

33 Hennessey, D, Hurley, M and Squire, P (2008) Winning large complex sales activities at Hewlett-Packard, *Velocity Magazine*, **10** (4), pp 31–33

34 Consalia 2009

35 https://www8.hp.com/us/en/hp-news/press-release.html?id=170269 (archived at https://perma.cc/2LQH-VT8P)

36 https://www.zdnet.com/article/unilever-in-675m-hp-outsourcing-deal/ (archived at https://perma.cc/XTE8-DRNS)

37 https://www8.hp.com/us/en/hp-news/press-release.html?id=171441 (archived at https://perma.cc/WP4H-BVBK)

38 Dweck, C (2017) *Mindset: Changing the way you think to fulfil your potential*, Random House, New York

07

Principle one: the value of authenticity

So how did we end up with the word authenticity and not, perhaps, integrity as the *lead* core value for salespeople?

It's worth spending a short while just exploring their meaning. Authenticity means the quality of being real or true.[1] Arguably the word also has a dimension that goes beyond 'fact'; the word also infers a richness. It originates from the Greek *authentikos*, which means original, genuine. The word integrity means a steadfast adherence to a strict moral or ethical code. Both these 'values' are hugely important to customers and are referred to jointly in our descriptors in the Appendix.

Whereas moral and ethical codes have different nuances depending on culture, authenticity can be used universally and consequentially. We found it to be universally accepted, globally. It appeals to Eastern cultures, which can be cynical about some of the Western proposed approaches to sales training, and also appeals to those in Western cultures who like the freedom of a less prescribed approach. Finally, we liked the link to the word 'original' and from that originality. The authenticity 'principle' allowed salespeople the 'space' to explore 'individuality' with 'originality' at every stage of the sales cycle.

This has important implications for the way in which salespeople are trained. Any sense of scripted conversation suggests unoriginality, inauthenticity and therefore erodes trust. As we stress: the research suggests that customers look beyond the spoken word, to seek the inner persona to understand how this person will act or not react during a sales cycle.

At a personal level I am sure we can relate to the fact that if we are meeting people for the first time, we often look beyond the spoken conversation to understand more about how they tick. Likewise, do not expect a sales conversation to progress unless the customer is satisfied that the account manager can be trusted.

People's reliance on intuition to make decisions

Judging whether or not someone can be trusted is not a precise science, and much relies on intuition – rightly or wrongly.

We will first explore the role and importance of intuition using a non-sales example. Here's an interesting account of how intuition led to the correct assumption – what's real and what's fake – based on two textile conservators working on a very valuable iconic talismanic robe for a national museum in Asia.

The curator of the museum had bought a robe from a well-known and reputable New York dealer, who had had the robe authenticated by a textile expert, as is normal practice.

At first there was no reason to believe that the robe was a fake. Indeed, it's understandable that textiles that are hundreds of years old are repaired – sometimes quite extensively – in order to extend their use, such as the case with this robe. However, in spite of the garment being sold by a reputable dealer and bought by a well-respected museum curator, the conservators had this 'sense' that there was something slightly wrong about it. Neither spoke to the other about their concern at first.

However, on further investigation there were a number of things that just did not quite work. For example, the lining of the costume did not fit properly. The stains they saw were too consistent a pattern – 'they did not seem accidental enough'. By this time they had spent one and a half days analysing the robe and they were definitely of the view that this garment had been heavily altered or re-stitched.

Even then it had not occurred to them that the whole robe might have been fabricated or faked – they just thought at this stage that it might have been over-repaired, which sometimes happens.

Then one evening one of team woke up: 'It was like a bolt of lightning. I realized that the staining was deliberate and had been painted on.'

Once they realized there was an intentional act to distract or deceive, they then decided to look at the garment again – through an entirely different lens. This time it all just slotted together. They realized, however, that they needed to test an adhesive that was used extensively on the garment. It was then confirmed that the adhesive was less than 20 years old, which proved the robe was a 'fake'.

The journey of these two conservators started with intuition; something was troubling them that it was not quite right. Then they used their experience to try to fit the pieces of the jigsaw together. The major breakthrough in their analysis of the garment was based on the *concept of intent*. When they looked at the same robe, but now through an 'intent to deceive' lens, not an 'intent to repair' lens, their analysis made sense.

All the evidence they considered confirmed quite clearly that the museum had purchased a fake textile. Those who had fabricated the robe had done so to profit through deceit. This analogy can be used very much in the sales process, with both salesperson and buyer looking for the other's 'intent' behind the spoken word, the way questions are phrased, the body language.

Is the buyer just wanting to get a better price from their existing supplier by inviting us to tender? Is the seller telling us everything we need to know or withholding information?

The fact that they used the word 'sensing' and 'not quite right' immediately upon seeing the textile is an example of how humans have the mental capacity to figure things out, even when we may not have data held in a conscious way.

Malcolm Gladwell expands on this theme in his book *Blink*.[2] The opening chapter of his book describes the celebration of a hitherto unknown Roman statue purchased for millions of dollars and subjected to a forensic test to assess its authenticity, which it passed. Well, it may have passed the laboratory tests, but it failed the test of the two eminent art historians who came to the opening private view and within a few seconds both said they thought it was a fake. Their instincts were later proved to be right.

It's interesting that it's often the emotional side of our brain that makes the decisions, and sometimes illogically. Daniel Kahneman[3] of *Thinking, Fast and Slow* fame, who received his Nobel Prize for his work on judgement and decision-making, describes two systems of thinking. System One is more instinctive and sometimes takes shortcuts in arriving at decisions. The other, System Two, takes more effort and is more logical. Humans, he argues, struggle to think statistically. We fail as a race to associate reasonable probabilities with outcomes.

This has important implications when selling. The use of 'structured logical reasons and insights' as to why our solution may be best, without appealing to the emotional context of a relationship, is dangerous – particularly if we agree with Kahneman that most humans make decisions using System One thinking.

Let us also revert to Professor Julian Birkinshaw's hypothesis described in Chapter 3, that we are perhaps entering the post-knowledge era, where 'emocracy' is a source of competitive advantage – emocracy being the emotional attachment to a brand or person that represents that brand. If we accept this as true, it's important that we are completely in tune with the emotional, sometimes unspoken, discourse that takes place between ourselves and buyers. Whether or not a buyer formed the right or wrong assumptions about the values of a salesperson, their perceptions are their reality. This requires considerable self-awareness and being in tune with the real you, the authentic you. It also requires you, as you assess your customer, to be consciously in tune with any bias that may filter incorrectly your judgement of customers.

In the same way that the conservators sensed something was odd about the robe, buyers sense the authenticity of salespeople. Their experiences with mis-selling or poor salesmanship will influence the lens through which they evaluate people, often coming to points of view on character that are based on no seemingly obvious logic.

The difference is, though, that unlike the experience of conservators, who rarely work on deliberately faked textiles, buyers have for centuries experienced salespeople who have over-sold and under-delivered. This poses a big challenge for salespeople. The lens through which buyers first evaluate salespeople is often an 'intent to deceive' lens, making it even more important that the salesperson builds trust.

Once trust is broken, it takes a very long time for it to be rebuilt. Buyers have been so scarred from poor experiences of salespeople that those salespeople who are good have to work very hard to overcome the initial cynicism that exists at the outset. It is a guilty until proven innocent process that makes selling, particularly to new customers, so much harder.

Authentic self

The question now is, 'how do we build awareness of what our authentic self is?' For this we again have to refer to our core beliefs and values. Remember that what customers will observe is behaviour, and behaviour is just the tip of the iceberg. Values lie hidden (Figure 7.1). Customers' perceptions will be influenced by what they see – it's not what you say that matters, it's what you do!

When asked, 'what are your values?' we encounter two responses. One, 'I have never really considered what they are.' The other is a quick, clichéd, more superficial response, with words such as integrity, family and honesty.

How best to assess your lived values

In order to determine your core belief systems and values, we have found it helpful to spend a considerable amount of time in reflecting on your actions and reactions in order to determine your underpinning values. To do this

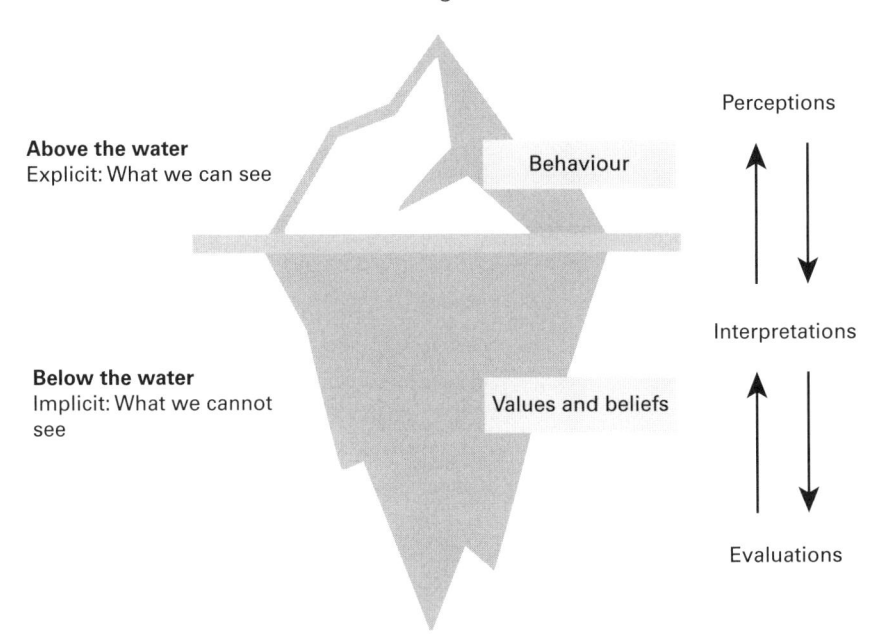

FIGURE 7.1 Values and behaviours iceberg

Above the water
Explicit: What we can see

Below the water
Implicit: What we cannot see

Behaviour

Values and beliefs

Perceptions

Interpretations

Evaluations

effectively you need to consider your lived values. It's important to define what we call lived values, as these are the values through which others will judge you.

We will demonstrate a fast way of addressing this question and then a more reflective way. Let's look at the fast way first.

There are a number of methods that can be used. The method below provides a list of 105 values (see Table 7.1) and asks you to form your point of view from this list. It's in two parts – the first part is to explore your personal values; the second is to explore your work values. Have a go!

Part A: Explore your personal values and mindsets

1 Look through the list and identify up to 15 that are your strongest values in life. This is not about work – it's about your personal values. Then choose your top five.

2 Can you identify one or two encompassing mindsets that reflect those values? (For example, family and friends are the most important thing; how other people view me is how I measure my own value.)

3 Consider as you do this what influences in your life may have helped develop these values and mindsets.

TABLE 7.1 105 values

1	Ambition	36	Responsibility	71	Respect
2	Service	37	Dedication	72	Fun
3	Equality	38	Creativity	73	Intuition
4	Integrity	39	Intelligence	74	Self-control
5	Charity	40	Pride	75	Enjoyment
6	Competence	41	Self-confidence	76	Environmentalism
7	Individuality	42	Kindness	77	Punctuality
8	Loyalty	43	Bravery	78	Faithfulness
9	Credibility	44	Empowerment	79	Reputation
10	Honesty	45	Religiousness	80	Comfort
11	Innovativeness	46	Capability	81	Passion
12	Teamwork	47	Humility	82	Health
13	Excellence	48	Empathy	83	Audacity
14	Accountability	49	Selflessness	84	Ingenuity
15	Quality	50	Sustainability	85	Dependability
16	Efficiency	51	Contentment	86	Open-mindedness
17	Dignity	52	Happiness	87	Trust
18	Collaboration	53	Cunning	88	Directness
19	Accomplishment	54	Knowledge	89	Composure
20	Courage	55	Challenge	90	Persuasive
21	Wisdom	56	Family	91	Spontaneity
22	Independence	57	Nurturing	92	Imagination
23	Security	58	Truthfulness	93	Frugality
24	Challenge	59	Freedom	94	Modesty
25	Influence	60	Spirituality	95	Politeness
26	Learning	61	Affluence	96	Encouraging
27	Compassion	62	Recognition	97	Being the best
28	Friendliness	63	Strength	98	Wealth
29	Discipline/order	64	Effectiveness	99	Curiosity
30	Generosity	65	Beauty	100	Tact
31	Persistency	66	Altruism	101	Duty
32	Optimism	67	Approval	102	Resourcefulness
33	Dependability	68	Instinct	103	Rationality
34	Flexibility	69	Development	104	Assertiveness
35	Logic	70	Leadership	105	Cooperation

Part B: Workplace values and mindsets

1 Now look through the same list and repeat the activity – only this time think about your values in your workplace. As before, now choose your top five.
2 Can you identify one or two encompassing mindsets that reflect those values and beliefs?
3 What influences in your work life may have helped develop these values?
4 Reflect on the differences between the two lists and identify possible reasons.

Sharing and discussing your results with those who know you can also help clarify your values. Remember, the truest judge of your lived values will be *how others* see you. Your customers, peer group, friends and family's points of view will help shape and deepen your understanding of your own core values and lead to considerable clarity.

There is no right or wrong answer and we have found it is perfectly possible to have different work values from home values. In most cases, though, there is an overlap.

Now link the values that you have determined for yourself and compare those with the values that customers want from salespeople. Are there values not listed or selected that you would like to develop? This process will certainly raise consciousness about how you perceive yourself and how others perceive you.

A second, more reflective approach is to consider 'critical, memorable, poignant, crisis' episodes in your private and work life. Explore *deeply* how you felt at the time and *consider what action you took or did not take* following these episodes. Then ask yourself: what do these actions, non-actions and feelings expressed at the time tell you about your values? What evidence is there to confirm these values are true? The process requires what we call critical reflection.

Critical reflection – a core competence for salespeople

Adopting the four 'principles' potentially requires new thinking and developing new habits – in this case, habits to improve sales practice. The challenge for salespeople is that there is often not enough time to think, let alone read, or to think critically about problems.

The term critical reflection is widely used in education; master's projects, for example, are assessed and scored on the ability of sales managers or salespeople to critically assess situations and problems.

The skills of critical reflection are helpful in solving problems or diagnosis and in that sense this skill is of real value to customers – a salesperson who can critically reflect is more likely to listen more carefully, understand 'my' needs more thoroughly. Yet it's not a word that is often used in traditional sales competence frameworks.

Critical reflection is absolutely key in this fast-changing world in which we live. Customers respond well to salespeople who can think deeply about problems or opportunities, as this provides reassurance that their needs will be properly considered and better solutions provided.

What is critical reflection?

It's a reasoning process and it takes into account what happens before, during and after an experience. It goes beyond a description of what the experience was. It questions why, the feelings that were felt at the time, asks 'what if' questions, and challenges us with thinking about how something could be done differently.

A number of critical thinking methods and frameworks will be introduced in later chapters. Gibbs'[4] reflective cycle (Figure 7.2) is one that is particularly well suited when reflecting on experiences. It comprises six steps. Often in time-scarce situations, the second and third steps are missed entirely or not conducted thoroughly.

The steps are described in more detail below.

1. DESCRIPTION

- What happened? Briefly describe the event as objectively and concisely as you can. Where did it happen? Who was involved?

2. FEELINGS/THOUGHTS

- What were you thinking and feeling at the time?
- What were you thinking and feeling afterwards?

3. EVALUATION

- What was good and bad about the experience?

FIGURE 7.2 Gibbs' reflective cycle

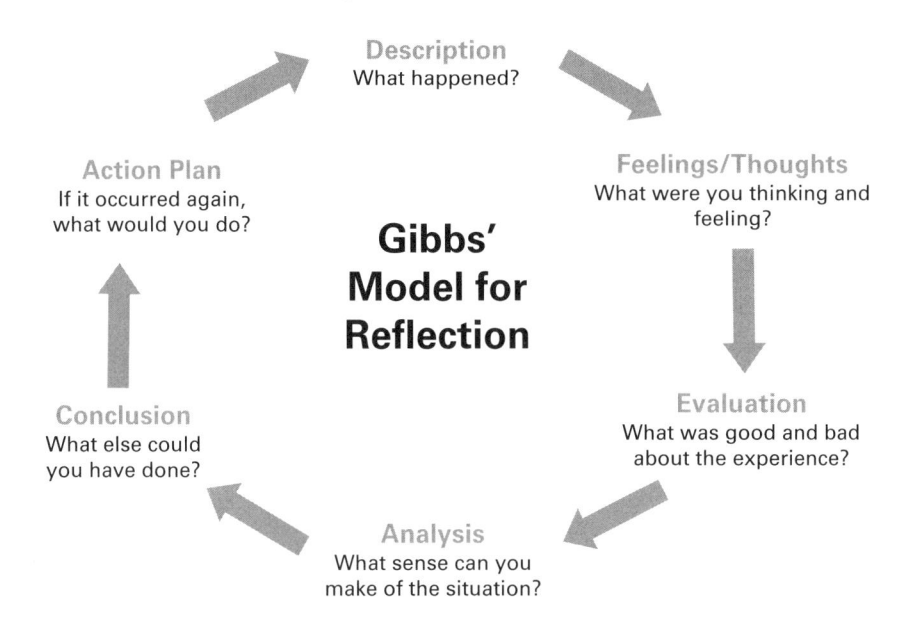

Gibbs' Model for Reflection

- **Description**: What happened?
- **Feelings/Thoughts**: What were you thinking and feeling?
- **Evaluation**: What was good and bad about the experience?
- **Analysis**: What sense can you make of the situation?
- **Conclusion**: What else could you have done?
- **Action Plan**: If it occurred again, what would you do?

4. ANALYSIS

- What sense can you make out of the outcome?
- What were the factors that affected the outcome?
- What helped and hindered?
- Why did it happen?

5. CONCLUSION

- What else could you have done?
- What might have been some alternative actions or approaches?
- What could you have done differently?
- If a negative event, could it have been avoided?
- If a positive event, could it have been even more effective?

6. ACTION PLAN

- If it happened again, what would you do?

- What would you do differently?
- What would you do differently in light of this understanding?

The following example shows how Gibbs' reflective cycle can be applied. It takes an example of someone who is wanting to link personal values with the values of selling. As values are often shaped in our early years, we take an example of someone reflecting on a pivotal event at school to better understand their values.

> I often think of Peter. Surprising, really, because he wasn't that much of a friend. I rarely think of Martin, the boy who bullied him. I was around ten at the time and since the age of nine had been sent to boarding school. As younger boys we slept in larger dormitories of 12.
>
> Maybe the independence helped – the independence that you get when you have to make do with what you've got; the independence you get when you have to fight your battles to survive the local playgrounds.
>
> The time before lights out was for reading. I don't know why on this occasion Martin decided to get out of bed with a container. We could hear the dorm master ringing the bell on the floor below for lights out, so I guess he felt it was safe.
>
> Peter was tall, quite lanky, pasty looking with reddish brown hair. He kept himself to himself and had few friends. He slept in the bed next to mine.
>
> Martin, on the other hand, was popular, very good at sport and was looked up to. I can't recall exactly what Martin said about Peter and why, was it about his red hair? Was it about the fact that he was shy? He started to go around the room telling the others, 'spit ... spit into the container', which they did.
>
> I remember looking across the dormitory, watching as the other boys, laughing quietly, spat into it, jeering across at Peter. I could hear him beginning to cry.
>
> Experience or feelings
>
> I felt this knot inside me, a knot of fear and anger, not knowing which of these two would surface. Fear – wondering how I would respond to Martin when I was instructed to spit – he was a much bigger boy than me. I was physically terrified of him. Anger at what he was doing to Peter, anger at how he was manipulating the other boys to follow his example. Anger at the injustice of it all.
>
> I looked into the potty and the spit, and something went inside me. Something quite terrifying as it was not in my control. With uncontrolled rage I punched Martin hard in the face. His head flew back. The potty smashed to the floor. He arched back and fell to the ground. The room went silent – save for

Martin sobbing by his bed. Me shaking from the horror of it all, surprised and shocked at my fury. Peter and the other boys in stunned silence.

The master ran into the room. Saw Martin on the floor. The matron was called. I was sent to the head master and was punished for what I had done.

Evaluation

I did not blame the school for the punishment. I felt they had no choice. But surprisingly I found that the hate that existed before between Martin and me developed into cautious respect. He never repeated that action again; he never goaded Peter. We never spoke about it. Peter was never again bullied to my knowledge.

I felt very uncomfortable with the lack of control and that the lack of control could be dangerous. But what triggered the anger? If I could find the root cause of the anger, I could avoid this in the future.

Analysis

Where did this fury come? It took some time to figure it out. It took me back to an experience some years earlier.

I was six or seven years old at the time. For some reason John, who was much older than me, picked on me – I have no idea why. Perhaps it was to show off? Perhaps he saw me as a threat? He organized an area next to the flats where I lived at the time. He ordered me to meet him for a fight. He got the other children from the compound to come and watch. He threatened me not to tell my parents. I fought him two or three times. I explained the cuts and bruises to my parents as falling off my bike. Then on one occasion John tripped, fell over and badly cut his head. On returning to his home he said I had deliberately tripped him up. Quietly I wished I had.

I found myself being asked by my parents, who were told of the incident, to explain myself and later was told I had to apologize.

Experience or feelings

I did not like being cornered or bullied. I felt it was okay to react as I did with Martin. I felt it was okay to stand up for others, as I had experienced what it was like to be on the receiving end. I felt there was injustice yet justice in how events panned out.

> Conclusions
>
> What values do 'I' possess from my reflections?
>
> - justice;
> - fairness;
> - courage;
> - loyalty;
> - independence;
> - resilience;
> - responsibility;
> - passion.

This process of understanding one's values can then be linked to the values customers look for in salespeople. In the example above:

- Courage supports 'audacity'.
- Justice and fairness support a moral code and therefore 'authenticity'.
- The lack of control of emotion, ie the fury that was expressed, is perhaps something to work on. Could 'tact' be missing? Could a more considered and controlled approach be more effective? Might 'independence' be a problem when working for a corporate?
- Passion is what customers look for from salespeople – with belief.
- Tenacity and resilience are key attributes for salespeople and linked with proactive creativity.
- Loyalty to Peter is linked to client-centricity.

Code of ethics

As mentioned earlier in this chapter, the principle of being authentic implies a moral code through its link with the value of integrity.

The Covid-19 pandemic clearly tested the ethical values of both sellers and buyers and we witnessed good and bad extremes on both sides.

Take the Harley Street doctor who made £2.5 million in a week by selling testing equipment at inflated prices. Take procurement, who are using the pandemic to call for price reductions, as witnessed on a recent sales conference call.

The Association of Professional Sales (APS), a not-for-profit body, has through consulting with its members set up a code of ethical practice for salespeople. Those signing up for membership of the APS effectively sign up to the following:

1 Maintain the highest standards of integrity in all business relationships.
2 Provide customers with a buying experience in which sales 'do the right thing in order to get the right results'.
3 Promote and protect good sales practice.
4 Always act in line with my organization's codes and within the law.

For those interested in testing their ethical sales approach, it's possible to conduct a short test.[5]

Mental health and stress

Finally, a few words on values and mental health – some observations and a word of caution.

The process of self-reflection to properly challenge and develop personal values, to find your authentic self, can result in what we call 'living contradictions', meaning that salespeople are sometimes asked to do something by their managers that clashes or contradicts with their personal values – in extreme cases it can lead to high levels of anxiety and mental health issues.

This could be expressed in, say, a manager putting extreme pressure on a salesperson to close a particular deal in advance of it being properly qualified. Or a salesperson being asked to sell a product that is inferior to one that is superior and soon to be launched. Or a salesperson who is being asked to recognize, in a forecast, sales revenues on deals that have no chance of being closed, in order to meet pipeline targets.

The point at which these contradictions cause too much stress is the point at which one leaves an organization.

Your values become your guide and as such govern your personal practice. Defining the authentic you is a foundation block for the next three chapters.

Endnotes

1. https://dictionary.cambridge.org/dictionary/english/authenticity (archived at https://perma.cc/3WC2-G3JW)
2. Gladwell, M (2005) *Blink: The power of thinking without thinking*, Penguin Culture, New York
3. Kahneman, D (2011) *Thinking, Fast and Slow*, Penguin, New York
4. Gibbs, G (1988) *Learning by Doing: A guide to teaching and learning methods*, Further Education Unit, Oxford Polytechnic, Oxford
5. http://store.professionalacademy.com/aps-professional-sales-registration-sales-code-of-conduct/ (archived at https://perma.cc/N3CR-ZA5H)

08

Principle two: the value of client-centricity

It's not just about the customer; it's their entire ecosystem, including partners, suppliers, customers, competitors. Client-centricity requires curiosity, interest, passion to do the right thing for the client, going the extra mile to find out more, going the extra mile to leverage more value for the customer, demonstrating non-autobiographical listening skills. It's consistently searching for new knowledge of the customer's business and looking for ways to add value to their business.

This chapter describes in a case study a particularly clever way the value of client-centricity was lived with an account team who had very little customer knowledge at the outset of a buying cycle but who ended up winning a large sale. We then describe a number of analytical tools that deliberately test our understanding of our customer's business. These tools can be used to elevate our knowledge of the customer and influence the questions asked of customers during client interviews.

A global mining business study – using a client-centricity mindset to win a new account

This first case stands out as an example of how the mindset of client-centricity was used to win a major new account. A 'win' came from nowhere and against all odds.

The chances of winning a new customer through a formal request for proposal process are pretty low. Eighty per cent of the time such contracts are awarded to the incumbent supplier. In this case an RFP from the mining conglomerate referred to as Allied Mining was emailed to Technology Services Company (TSC). The challenge for TSC was that they had no account manager assigned to this account.

The lead came through to the special bid team, who then organized a meeting to evaluate the RFP. The sales opportunity was to run Allied Mining's data centres globally. Allied Mining had made it clear they really wanted TSC to bid. TSC were very excited about the opportunity; technically they knew they could deliver a great solution.

But here was a sales opportunity from an organization that they knew very little about. They knew about the risks involved. They knew that in pre-sales costs alone, to respond and take part in the bid would be circa $1 million. Furthermore, there is the opportunity cost to consider. Committing a team to work on this deal exclusively for six months would be at considerable opportunity cost. But then again, with a deal value of over $250 million over five years, surely this was worth pursuing.

Traditionally – and desperate to win new business – the team would normally have signalled their intent to respond. They were under huge pressure to hit the aggressive sales targets set. Plus they had access to pre-sales funds for such a project.

This is what happened. They wrote a letter, emailed it to the Allied Mining contact who was running the bid and said words to this effect:

> Dear Sir, we really appreciate the opportunity you have provided us to respond to your RFP. We have noted your comment that you would really like us to bid. We have taken this opportunity seriously indeed; we brought together a team of our most experienced solution architects and project managers to review the RFP. Our conclusion, having studied the bid, is that we feel that whilst TSC is indeed extremely well placed to respond, we feel that in this case we can't. So it is with regret that we will not respond.

The view was taken by the sales team that Allied Mining could take one of two actions:

- If Allied Mining were serious about TSC being one of the bidders, they might come back.
- If, however, Allied Mining simply saw TSC as being a means of knocking down the prices of the incumbent, they would probably just acknowledge their letter and not care to follow up.

It was a gamble, but the team knew that unless they were allowed to build relationships with the client and really understand the client's business more intimately, there was no chance of winning. Relationships can't be built at arm's length. Here the team was considering very seriously the client-centricity value, hoping the client would come back in some form, but not expecting them to do so.

The gamble started to pay off. The project lead for the account team got a call from Allied Mining:

> Given what you wrote in your letter, why did you not respond? We were frankly a little disappointed.

To which the project director replied that they did not take the writing of the letter lightly; they did indeed want to pursue the RFP but felt that as they had no account manager on the account and therefore no serious relationship with Allied Mining, they knew the chances of winning were small. The project director ended by saying:

> If we had a relationship with you, our response would, we are sure, have been different.

At which point Allied Mining asked:

> Well, what would you like to know about us and how can we best achieve that?

Anticipating this question, the project director said:

> It's quite simple: we would really like some time talking with your technology team to get a perspective, ideally globally, of the issues you face. We really want to understand better the context for the reason the RFP was raised. In fact, we think the incumbent perhaps has an unfair advantage over us as they have information and relationships we lack.

The Allied Mining contact responded by inviting two of the TSC team to a meeting of their global CIO managers a couple of weeks later. Of course TSC agreed and the two of them went to the meeting. Indeed, it was very productive. They sensed that those present were keen to get to know TSC; they also picked up in some of the nuanced conversation that the incumbent was not doing a great job and that Allied Mining did not altogether trust them.

They returned to the office, convened a meeting and optimistically reflected on what they had learned. However, they concluded that there were still some serious gaps in their knowledge. They did not know what the IT department's 'customers' really cared about – without that knowledge, they were still very vulnerable. Whilst they had gained some more insights and started to get some trust in the client and vice versa, they felt they needed to know more.

So, what did they do? They wrote another letter saying that they hugely appreciated the chance to meet the team and that meeting them made them feel much more comfortable about responding; however, they were still of the opinion they were not in a position to bid. They would like, if possible, to visit some of the mines in order to better understand how IT supported the mines themselves. If they could do this, they would respond. Allied Mining readily agreed to set up some meetings and the TSC team kicked into action. They visited three mines at various locations in the world.

This is where the story gets interesting.

The account team quickly realized how vast these mines were. It could take hours to get through security and to the HQ for the mines. They realized, just in this small detail alone, that what was being asked of the IT vendors, in terms of service level agreements, was impossible to deliver on. A two-hour KPI to service or respond to an IT problem was unrealistic.

Furthermore, in speaking with one of the mines' general managers (GM), one of the TSC team discovered that what kept the GM of the mine awake at night was keeping the mine working at all times. Down time is lost profits. Keeping track of assets in a mine, particularly the people working in the mine, was critical. If any person became unaccounted for, the mine would have to stop operations.

This interest in understanding the 'customer's customer' produced a much deeper understanding of Allied Mining's business context. Fresh insights were providing hugely important information – information that would be used later when returning to the UK to swing the deal in TSC's favour.

As far as the client was concerned, TSC were demonstrating uniquely high levels of client-centricity. No other vendor had taken this approach.

By this stage TSC had realized that they had effectively created a competitive advantage in this pursuit. During their update calls with the customer, they sensed that the customer was excited about the efforts TSC were making to get to know them.

On the team's return, what did they do? They met Allied Mining, shared their experiences and said that the RFP was not written as well as it needed to be, as no vendor could deliver to the terms set. Furthermore, they said:

> We learned that one of the things that keeps the mines shut down is not knowing where their assets are. We have some asset-tracking technology being developed at our laboratory that we think you should take a look at. We know

this is not part of your RFP requirement, but we think you have nothing to lose by the visit.

As a result of the initiative, TSC were asked to rewrite parts of the tender. They knew, then, they had the upper hand in the sales process and now had earned the right for a deeper level of collaboration with the customer in their buying cycle. TSC ended up winning the confidence of this new client in a relatively short time – just seven months – and with that confidence knew that they had won the deal.

They almost doubled the contract value as, along with the server deal, they won an additional telecoms opportunity.

This interest in the client was the defining moment – but what took the thinking beyond most account teams' horizons was in defining who the client was. The moment they realized that the client was not the IT department but the IT department's customers, ie the mines, they began to differentiate their approach from the competition. This genuine curiosity and desire to align the right solution to serve the operational units of the mine was reflected not just in redesigning the tender document, but also in the language in which the business outputs of their solution was framed.

The learnings from winning the Allied Mining deal helped to develop a more client-centric culture across the organization. All sales executives were asked to assume that whatever they knew about the customer was not enough. Sales teams were encouraged to continuously research the customer.

Client-centricity involves knowing not only your customer and your customer's customer but also the industry of your customer. But what tools and resources can be used to build our knowledge of the customer?

They will vary from more simplistic techniques, such as simple internet-based research and qualification questions used to define the customer's requirements asked during meetings, to more strategic tools used to delve into much deeper levels of knowledge.

Cracking the industry code

I was fortunate enough to work with two renowned professors at IMD[1] – both specialists in global account management. They argue that in today's competitive landscape, it's not enough to know your customers and their customers; it's also essential to know of the industry in which the customers operate.

For example, knowing the critical factors that drive profitability in, say, the automobile sector would help sales teams selling into that sector. The flooding in Thailand[2] caused factories as far away as Kentucky to close temporarily to conserve parts. There is so much economic interdependence globally. Whilst driving down cost of production by setting up factories in different countries could lower cost, it could also increase risk. The Covid-19 pandemic vividly demonstrates the risk associated with interdependence of key elements of the supply chain.

Just having this level of industry knowledge can help generate those priceless insights that can lead to making significant contributions to winning value propositions – as seen in the example below.

One of the world's largest manpower services providers, referred to here as MSP, was looking for a new enterprise resource planning (ERP) software solution to transform their business efficiency.

The sales team assembled to study the opportunity realized they knew too little about this customer and, on this occasion, we invited a financial investment analyst to dial into a workshop we were facilitating. Analysts are an incredibly useful source of data – they spend all their time studying an industry and the major players within it. An hour of their time is priceless in getting to know more of the drivers that affect a business.

It was here, during the MSP deal, that we realized that the focus on the customer's customer is sometimes not the answer.

The analyst explained that MSP's business is very cyclical; these cycles sometimes last years, and it's to do with finding labour and staff to fulfil demand in some cycles and then finding clients in other cycles. The issue for MSP, the analyst said, was not about the customer wanting to find customers to grow its business; it was about making it easy to find temporary staff to place. Demand was high – no shortage of customers – but supply was weak. This insight on the supply chain led to a completely different understanding of how to position their solution. What the team did was to offer their knowledge of web portal development in addition to the ERP software as part of the solution. Their creativity and client-centricity were rewarded with a contract.

Account teams, according to Hennessey and Jeannet (2003),[3] need to learn their client's requirements for success in their specific industry. They need to 'crack the code' of the industry.

The industry code is the behaviour required from an organization to assure long-term success. It must be met to achieve profitability and success. Violating this code would endanger a business's profitability.

The code needs to contain a collection of 'musts' – things that a company must do. These are different from core competencies, which just describe what a company does well. Musts are important for a company to know because they are the factors that will influence long-term success.

Included in the industry code are key success factors (KSFs). These are the basic competitive requirements that an industry participant has to master for long-term success. Typically, key success factors describe basic actions or industry behaviours that winning companies must master. They can be categorized into:

1 qualifiers – which determine if a participant is able to 'play' in an industry;

2 differentiators – which set players apart from others.

All industry participants must comply with the qualifiers, but only some may perform on differentiators.

Tool 1: for cracking the code

1. What are the 'must segments' for the customer?

Must segments are those segments in which a company must be present in order to be a major player. These segments will be important due to factors such as their relative size, above-average profitability, growth, technical development, etc.

2. What are the 'must combinations'?

Must combinations, or bundles of segments, represent the next level of understanding. Many industries frequently need to be in several segments, not just one. The choice of segments is vital. The company needs to be able to assess the bundle of segments that best fits its requirements.

3. What is the minimum amount of coverage required?

What is the minimum amount of market coverage needed in order to reach strategic goals? For example, a company may need to have access to 60 per cent of the total market opportunity to be a leader, but it could reach its strategic objective with less.

4. What is the required critical mass?

This is the minimum size required to be competitive or successful. Critical mass may occur around a company's entire volume, or may be more relevant if assessed by segment, country/geographic unit or key function (eg minimum research and development budget).

5. What is the required level of integration?

The industry code may require different levels of integration to be successful. Forward integration deals with the ownership or control of the downstream part of the industry. Backward integration concerns the upstream aspects of ownership or control. Understanding the relevant amount of integration and its impact on profitability is an important part of sizing up the industry.

6. Identify focus and/or restrictions

Identifying the required focus, or restrictions, on selected activities can be an important part of the industry code. Where should a company focus? Focus dimensions might include integration levels, range of products, range of segments, geographic spread, range of technologies, etc.

7. What are the strategic dilemmas being faced?

Strategic dilemmas are critical questions being faced by company CEOs that cause senior executives to lose sleep at night.

8. What are the major dilemmas being faced by the industry?

Dilemmas could be centred on forward or backward integration, segment focus, bundles of segments, mastering of single or multiple technologies, etc. Dilemmas manifest themselves through choices or decisions to be made – or determining which 'forks in the road' to take.

So how can we test how well we know the customer?

Tool 2: the customer pulse check

The customer pulse check is a checklist of questions that can help determine how well we know the customer. It's described as a 'pulse check' because the customer's situation changes or can change so quickly. It is based on the EFQM (the European Foundation for Quality Management). The fundamental concept of EFQM is based on the following seven pillars:[4] driving performance and transformation; stakeholder perceptions; leadership strategy and constancy of purpose; strategic operational performance; organizational culture and leadership; stakeholder engagement; and creating sustainable value.

They enable us to look at and assess a customer's business as if we were management consultants. It is a microscope we can use to examine their business and it provides a great test of how well we know our customer. These questions are asked in the context of the current economic environment – clearly in challenging Covid-19 times, priorities will have dramatically changed.

Driving performance and transformation

1. What is your customer's current financial situation? What do their balance sheet and income statements reveal? What is your customer's cost structure and cash flow?
2. Is your customer financially/fiscally 'healthy'?
3. What does your customer think would improve their financial position?
4. What are the sticking points or challenges with their financials?
5. What are your customer's long-term financial goals? Where do they want to be in a year? Three years? Five years?
6. What are your customer's business and individual performance metrics?
7. What is their source of competitive advantage?
8. How has your customer been performing for the past three years?
9. What are the metrics for the next three years and how do they plan to achieve them?
10. What would help your customer to increase performance against these metrics?
11. How will your offer help your customer meet and exceed their financial objectives?
12. How will your offer help your customer to reach their near-, mid- and long-term strategic goals?

Stakeholder perceptions – the customer

1. How do customers (end-users) talk about your customer?
2. What type of company is your customer perceived to be?
3. How does your customer want to change these perceptions?
4. Why do end-users switch to one of your customer's competitors?
5. Why do end-users remain with your customer?
6. What attracts new end-users to your customer?
7. Who is your customer's end-user (demographics, psychographics)?
8. Who are the 'hot' end-users? Today? Tomorrow? Why?
9. How is the end-user changing?
10. How much does your customer spend on customer acquisition?
11. How does your customer listen to their customers to obtain actionable information?
12. How will your offer improve your customer's ability to improve the way they interact with their customers?

Leadership strategy and constancy of purpose

1. To what extent is the customer a purpose-led organization?
2. What is their purpose?
3. What are their stated values? How committed are they to their values?
4. How has this changed?
5. What are your customer's strengths and weaknesses in creating the future?
6. What is 'success' for your customer? What is driving this definition?
7. How does your customer plan to achieve this success? What would help them?
8. With what does your customer feel comfortable and what are their concerns?
9. What change initiatives are going well and what is not going well for your customer?

10 What are the C level key performance indicators? (Understanding C level key performance indicators helps you to know the priorities of the C suite. If your solutions can be shown to positively impact these KPIs, they will be seen as being highly relevant.)
11 How will your offer improve the way you support the organization's purpose?
12 How will your values align with the customer's values?

Strategic operational performance

1 How does the customer seek to increase operational efficiencies?
2 How does the customer seek to reduce operational costs and to what degree?
3 What are the key metrics to measure operational performance?
4 How does the customer's supply chain flow?
5 What and where are the customer's critical supply chain challenges and vulnerabilities?
6 What is the customer doing to improve supply chain performance?
7 What systems and technology does the customer use to enable their operations and supply chain? What is their online strategy?
8 How does your customer ensure that their suppliers are qualified and positioned to enhance performance and increase customer satisfaction?
9 How does your customer evaluate supplier performance?
10 What is the customer's situation with suppliers – eg is the market dominated by a few large suppliers, are there many suppliers or is there one key supplier on which they depend?
11 Can the customer be flexible with suppliers or are they constricted by high switching costs?
12 How will your offer improve your customer's processes to reduce cost or increase revenue or margin?

Organizational culture and leadership

1 How is your customer organized to achieve and sustain their vision?
2 What capabilities and competencies do they need to develop to implement their strategy?

3. How does your customer recruit, hire, place and retain new members of their workforce?
4. How does your customer manage and evaluate organization and people performance?
5. How does your customer prepare their workforce for changing capability and capacity needs?
6. How does your customer develop a high-performance organizational culture?
7. What commitment do they have to continuous learning?
8. What is their organizational culture?
9. How empowered are employees?
10. What do ex-employees say about your customer?
11. How in tune with their strategy is their culture?
12. How will your offer impact the customer's employees?
13. How will your offer impact the decision-makers' reputation?
14. How will your offer impact their culture?

Stakeholder engagement

1. What ecosystem does your customer rely on to compete?
2. What is their partner strategy? Who are their key stakeholders?
3. What percentage of the customer's income comes from channel partners?
4. How important are partners to your customer?
5. How do they segment their partners?
6. What support do they provide their partners?
7. What is the risk in their partner channel?
8. What other associations or public bodies are they connected with?
9. What entry/exit constraints exist for these segments?
10. How does your customer plan to retain their partners and acquire new end-users and markets?
11. What political influences do they have?
12. How can your offer or your organization impact their stakeholders?

Creating sustainable value

1 What is their corporate social responsibility (CSR) strategy?
2 What environmental policies do they have? How committed are they to achieving these?
3 What goals and targets do they have in achieving their CSR strategy? To what extent are these being reached?
4 What are their diversity targets?
5 How can your company's products, services and support help your customer to enhance their brand position with these end-users and in these markets?
6 How is the customer's brand perceived?

The Allied Mining case study is about how to win new business using a highly customer-centric approach. But how does an organization begin to transform its culture from being supplier-centric to customer-centric, and how might 'this' translate into business performance at an account manager level?

What follows is a great example of how one organization is transforming its culture from one that is based on technical excellence (we are technically great at what we do) to a culture based on customer-centricity.

Professional services technical consultancy group (ConstructXion)

This case study explores two questions:

1 What initiatives might be taken to transition from a product-centric to a client-centric culture?
2 How might this culture impact on sales performance transformation at an account level?

1. How to transition to a client-centric culture

ConstructXion is a multi-billion-dollar professional services consultancy operating out of more than 100 offices worldwide, and employing over 10,000 people. Their projects vary in size from the hundreds of millions to the thousands. Until very recently they had no account management structure. They have won business through technical excellence, the winning of awards and word-of-mouth recommendation.

These are the key initiatives they took.

LISTEN TO THE VOICE OF THE CUSTOMERS

The journey started with video interviewing and researching a number of their customers about how they were perceived. They found that customers were asking ConstructXion to leverage more of their considerable expertise to bring value to them, to be more overtly confident in their ability. These 'voice of the customer' interviews were to become a critical catalyst for the cultural change the organization was then wanting to make.

One of the challenges they faced, as with many professional services companies, was to make a shift from working in the business, ie on short-term projects, as opposed to on the business, ie developing the business for a sustainable future.

DEVELOP APPROPRIATE KPIs

Many lawyers, accountants and other professional organizations face this challenge. Their focus on billable hours stops them from standing back and taking a more strategic view of customers, ie spending the time to look for servicing the customer requirements at a holistic level. A consultant who has a particular discipline would be very good at projects on which that discipline would be required. An energy expert would look for energy projects and not look for transportation opportunities or smart city projects. This model did not lend itself to driving a client-centric approach. The organization created a remuneration system that allowed these account managers time to manage their accounts without being penalized.

It was to prove quite a challenge to ask the consultants working on client projects to stand back and strategize and have a more traditional account management role with existing clients.

ENSURE EVERYONE HAS THE APPROPRIATE TOOLS, SKILLS AND COACHING SUPPORT

A global WVP® development programme[5] for the newly selected 150 account managers was instigated. These programmes took account leaders through the customers' perspective of ConstructXion, using the 'voice of the customer' interviews. They were also trained on the mindsets, tools and thinking frameworks; peer coaching sessions encouraged the sharing of learnings across different regions.

In parallel, a number of what they call high premium accounts were selected for special focus. These were the accounts that they felt would particularly benefit from the mindsets approach and where there was high potential for growth.

The high premium account leaders meet collectively with the main board directors on a biannual basis. They report back on progress made and share ideas to discuss any additional resourcing requirements to grow the account.

SET UP A PROJECT TEAM AND ADOPT A CHANGE MANAGEMENT APPROACH

What has enabled this organization to succeed is that they have approached this from a change management perspective. The Kotter[6] model was the framework they used to drive the cultural change. Using the model they:

- created **urgency** by asking customers what they wanted of Construct-Xion's account management approach – this compelling need to change was the call to action;
- formed a **powerful coalition** by asking a team of senior executives to work with the main board to drive the change;
- created a **vision for change** through a rebranding exercise that put the customer at the centre of all their activities;
- **communicated the vision** through workshops run globally;
- **removed obstacles** through board sponsorship and adapting internal time sheets to ensure the account leaders were not penalized for spending time on client development activities (rather than billable projects);
- looked for the **short-term wins** through a particular focus on the high premium accounts and celebrating wins through the prestigious Chairman Awards;
- **built on the change** through ongoing training;
- **anchored the change** through a well-established awards programme, regular updates on wins, and in working with HR to establish account leadership as a fast-track career development option.

2. How a new culture achieved sales transformation at an account level

We now pick up a story relating to their Asia-Pacific subsidiary. The board had recognized that their organizational structure did not lend itself to being client-centric. It was formed of separate technical practices led by consultants who were focused on searching for projects that would keep them busy and their billable hours up. Whilst this resulted in winning a number of discrete projects, it wasn't a scalable strategy. They were not winning the larger deals.

The board decided to appoint a new leader of a transport sector that would be responsible for developing a commercial strategy across all transportation disciplines. John joined ConstructXion at the time the company was starting the account leader programme in earnest and then became the new transportation sector leader. At the same time, an Asia Pacific-based public sector transport agency was selected to be a high premium account.

CHANGING THE SALES TEAM'S BELIEF: CAN WE WIN LARGE DEALS?

The first important challenge John faced was how to change the team's mindset, as few of his current team, in the early stages, 'really believed ConstructXion could win large deals' because they were used to hunting out the discrete projects referred to earlier.

The issue was not whether the larger deals existed or not; it was how best to build the team's confidence that ConstructXion could win these opportunities. Much of that depended on the confidence that 'our' customer had in 'us'. ConstructXion had to earn the trust of the customer and earn the right to compete in the large deal space.

Challenge our knowledge of their business 'We really discovered how little we knew of the customer – we did not know of their vision, we were not that well known to key decision-makers.' So, every time a new project came up, John explained, 'we challenged our understanding of their business through the strategy grid, and it took the best part of a year for us to feel that we really understood the vision of Transport Agency.' This is not totally surprising given that Transport Agency is a complex, matrixed organization employing several tens of thousands.

A major realization came to the account team. While they were thinking about roads, trains, light rail, etc (ie from a perspective of their technical disciplines), this was not the language that Transport Agency were using. There is nothing expressed in their published values that talks about roads and trains:

- **Consumer focus:** We place consumers at the centre of our business.
- **Innovation:** We deliver innovative and sustainable solutions.
- **Team work:** We respect each other. We create better outcomes by working together.

- **Integrity:** We take responsibility and communicate openly.
- **Safety:** We prioritize safety for staff and consumers.

Focus on customer experience – Transport Agency customers' experience As John explained, 'It's not about designing a road or a tram line for them – it's helping *their customer* get from A to B and giving them a good customer experience.' Once the team had deeply understood what Transport Agency cared about, they were better placed to align the rail or road projects that emerged as RFPs with the vision of Transport Agency. This was to influence *everything* the team did in their response. Design proposals were linked to efficacy and the customer experience: 'we talked more about the value of our proposals rather than our services.' Their approach was less about selling ConstructXion and more about the value they would bring to the customer's customer, together with an alignment of ConstructXion's values with theirs.

Focus on the customer's customer This shift in mindset to focusing on the customer's customer and then working back to consider 'what do we have in our portfolio that would impact what our customer cares about?' is fundamental to developing a client-centric approach. Many salespeople, though, start with the question, 'what do we have that we can sell to a customer?' and 'how will we sell it?' This supplier-centric approach is the instigator of many of the behaviours that relate to the negative values/mindsets described in Table 5.1 in Chapter 5.

CREATE A VISION FOR THE ACCOUNT

The vision statement for the account created by the ConstructXion account team reads as follows:

> Supporting Transport Agency with our national and international expertise across multiple disciplines **to focus and understand their customers' needs** and provide safe, reliable, efficient and affordable transport systems.

As you can see, it sets the direction for all account selling policy. The team's focus on the customer's customer is used to guide their response to all opportunities that they pitch for.

LEVERAGE INTERNAL RESOURCES

Up until 2016, Transport Agency were awarding ConstructXion small projects worth less than $80,000. In 2017 they won their first big order for

$100 million. This was attributed to a highly collaborative team effort, both locally and globally, as John and his team leveraged the ConstructXion capability in other regions to bring value to the agency.

Salespeople's perspective is often that it's harder to sell ideas internally than sell to customers. Being client-centric requires considerable creativity and influencing skills in leveraging internal resources to maximize value for customers.

For example, metro/subway developments in other countries provided the evidence of ConstructXion's capability for handling a project of this magnitude.

The multiplier effect It was clear that ConstructXion was now beginning to be seen by Transport Agency as a trusted partner. Furthermore, this larger contract enabled them to broaden and deepen relationships across Transport Agency and increase their understanding of 'what Transport Agency was all about'. It was to become the catalyst for further change and developments.

Another unexpected and major breakthrough came when Transport Agency voiced some frustration about the efficacy of their procurement process. As ConstructXion was developing the designs for the 'Metro', the client was invited to their office and was able to comment in real time on the designs proposed, using their digital design technology. It allowed the two-week design decision-making process to be reduced to one day. As John elaborated, 'It also meant that we did not have to print hundreds of drawings.'

Seeing this technology in action made Transport Agency want to apply the technology elsewhere. Over time, Transport Agency were enabled to run focus groups with consumers, providing them with 3D images of station layouts. Amendments to design could be made in real time.

ConstructXion became more and more integrated with Transport Agency, even to the point that they now have, as with other clients, managers working on the client site permanently, leading a team of Transport Agency employees focused on 'digital engineering'. This level of collaboration was unprecedented.

Business impact

So, what has transpired since is remarkable. Although there are no major infrastructure projects to bolster revenue, such as the Metro project,

ConstructXion has been rewarded with other consulting projects and seen their net revenue rise six-fold over four years.

Furthermore, the client feedback was positive:

- ConstructXion 'think differently' – they bring innovation and are not afraid to challenge.
- ConstructXion are not constrained by sectors or practices – they deliver as a holistic organization.
- ConstructXion invest in what they care about.

While this case study shows that it takes time to develop a strong and trusted brand, it also shows what can be achieved in a relatively short time by taking a more strategic and client-centric perspective of a client.

It also demonstrates that even in the public sector, where salespeople say 'the winning of bids is only about price', it's possible to develop a more strategic and value-enhanced relationship for both parties while at the same time respecting the ethics of a rigid procurement process.

Sales transformed

The before and after comparisons demonstrate just how transformative the journey has been. ConstructXion's competitors could have done the same as ConstructXion, but didn't.

This account team, with the right mindsets applied in their daily account-supporting activities, has become the source of competitive advantage.

The case study is an extraordinarily good example of the right mindsets applied as lived values and is now an approach that will be replicated on other accounts.

The following sequential steps can be observed in their approach:

1. **You:** The team first focused on the customer as 'you' – a study of the customer's values helped them realize that consumer experience was their primary concern.
2. **Us:** They then took a careful look at what services they had that could provide value; they were creative enough to consider assets they had that were not mainstream products, such as procurement.
3. **Connect:** They were careful not to pitch for business that was not their core competence; they connected their expertise with the customer.
4. **Evidence:** They leveraged experience as case studies from across the group to prove their ideas could be implemented.

TABLE 8.1 Before and after

Before the WVP® development programme: supplier-centric mindset	After the WVP® development programme: customer-centric mindset
Small-deal mindset	Large-deal mindset
What services can we sell?	What value can we bring?
What can I do?	What can *we* do?
Respond to client tender	What new ideas can we bring?
No understanding of customer vision	Deep understanding of customer vision
Team located at ConstructXion's office	Team located at the client site and ConstructXion's office
No contact with Transport Agency end customers	More engagement with Transport Agency end customers
No key account plan	Collaborative key account plan
No leverage of global resources	Much support leveraged from ConstructXion globally

Table 8.1 provides a summary of the transformation that has taken place, showing how the account team applied the organization imperative to become client-centric.

This chapter has focused on client-centricity – the second of the two positive mindsets. As we have said earlier, authenticity and client-centricity are the baseline for developing trust, but it's the next two mindsets that take relationships to a much higher level of strategic engagement and will earn the right of the account team to get into the winner's circle. The next two chapters suggest how this can be done.

Endnotes

1   Hennessey, HD and Jeannet, JP (2003) *Global Account Management Creating Value*, John Wiley & Sons, Chichester
2   https://www.reuters.com/article/us-toyota/thai-flooding-impact-spreads-across-world-for-toyota-idUSTRE79Q43I20111027 (archived at https://perma.cc/JGN6-U54H)
3   Hennessey, HD and Jeannet, JP (2003) *Global Account Management Creating Value*, John Wiley & Sons, Chichester
4   https://www.efqm.org/index.php/efqm-model/ (archived at https://perma.cc/K3Z4-3C8L)

5 WVP is a programme developed to help account teams win large deals and develop large accounts. It uses the specific Consalia mindsets as the basis for developing selling strategies and tactics.
6 https://www.kotterinc.com/8-steps-process-for-leading-change/ (archived at https://perma.cc/WU8A-GZKR)

09

Principle three: the value of proactive creativity

Proactive creativity requires a more strategic thinker, being one step ahead, coming up with ideas that the customer has not thought about before, believing that through collaboration new ideas can be formed – using subject-matter experts where they see they lack key knowledge from both inside and outside their organization. These could be big ideas or little ideas or even crazy ideas – as long as these ideas are grounded in the first two values described above. Lead with the relationship; once trust is built, it's easy and more believable (from the customer perspective) and the salesperson will not be seen as complacent.

The genesis of the value of proactive creativity as a value came from the Starbucks case study. Starbucks created their value proposition for the multi-million-dollar vendor investment in internet capability by realizing the value of their 'third place' and selling this value to vendors like HP/Compaq. As their strategy was based on creating an environment so their consumers would want to visit their Starbucks store, they knew everything about their customers. Consumer demographics could include age, gender, geographic, average spend, average amount of time in store, when this time was spent in store, how frequently each customer returned to the store through loyalty cards, etc. These were the very customers the mobile telephony companies wanted to sell to.

Figure 9.1 explains their thought process. They started with the question, 'What do we care about?' They then asked the question, 'What do we have that our vendors/suppliers care about – ie the third place?' Finally, 'How do we value what we have?' And then, 'How do we pitch this idea?'

But we asked what would have happened if the idea had originated from one of the vendors *before* Starbucks had even thought of it (Figure 9.2)?

FIGURE 9.1 Third place thinking from the buyer's perspective

Starbucks started here...

Step One
What do we care about?

- Customer loyalty
- Market share
- Increasing global footprint
- Our brand
- Delivering shareholder value
- Our reputation
- Our value proposition to customers
- Our cash flow
- Investment risk
- Health and safety

We worry about:
- changing consumer behaviour
- the threat of new entrants (at the time internet cafés)

How will we fund the capital investment required?

They then went here...

Step Two
What do we have?

Third place: our stores and our customers

- We have millions of customers.
- They have a certain age profile.
- They represent a certain economic grouping – young professional, etc.
- They are located in this geographic/demographic.
- This is their average spend.
- This is their loyalty.
- This is their frequency of purchase.

They care about:
- being in a cool place
- drinking great coffee and quality food hygiene
- no effort
- consistency

They care about Starbucks' corporate sustainability and responsibility policies.

A great place to work and catch up with friends and great access to the internet.

They then went finally here...

Step Three
How do we put a value on what we have and how do we pitch this idea?

The value proposition to potential suppliers:

Invest in us through your technology and we will enable you to get your brand in front of our customers, our consumers – a market you have absolutely little knowledge of. You can leverage our knowledge of this market to sell your mobile telephony solutions.

FIGURE 9.2 Third place thinking from the seller's perspective

What if we, the vendor, started our thinking here in the third place...

Step One
What do Starbucks customers care about?

They care about:
- being in a cool place
- drinking great coffee and quality food hygiene
- no effort
- consistency

They care about Starbucks' corporate sustainability and responsibility policies.

A great place to work and catch up with friends and great access to the internet.

Then went here...

Step Two
What do Starbucks care about for themselves?

- Increasing customer numbers
- Improving their demographic of customers – young, professional, tech-savvy
- Increasing average spend
- Improving loyalty
- Increasing market share
- Increasing global footprint
- Delivering shareholder value
- Improving reputation
- Developing value proposition to customers
- Increasing cash flow
- Reducing investment risk
- Health and safety

Deal with changing consumer behaviour – the tech-savvy.

Manage the threat of new entrants (at the time internet cafés).

Concern with losing market share and great access to the internet.

They finally went here...

Step Three
How do we put a value on what we have and how do we pitch this idea?

The value proposition to Starbucks:

We can work with you to build on the third place environment that will encourage your most profitable customers, the young professionals, to spend more time there through our XXX solution, increasing the chance to increase the average spend per customer and decrease the risk of them spending time at the newly emerging internet cafés. This will also help increase traffic at the stores at less busy times, as a new customer segment – the remote work professional – will seek out the store to work from and meet customers.

We also see the potential in a technology partnership that co-creates new concepts in mobile telephony.

Tool 3: the third place from the seller's perspective

Being proactive requires thinking more reflectively and deeply about the customer. Starting the thought process, in this example, from the customer's customer perspective forces a more client-centric approach and provides the intellectual space for creativity from which new ideas can be developed.

The Summit Value Group, a sales consultancy group based in the USA, coined the term 3rd Box Thinking™. It neatly captures the process suggested above: the third box relates to the customer's customer, the second box the customer, the first box the supplier.

The biggest blocker to creative thinking is the way salespeople traditionally approach sales opportunities. They start their thought process in the wrong place, ie the first box.

Breaking with tradition

Most salespeople naturally have a thought process that is based loosely on the following 'cycle'. What are my sales targets, and how do I sell my portfolio, ie products, to prospective and existing customers in order to hit my target? Such is the pressure to meet or exceed targets that it becomes an all-consuming past time. It's all-consuming as sales reps are bombarded with calls from product managers keen to have the latest data on how their products are selling and sales managers who maybe don't care about what products are being sold as long as the overall revenue targets are being met. This pressure transmits from the management to the salesperson and then to the customer.

Customers sense the pressure through the questions being asked, the readiness to offer discounts in order to clinch deals, particularly at quarter end, and the relentless phone calls. In extreme cases, the phone calls to the customer come from the rep's manager trying to clinch a deal. It's easy to understand the sales culture of an organization from this kind of approach. It's not pretty – as one customer said of a salesperson, 'the pressure is so intense it's almost hormonal.'

To live the values of proactive creativity, this 'cycle' *has* to be broken. It's not easy to break as it's counterintuitive for many – but for those who master the cycle, they enter the winner's circle, and will find it easier to close deals, develop a healthier pipeline and broaden and deepen relationships.

Let's contrast two sales approaches with the same opportunity

Boohoo is one of the world's fastest growing etailers. Headquartered in Manchester, UK, they have a fast-growing international business. Sales are increasing at 44 per cent per annum.[1] They sell great-quality clothes, shoes and accessories at unbeatable prices. They are an online retailer; they lead the fashion e-commerce market for 16–40-year-olds around the world. As at 31 August 2019, the boohoo group had around 13 million active customers.

Any orders placed before 11pm will be delivered the next day. Their investment in new warehousing and logistics centres enables them to provide a state-of-the-art supply chain solution, but they rely on parcel delivery to deliver their customer promise. This investment also helps future-proof a dramatic global sales increase. They have capacity to support a £3 billion turnover business (as of the 2019 accounts, turnover was £856.9 million).

Their 2019 accounts revealed they shipped over 30 million orders – an increase of 128 per cent over the year before!

Clearly this would be a significant opportunity for a parcel collection and delivery vendor. So given this data and the chance to win a lucrative contract, what would be the traditional sales cycle for a potential parcel logistics salesperson?

This is a traditional thought process.

The salesperson will ask, 'What is it that we have that could help us create the best competitive offer?' The sales team may come up with arguments to win that include: we do national delivery; we can offer a pick-up service from your depots during the night to meet your next-day delivery process; we offer a state-of-the-art tracking service so you and your customers can track where the parcels are at any time; we offer very competitive prices; we have customers who have similar logistics requirements so we can cope with a project of this size and complexity; we have a very good NPS (net promoter score), etc.

The problem with this approach is that creativity is immediately curtailed as the lens through which the sales team is reviewing the opportunity is already limited through what we call supplier-centricity bias.

As most suppliers will respond in this way, boohoo's procurement department will receive proposals with similar arguments from all the major parcel delivery companies. No one can blame boohoo's procurement department for selecting the vendor with the lowest price.

Those in the winner's circle will not play that game. This is how they can break with tradition.

Focus on 'the you: customer's customer'

Clearly a more creative and reflective thought process is required. Starting with the mindset of the customer's customer, think first: 'What value does boohoo need to *create for its customers*?' This question matters more to boohoo than the commodity service of logistics, ie parcel delivery.

Whilst boohoo will want a reliable and cost-effective solution, what they most care about is delivering on their promise to their customers – these being the 16–40-year-old consumer segment located predominantly in the UK, Europe and the USA.

Because boohoo's target customers have little disposable income or don't want to spend much, many leave their purchasing decision, say a dress for a party, to the last minute to maximize their personal cash flow situation. Customer experience for them will be getting a great-looking dress at an unbeatable price delivered *the day before the party*.

As explicitly explained in boohoo's annual report and accounts: they understand the importance of a 'great customer experience' and getting products to their customers when they want them, with minimal effort. They also offer 'free returns' and make sure the customer services team is available to help at all times through a range of different channels.

Reliability is key. Interesting to note, therefore, that reputable damage is highlighted in the boohoo annual report and accounts 'risk register', where they cite 'refund disputes' or poor customer service could 'damage reputation'.

The you: the customer

Now let's consider the question, 'What is the value that boohoo wants to create for itself? What kind of metrics do they look at?'

In addition to the standard financial metrics such as turnover, turnover growth, gross profit margin, cash flow, etc, we can conclude from desk-based research:

- The number of active customers is important.
- Conversion ratios from web searches to orders are key.
- Order frequency is critical.
- Numbers of social media followers are important.
- Average spend per customer drives revenue and profit.

It's also always beneficial to research the values of the company. In boohoo's case, they are:

- passion;
- agile;
- creative;
- team.

Refer to or use these values as the response is formulated – boohoo probably expect their strategic suppliers to reflect their values as a sign of how the parties might work together. One phrase used to describe their 'creative' value is noticeable – 'dare to be different'. Account teams have an open door to do just that – they are actively wanting people to be proactively different.

So it's only now that we finally start to consider the question, 'What is it we have within our product or services portfolio that can impact what the customer cares about?'

The 'us'

Consider both the tangible and intangible assets. But don't just think about your core products and services – we refer to these as 'tangibles' – also think of the 'intangibles'.

Intangibles are any aspect of your organization that could potentially add value to a customer – for example, it could include your brand, your knowledge of international markets, your logistics knowledge, your CSR policies, your social media presence, your advertising programme, your marketing research, your internal educational programmes, your customer base, your R&D programme, your real estate management capability, your ability to develop partnerships, your omni-channel knowledge. Often these intangible assets are taken for granted and become an under-utilized aspect of your sales approach.

Think of the Allied Mining case study we shared in the preceding chapter – the Technology Services Company invited the mining company to check out the emerging intellectual property (IP) from their laboratory. ConstructXion invited Transport Agency to share their environment initiatives and join parliamentary groups looking at this area. None of these suggestions would result in an invoiced sale, but both examples would contribute to a perception of value potentially far greater than the provision of the core service.

The 'connect and the evidence'

In boohoo's case the account team now can consider the question, 'How can we connect what we have to what the customer cares about?' – to search for the synergy between the two companies.

Armed with this more considered research, the account team can be much more client-centric and creative in their response. For example, the parcels company might come up with the following ideas. Please note these are used for illustrative purposes:

- We know refunds management is key. We can help facilitate the pace at which refunds are made through our XXX technology and partnership with Y bank. The moment, for example, a return is picked up by this will trigger a refund into the customer's account. This will potentially enable the customers to reorder more quickly, therefore increasing the number of orders per customer and reducing any potential negative disruption from an otherwise unhappy customer. We know this has never been done before but would like to partner with you to make it happen. You would certainly be the first to do this.

- Whilst this proposal is for the UK market, we understand that the international market is growing at a faster rate and is likely to be where your future sales will mostly be generated from. We would be interested in talking to you about reducing the cost of parcel delivery, if we can increase the scope of the project to cover your international operation.

- Our NPS scores are ten basis points higher than those of our competitors. Two in three online customers are likely to purchase if they know we are delivering.

- We are working in partnership with many of the UK's leading etailers on a government-sponsored research programme to explore how to develop efficiencies in supply chain and omni-channel marketing programmes – we would be delighted to sponsor your joining this group.

- Clearly these ideas are in addition to the core proposal of a competitively priced parcel delivery solution with a service delivery model that meets boohoo's exacting service level agreements.

It's possible boohoo's procurement department will still just buy on price, but there will be more chance of getting through to the next round if creative, relevant and challenging ideas are proposed.

So to summarize – a supplier-centric bias can be avoided by doing the following:

1 Focus first on the '**you**' – think customer's customer first, ie what value do they seek from your customer, then consider the value the customers seek for themselves.
2 Focus next on the '**us**' – think what it is we have that can impact what the customer cares about. Consider the tangible and intangible assets in your brainstorming.
3 Focus then on the '**connect**' – consider how the ideas above connect what your customers care about.
4 Finally consider the '**evidence**' – how will you articulate your value proposition and what evidence can you show that reduces the risk of your proposal?

Tool 4: customer strategy grid

What we refer to as the customer strategy grid (Table 9.1), adapted from the nine-box model,[2] helps to analyse the current market environment and the impact on an organization's strategies and objectives. It helps to increase understanding of a customer, the environment the customer is working in and the *reasons* for their strategies.

Where the customer strategy grid does particularly well is that it both requires a deep knowledge of the client and invites you to apply the values of proactive creativity and tactful audacity. Let's explain how.

To use the grid, first identify the customer's objectives, then complete a SWOT (strengths, weaknesses, opportunities, threats) analysis. The SWOT forms a matrix against which the organization's *potential* and actual strategies can be identified and analysed.

Stage 1: Company objectives

What are they trying to achieve? Financial, vision and in what timescale? Information for this can be gained through careful study of the company's report and accounts. Consider the CEO and chairman's statements, seek analysts' reports, and consult with the client if the existing relationships permit.

TABLE 9.1 Customer strategy grid

Customer objectives	Customer strengths	Customer weaknesses

Customer opportunities	Attacking strategies	Daring strategies

Customer threats	Crushing strategies	Protecting strategies

Stage 2a: Company capability

What **strengths and weaknesses** does the company have, relative to the competition, and what do customers expect? Analysts provide a more objective view of a company's capabilities – they may not be right, of course, but their reputation is at stake if they get it wrong. There are other sources available, such as consumer blogs, end-user group associations and trade press. All of these can paint a picture of the capabilities of the organizations.

Stage 2b: Company environment – opportunities and threats

What external **opportunities and threats** derive from the macro environment and industry forces that the customer operates within? As above, the analysts' reports will be helpful. Sometimes companies publish forward-looking risk statements that suggest threats.

The **grey boxes** (in Table 9.1) are the result of looking at the SWOT information and where they intersect. By completing the 'strategies' to the best of your ability, you will be living the values of proactive creativity and tactful audacity:

1 **Attacking strategies** are for opportunities in the area of company strengths. These are areas where the company can aggressively go after opportunities, where they will focus resources, both people and investment.
2 **Crushing strategies** are for areas where the company is strong but there is a market threat. These threats need to be aggressively crushed and this is often via aggressive pricing, promotions, product development, etc, that crowd out weaker or potential competitors.
3 **Daring strategies** are for areas where the company is weak but there is an opportunity. The company can do something high risk – but with potentially high returns. These are step-outs and more speculative.
4 **Protecting strategies** are for the areas where there is a threat and the company is weak. Classic strategies here are business simplification, process re-engineering and reorganizations. Strategies can also include selective price reduction.

Table 9.2 shows how the strategy grid has been applied to Delta Airlines. Customer objectives have been taken from their annual report. The grid has been completed for illustrative purposes.

We have seen considerable success with the customer strategy grid when account teams have first completed the grid and then shared their ideas with the customer. Even though some of the conclusions may be wrong, customers will in most cases appreciate the effort the sales team has made in thinking at this level with their customer.

TABLE 9.2 Customer strategy grid applied to Delta Airlines

Customer objectives	Customer strengths	Customer weaknesses
Maximize prosperity	Excellent reputation for service	Poor awareness
Global force for good	Convenient flight schedules	Business flyers doubt Delta Airlines' capability of meeting business needs
Increase operating profit from 11 to 14 per cent	Wide choice of destination	Not well known for international routes
Increase earnings per share from 10 to 15 per cent	Safe and reliable journey	Poor liquidity due to financing new planes / net debt down from $19 billion to $9 billion
$6 billion operating cash flow	Sensitivity and understanding towards passengers	Liability to asset ratio is still an issue but cash flow is quite strong
Reduce net debt to $5 billion by two years	Adaptability to needs of its flyers	
	Lack of advanced purchase requirements for international flights	
	Employee relationships with management	

Customer opportunities	Attacking strategies	Daring strategies
Business travellers spend 2–3 times more than leisure travellers	Review its business travel value proposition	Create an innovative social media campaign to raise awareness
Loyalty with business traveller	More innovation around the business traveller value proposition	Can they create a bold, break-away advertising campaign?
A large segment is untapped – the business traveller	Relaunch the brand promise for the business traveller	Link this to loyalty programme
Customers do know and appreciate the quality of Delta Airlines	Invest in wider seats for economy – $750 million	Different planes for different level of service
Setting up of on-board offices for business travellers		

(continued)

TABLE 9.2 (Continued)

Customer threats	Crushing strategies	Protecting strategies
Companies moving towards cheaper alternatives to business	Aggressive pricing	Continue to focus on you – 'you' the employee, 'you' the customer – this is personal
37–46 per cent decline in business travel (general stat)	Launch of low-cost airline or acquire new low-cost airline	Lobby Atlanta to provide improved airport infrastructure services
Highly competitive		
American Airlines: first-class meals for business		
Provision of higher-quality lounges by BA		

Tool 5: whitespace analysis

At the beginning of a joint visit with a salesperson to a telecoms operator in Norway, the salesperson said that the operator was their largest customer and very important. To which the operator replied, 'We may be very large to you, but in overall spend you are not that important to us.' It was a comment about relevance – being relevant and staying relevant and not being complacent.

Complacency sometimes occurs when salespeople sell what they have traditionally been selling to customers over time. It takes little effort to sell repeat orders: arguably this is not what salespeople are paid to do.

Whitespace analysis is a process that considers the overall spend a customer may have and invites the salesperson to consider what the addressable market is. This is a supplier-centric approach; however, the process prevents complacency when considering the customer's needs and requirements by inviting the salesperson to consider the customer's requirements more holistically.

If sales revenue is the only measure of sales success, there is an inherent danger that the sales teams become complacent.

Questions that enable us to review the whitespace are:

1 What is the total market spend? This is the total addressable market for your products and services.

2 What is our customer's spend with us?

3 What is the addressable market? There might be a difference between the total market spend and the addressable market. There may be reasons why you cannot serve the total market spend – sometimes the regulatory environment restricts sales to customers. For example, the big four consultancy firms cannot be selected by their customers to both conduct audit and provide consultancy services – even though they can do both.

4 Size of the prize: this would be the stretch goal set for the account.

Whitespace analysis helps consider the question, 'What do we have that could impact what the customer cares about?' And by doing so, 'What resources do we have as a company that we can leverage?'

To what extent can a national culture be encouraged to live the positive mindsets?

So whilst the two case studies reflect great practice of tactful audacity at an account manager level, this next section combines a national transformation story with an entrepreneur.

Whenever I touch down at Incheon Airport, I am reminded of my father – he fought with the British Army in the Korean War (1950–1953), in which it is estimated that 2–3 million civilians died.[3] It's regarded by many in the military as being one of the most hard-fought wars. Entire towns and cities were destroyed. Seoul itself changed hands four times during the conflict. The war ended in a stalemate.

It's all the more incredible, therefore, to see how South Korea has emerged as the 12th largest economy in the world as measured by GDP. In 1960, for example, the GDP was $158.21 per capita; in 2018 this had grown to $31,362.80. It is currently the 12th richest country in the world.[4]

Much of this growth can be attributed to the reforms introduced by Park Chung-Hee. Park, who came from a military background, seized control of the government in May 1961. In 1963 a government was formed, following which South Korea's dramatic progress started – it is referred to as the Miracle of the Han River.

Park set about encouraging entrepreneurs to lead the charge. Huge infrastructure projects were awarded to an emerging group of entrepreneurs from which the great chaebols (industrial family-controlled conglomerates) were created. His focus was on export-led economic growth. Samsung, LG,

Lotte SK and Hyundai were some of the chaebols created. Many of these are now global brands. What makes the story more remarkable is that South Korea has very little in the way of natural resources. It had to be inventive and tactfully audacious in the way it grew.

I came across Chung Ju Yung's name when on a business trip and heard a remarkable story of how one man's vision led to the creation of the world's largest ship manufacturing business (amongst others!) on the back of a bank note and a photograph of a beach.

He came from a very poor peasant family based in North Korea and made three attempts at an early age to leave home and make his way to the South. By the time this story starts, just after the liberation of Korea from Japanese control, he had created Hyundai; following the war he managed to pick up post-war construction projects through his Hyundai Civil Industries business.

I owe much of my research on Chung Ju to Donald Kirk and his book *Korean Dynasty: Hyundai and Chung Ju Yung*.[5]

Well before President Park was looking to develop an industrialization policy in Korea in the 1970s, Chung Ju had set his sights on ship-building. He initially explored the idea of doing a joint venture with Mitsubishi. Mitsubishi were concerned with Korea's lack of technical skills and proposed the largest ships that they should build were 50,000 tonnes and that all management control would be with the Japanese.

Chung Ju felt that the Japanese were simply wanting to manage the threat of Korea developing a new business to challenge their own. He decided to come to the UK to look for technical and financial support. He visited two ship-builders – Appledore and Scott Lithgow. He offered $1.7 million for their technical support and a commission of 0.5 per cent on sales. Longbottom, the chairman of Appledore (who was later to become quite pivotal in Chung Ju's success), was, like Mitsubishi, very sceptical of Korea's ability to build 250,000-tonne ships; after all, the largest ships built in Korea were around the 17,000-tonne mark – the labour force simply did not have skillsets required. It was when Longbottom challenged Chung Ju that he pulled out a 500-won note.

This particular note has imprinted a picture of the very famous Admiral Ji (1545–1598). Without any naval training he defeated the Japanese in at least 23 naval battles without losing a single ship.[6] Also printed on the 500-won note was an image of the Turtle Ship. These were iron-clad ships and were to be hugely important in the war, deflecting the fired burning arrows and having a much superior canon-firing power.

Chung Ju's response to Longbottom was that 'the Koreans had been building iron ships since the 16th century, long before the British started its ship-building industry'. He then went on to convince Longbottom that 'where there is a will there is a way'. If others had not set their sights on building very large ships, it was because they simply did not believe it could be done. As he believed in his vision, he would make this happen. His conviction persuaded Longbottom.

Now there was the next formidable challenge of raising significant finance – $60 million. Longbottom, at Chung Ju's request, wrote a recommendation letter to Barclays Bank. Barclays agreed to the loan but only on the basis that Chung Ju was able to get an export guarantee to cover the loan. On his return to Seoul, he was told that whilst he could obtain such a guarantee from Seoul's Export Import Bank, they could only provide the guarantee against sales orders. Now he needed buyers.

Here Longbottom was to help again – he put Chung Ju in contact with a UK ship broker, who in turn put Chung Ju in contact with George Livanos, a Greek shipping magnate. Armed with detailed drawings of the 250,000-tonne ship and a photo of the beach where the shipyard was to be built, he met Livanos and returned with orders for two ships!

The rest, as they say, is history. Hyundai built the ships in super-quick time, building the dockyard and ships in parallel. From these early beginnings Hyundai became the world's largest ship-builder.

(Chung Ju's motto was: 'Conviction creates indomitable efforts. This is the key to true miracles. Man's potential is limitless.'[7])

This is a great example of all mindsets at play, but in particular proactive creativity. It's the idea – and the conviction that went with it – that drove this extraordinary salesman. It's indeed amazing what you can do with a 500-won note and a photo of a beach!

South Korea can also lay claim to living the positive differentiating values through the policies of Park in the 1960s and 1970s that allowed the nation to rebuild its battered state. It can now reflect with some pride on its extraordinary achievements.

I wonder to what extent their nationalistic self-confidence is influenced by history? After all, the Silla Dynasty (57BC to 937AD) was one of the world's longest dynasties – providing political and governing stability. Gyeongju, its capital, oversaw a flourishing iron age and then gold age. Being on the northern track of the Silk Route, it was also a hugely important and wealthy trading post. It has had close ties with Persia for over 1,500 years. No wonder, perhaps, that global trade and technical expertise are in South Korea's DNA.

Whilst proactive creativity generates ideas, tactful audacity is required to implement the ideas. For example, the simple attempts to leverage a company's internal resources to bring value to a customer can sometimes require much more effort and courage than selling to the customer! In the 'injection moulding' example in Chapter 3, it would take tactful audacity to first approach the CEO with the idea that a different procurement strategy could result in reducing the time to market from 20 days to 4, particularly if there was no current relationship. There is a big difference in coming up with an idea as opposed to executing on the idea.

Endnotes

1 https://www.boohooplc.com/sites/boohoo-corp/files/all-documents/4412-boohoo-ar-2019.pdf (archived at https://perma.cc/55NC-NRE3)
2 Marcos, J, Davies, M, Guesalaga, R and Holt, S (2018) *Implementing Key Account Management*, Kogan Page, London, pp 77–9
3 https://www.history.com/topics/korea/korean-war (archived at https://perma.cc/N4ZE-ZRBC)
4 https://www.investopedia.com/insights/worlds-top-economies/ (archived at https://perma.cc/D9GF-GBM3)
5 Kirk, D (2015) *Korean Dynasty: Hyundai and Chung Ju Yung*, Routledge, Oxford
6 https://en.wikipedia.org/wiki/Yi_Sun-sin (archived at https://perma.cc/CR7P-DLB6)
7 Steers, RM (1999) *Made in Korea: Chung Ju Yung and the rise of Hyundai*, Routledge, New York, p 1

10

Principle four: the value of tactful audacity

Tactful audacity is the art of knowing how far to go without going too far. It's very difficult to do if parties are not known to each other – an unsolicited approach and tactfully audacious approach from a salesperson may well trigger a great idea, but the customer may then go and talk about it with their preferred incumbent. After all, they already have a relationship with them. It could also be seen as arrogant. What do you know about me or my business that makes you, the supplier, think you can help?

The word 'tact' is important, as we know many customers see salespeople, particularly those who represent major brands, as assuming a cloak of arrogance. No one wants to be controlled. So 'tact' is key; emotional intelligence coupled with the courage, ie audacity, to be bold and courageous in presenting new ideas or in the negotiating process in the right way will lead to salespeople being in the 10 per cent. No one likes to be challenged inappropriately.

There is a fine line between being seen as brazenly arrogant and being tactfully audacious. The values of tactful audacity can be seen in people who develop what Jim Collins and Jerry Porras have termed 'big hairy audacious goals'[1] – think Richard Branson as he formed Virgin Atlantic to take on British Airways or Virgin Cola as he took on Pepsi and Coca-Cola, or Jeff Bezos as he created Amazon to shake up retailing, or Travis Kalanick and Garrett Camp as they created Uber, which has disrupted the taxi business. As described earlier, tactful audacity is the art of knowing how far to go without going too far.

There are just so many quite inspiring people who do quite amazing things – though not all turn out to be successful. Virgin Cola, for example, failed in the USA. As Branson himself said,[2] the idea of using a Sherman tank to crush a wall of Coca-Cola and Pepsi cans in Times Square was perhaps a step too far in arousing the anger of Coca-Cola and Pepsi, which used their financial power and political weight to prevent Branson from using any of the distribution channels in the USA – Virgin Cola pulled out.

But not all failures fail. Indeed, consider the intriguing case of the Museum of Failure in Sweden, opened by Dr Samuel West. West wanted to make the connection between failure and innovation, and, as he subsequently shared at one of our global sales transformation conferences: 'Too often organizations punish failure to the extent that no one takes risk. It's important that organizations allow the psychological space to accept failure is a prerequisite for innovation.' Branson and most entrepreneurs would agree with this.

In fact, Google conducted research, referred to as its Aristotle Project, across 180 teams, including 65 sales teams, about what were the most important factors that contributed to high team performance, such as meeting a sales quota.

The most important factor, according to the analysis of both quantitative and qualitative data, was psychological safety. The Google report explains that psychological safety refers to an individual's perception of the consequences of taking an interpersonal risk.[3] Clearly there is a difference between those who see failure as a negative and those who see failure as a positive learning experience.

Whilst Branson failed with Virgin Cola, one of the biggest positives, he said, that came out of this experience was the launch by his co-founder of Innocent Drinks. The key learnings from this experience were the importance of a purpose-driven ideology and a superior product as being paramount for creating successful business.

And it's not just business-related. There are many examples of people who have created something out of a passion for something.

Clearly passion and inspiration are two fundamental attributes for tactful audacity. In the sales world, this passion could be driven through a salesperson's sense of purpose, ie their fundamental motivation.

Theirs could be simply self-centred motivation, ie the desire to make money, or self-recognition, ie to be top of the leader board. These salespeople will use their energy to sell more, to do more deals. But this type of motivation will, if not well disguised, lead to the adoption of negative values. Customers will quickly spot these values of supplier-centricity, manipulation, and sometimes arrogance.

Or it could be driven by customer-centred motivation – a passion to do what is right for the customer, to do deals with customers that maximize value for both parties. This passion will drive time spent on doing things that realize this aim.

This value can often result in what may be, on the surface, very simple actions, but can generate big results further down the line.

The following case study is an example of customer-centred motivation that required the account manager to seriously challenge his personal values and beliefs as he figured out a way to protect his business.

Sony Mobile: how can you increase market share from 8.7 per cent to 17.4 per cent in less than two months?

A sudden change in government regulations was going to decimate Sony's mobile phone market share. A series of tactful audacity strategies not only prevented this from happening, but doubled market share in two months.[4]

Sony Mobile had just embarked on a 'leading sales transformation' master's programme for its key account managers. Gustavo Mancera, one of the 12 selected to attend the programme, is based in Colombia and responsible for the largest carrier (telecoms operator).

This is his story of what happened *and the personal journey* he took to transform a problem into an opportunity. Many thanks to Gustavo and the *Journal of Sales Transformation* for allowing me to share the story.[5]

In July 2014, the CRC (Comisión de Regulación de Comunicaciones, or Chamber for Regulación de Communications Regulations) resolution 444 (2014) became effective. It mandated that 'permanence clauses' in mobile services contracts were forbidden in Colombia. As a consequence, carriers ceased subsidizing mobile phones, as they could not be confident a customer would stay for the time needed to ensure payback. This initiated a downward trend at the high end of the mobile market, which shrank 53 per cent versus the first semester of 2014.

Gustavo's client, the carrier, announced immediately that it would, following this announcement, be focused only on selling the low-end handsets. This would have a disastrous effect on Sony Mobile's market share, as its smartphones required the carrier's support.

It was in this context that Gustavo seriously began to question his personal values and mindset. What would it take of him and his account team to deal with this problem? As he commented, 'The rapidly changing market affected the entire team's mindset, including myself. We had fallen prey to negative mindsets while struggling to deliver the company's sales goals.'

His reflections, based on surveys with his managers and his team, highlighted that he had often adopted a supplier-centric mindset and used manipulation to try to get what he wanted. He was aware that he was seen by his team as demonstrating overt arrogance and complacency, *but was concerned that they saw many of what he recognized as bad mindsets as being good*. He realized that he had to change the entire approach of the team and also recognized that, in doing so, there was little risk – after all, it looked like no matter what they did, the client had made up its mind.

He also became aware that the tension-induced relationship prompted by his customer also helped drive the negative mindsets. The point is that our values and behaviours can be shaped by our customers: as we have seen, customers do not trust salespeople often, and it's also the converse – salespeople do not trust customers, particularly those in procurement.

He was convinced he needed a radical rethink of his personal behaviours and mindset if he were to succeed, and not at all sure that he would be able to change the mindset of his customer. He used a range of critical reflection techniques, such as the customer strategy grid, '5 why analysis', appreciative enquiry, and customer's customer thinking, to consider his customer position.

These were some of his first observations

The measure that carriers most care about is how to build average revenue per user (ARPU). 'The challenge of building ARPU growth is a goal that could only be achieved through *consumer experience* (Zhou and Rahman 2013) and one that could only be delivered with high-end smartphones such as Sony Mobile devices.'[6]

Gustavo and his team were convinced through research they had conducted that the Colombian consumers wanted a high-end consumer experience, and they would find ways to pay for this experience! It was Gustavo's view that playing in the low-price segment would result in a loss of long-term focus for the client; they have started to give away the more profitable, high-end segment. His client had to keep their financing model intact to maintain the dominant position in the marketplace.

Gustavo and his team thought this through from the consumer perspective, wanting the experience of the smartphone, and linked this to the stated goal of the carrier, which was to build market share through consumer experience. He realized they were making a big mistake. Stopping the smartphone segment would have a disastrous effect on the carrier's business and completely destroy all the differentiation they had built in recent years.

Gustavo and the team set about convincing the customer that:

1. Their decision was wrong; and
2. They could address the financial risk jointly by changing the barriers in the contracting terms with consumers and Sony supporting the financial risk.

This would only be done:

3. If Sony had an exclusive deal with the carrier to promote Sony's smartphones over and above others during the busiest Christmas trading period. (In return, Sony would ensure sufficient stocks were there to meet anticipated demand.)

Here we can see the passion, energy and belief that were all required to challenge the customer.

They approached the customer at multiple levels to persuade the customer to change their mind – as Gustavo commented:

> Articulating this to the client was not easy – the client was reluctant to admit they had made a huge mistake. They overcame this issue by convincing multiple levels of key influencers within the customer's organization that the financial model of how consumers bought phones had to be modified. After several weeks of discussions, their down-payment policy was changed and sales started to increase rapidly, contradicting their initial analysis that further price drops would be necessary.

The results were extraordinary. In the highly competitive mobile phone market, Sony's market share grew from 8.7 per cent to 17.4 per cent. Whilst other suppliers had accepted the market changes at face value, Gustavo was prepared to challenge the status quo.

SUMMARY OF TACTFUL AUDACITY IN ACTION – KEY LEARNINGS

Gustavo started by examining his personal values and those of his team and aligning these with the winner's circle mindset.

Rather than do as his competitors did, he challenged the decisions being made. The challenge was grounded in his understanding of the competitive advantage his customer was seeking to create.

> He connected his customer's desire to build their value proposition based on customer experience with the high-end smartphones that Sony were selling.
>
> Working in a collaborative way with different levels of management, they built a compelling value proposition to do a major campaign on the smartphone over Christmas, supported by financial investment on both sides, to make it easier financially for consumers to buy the phone.
>
> The senior executives at the telecoms operator finally accepted the logic. Demand was so high that no further financial incentives, ie discounting, were required to shift stock.
>
> Whilst the other handset manufacturers could have benefited from the smartphone sales, they were not prepared and had no stock to sell.

But what does it take to be bold and to have courage? It requires building a solid case, a compelling value proposition.

A number of frameworks and tools to define needs in a creative way have been covered in previous chapters. These include cracking the industry code, 3rd Box Thinking™, the customer strategy grid, and Gibbs' reflective cycle. There are a number of additional tools that help build a compelling value proposition.

The first is a way to consider the relevance and value to the supplier and the customer of the solution components being considered.

The solution development framework is very simple to use (Table 10.1).

Its application is for when considering the question, 'What assets do we have?', listed in the solution component column (consider both tangible assets and intangible assets). How easy is it for us to leverage this asset

TABLE 10.1 Solution development: solution value grid

Solution component	Feasibility	×	Value to customer	+	Value to us	=	Result Y/N	U

1 = Little to no value; 2 = Below-average value; 3 = Average value; 4 = Above-average value; 5 = High value; U = Uniqueness

scored in the feasibility column? What value does this asset bring to the customer and then to us? This provides a numeric score. A decision is made – yes or no. In the final column, how unique is this solution?

Note the use of the multiple. The value to the customer is a multiple of feasibility – the idea being that all the time the weighting of value is towards the customer.

In Gustavo's case, the solution components would have included:

- the Sony smartphone;
- investment in a financial model to help the local Colombian market;
- a campaign strategy for Christmas;
- customer experience data showing the connection between smartphones and user experience and loyalty, etc.

The brainstorming of ideas, careful consideration of how feasible it is when securing the necessary resources, and the discussion of value help to build the confidence required to be tactfully audacious in articulating the value to the customer.

The usage of the solution value grid is very helpful when brainstorming multiple components of a final solution and their relevance.

Win themes

In some complex bids, where the solution components are many, it's useful to consider grouping the components under 'win themes'. These win themes help when articulating the final value proposition. They can also be used at an early stage when building the campaign. Their use can help customers understand your offer. It's a bit like an advertising campaign.

For example: Donald Trump's message was 'Make America Great Again'/'Keep America Great' and 'Promises Made, Promises Kept'. Boris Johnson's message was 'Get Brexit Done'. Indian Prime Minister Narendra Modi's slogan was 'Good Days Are Coming'. Arguably these messages were effective in their communication and connecting with the public who voted for them. Short and memorable themes will help customers understand the value of propositions being made and again demonstrate authority and organization in the way value is articulated.

Here is an example of win themes being applied in action by a hypothetical application testing company.

The Valentine Break Up campaign

Not long after Australian NAB Bank launched its audacious Valentine Break Up[7] campaign, an application testing company was wanting to secure a relatively small but strategically important deal with the bank. If you have the time check out the link in the endnotes, there is a lot to be learned from NAB's campaign – which positioned NAB as breaking up what was perceived as a banking cartel in Australia between the major banks.

The team working on the opportunity used the customer's customer approach and themselves replicated, with arguably more tact, similar strategies to NAB in the way they crafted the win themes.

They video-interviewed NAB customers, both business and consumer, and built the three win themes as messages around their solutions. These were:

- Know me more.
- Invest in me.
- Make IT better.

Under each of the themes they had listed their solution components and then used the video clips to build a campaign reinforcing these messages. These video clips were embedded in presentation slides and on business cards. Onsite engineers also had polo shirts with the win themes on their sleeve. These invited comment from the bank and played their role, as with Boris Johnson and Donald Trump, in making a concise message memorable.

The application testing company won their largest order in the Asia-Pacific region with NAB Bank against competition from the major technology companies. Their proposal was seen as both innovative and bold. Clearly NAB felt there was a cultural fit between them.

Trust the foundation for tactful audacity

As we have seen from the customer interviews, customers like to be challenged, but only once trust exists and where the basis for challenge by a salesperson is grounded in a genuine desire to solve a customer problem in a new way. The extent to which a salesperson develops a deep knowledge of the customer, the industry in which that customer operates and the customer's 'consumers' is key. Knowledge develops confidence.

Often it's the fear of what people might think of you or failure that prevents people from taking action. They remain frozen. Smart people learn by being curious and objectively reflective and having an approach to failure that allows it to happen and to learn from it.

Confidence builds, as Gustavo has demonstrated, with developing honesty in understanding and challenging your own values and belief systems. Being comfortable in your own skin can take years, but arguably it's the most important gift of experience. Finding your authentic you is key to being tactfully audacious. That inner confidence – I'm okay, you are okay – is a baseline requisite.

But it's also about having good ideas and the ability to synthesize data and information – to evaluate connections for their relevance is also key to developing new insights. A tactfully audacious salesperson will also be a reflective practitioner.

Taking a research-led approach to solving problems develops confidence that all angles are covered, enabling bolder propositions.

Tactful audacity requires conviction, a 'just do it' attitude

Where do big ideas start? Quite often it's a spur-of-the-moment action: one where courage meets opportunity, a seemingly innocuous 'something' that can lead to an opportunity down the line. This is particularly relevant to those curious to know what lead measures result in lagging performance metrics down the line. Whilst deals can be recognized when closed, one should never forget where that journey started. If Zhang Qian of Silk Road fame and Zheng He of the maritime Silk Route fame had not started out on their epic journeys, the resulting economic development of the Han and Ming Dynasties would not have happened.

The start of the journey should be as 'celebrated' as much as the end. Starting the sales cycle is often the most difficult and it's always interesting to observe tactful audacity in action at this point. What earns a salesperson the right to get an audience with the customer and start the cycle? This is particularly true of the C suite.

It can be as simple as saying: 'I have noticed x and I think there is something you have not considered.' It's all about timing.

The following story charts an example of tactful audacity at the start and what it led to some months down the line.

John worked for one of the large professional services firms and was a newly appointed account manager. He realized that whilst his account had produced revenues for his firm over the years, 'the relationship was purely transactional'. The strategy grid analysis showed they did not know the account at all well. He had no relationships with the executive-level team and most contact historically was at lower and middle management levels. He decided to approach this as if it were a new account.

The context of the business environment of his customer was tough. Cuts had to be made. It was a very procurement-led relationship – certainly not strategic – that led to diminishing returns on projects won.

John encountered a significant amount of resistance internally. It was argued, 'Why focus on your account if they were considered difficult to work with, offered low-margin contracts, were resistant to change, and frankly unresponsive?'

John did not accept this; he believed that in the longer term this account would grow. It would, in his mind, be a mistake if they took a short-term view and did not invest the time to try to strike a new and transformed relationship. Clearly tactful audacity would be required, both managing the internal scepticism as well as trying to rebrand his company as being the go-to organization for strategic consulting work.

By chance John was at an event attended by the client's MD. Up until this point, his firm had had no dealings with either the MD or his reports.

Seeing the MD was alone for a moment, John introduced himself as the account manager and the person responsible for looking after his organization. He briefly explained the new account structure that his firm had established for looking after its strategic accounts and said, rather spontaneously, that he would very much like to set up a meeting with the MD and John's chairperson. He added there were some ideas that they had that could potentially help drive efficiencies.

There was risk in making this *first tactfully audacious* and unsolicited approach: it could well have irritated the MD. But the fact that John proposed a peer-to-peer meeting was instrumental in its success – furthermore the MD was impressed that John's company was clearly investing time in the relationship and was pleased to meet the chairperson of the company. He asked John to set up a meeting for a couple of months ahead. As John reflected, 'This was a spur of the moment thing… tactful audacity.' No one at the time predicted just how important this chance meeting would be.

This was the start of something 'really special'. The first meeting was extraordinary. In the hour they spent together, the MD just downloaded – he was very open in sharing the challenges that his company had, the downsizing and restructuring that were to take place.

This is what they learned: the MD's company had traditionally been structured with divisions focused on different sectors, each of these with their supporting departments. As part of the initiative to make the company leaner, cross-functional departments were being created to support all divisions. Redundancies would follow.

A structural change of this magnitude was fraught with risk. New processes would need to be created, new structures, new roles and a new, less siloed mindset. The upside, though, was that the newly structured company would work together more synergistically, which would lead to more efficiencies. This structure was set up to enhance collaboration to make better decisions more quickly.

They realized that they had to, in three months, come back with something 'new', considered, 'not expected' and strategically aligned. Otherwise, these meetings would just be a rather 'superficial exercise' and the relationship would probably 'peter out'.

They also realized that unless they engaged with the MD's direct reports in parallel, they ran the risk of being isolated – that the people they engaged with at a departmental level on a daily basis would be suspicious and resist any new ideas and changes being proposed. There is ironically a danger in selling at too high a level. Tactful audacity requires a high level of emotional intelligence.

John and his now less cynical team realized this was a change management exercise – whilst changing mindsets inside the firm is one huge challenge (more on this later), they recognized it was arguably a bigger challenge for an external party to suggest news ways of working. Their client was very conservative as an organization. This had to be a collaborative process.

Working with lower-level management in the three months, they proposed a new way of cross-departmental planning focused on a new digital platform, based on some technologies and processes that they had developed that would allow multiple departments to work on a plan in real time.

They were also able to leverage from their considerable global expertise to demonstrate, through case studies and client references, how these technologies and new processes could save 30–50 per cent in time.

The functional directors were very excited by its potential and, in working with John's team, agreed that the best way forward was to do a pilot project to test the idea. If this was successful, it would be rolled out for other projects.

The next meeting with the MD was crucial. Whilst they had done much preparation and internal selling, they had no idea how the MD would react. It was a nervous moment. In their preparation, John had suggested that the chairperson should be the one to get commitment to the idea.

As they entered the meeting room, they found that one of the divisional directors had also been invited. This was a good sign. The idea of doing a pilot was discussed; crucially, it was clear that it had the divisional director's support. The chairperson asked for the order: 'how do we proceed?' The divisional director answered, 'we should probably go through the procurement channels.'

This would have resulted in a substantial delay… on reflecting a little, the MD responded, 'No, we won't! We can single-source this project as it's a pilot. I can sort that.'

This was the first time a single-source tender had been won by John's company – the second time that tactful audacity had been demonstrated in (a) coming up with the big idea and then (b) having the courage to sell it, ie close on the idea, and it showed a certain amount of tactful audacity by the MD.

Furthermore, the MD proposed that he and the chairperson personally sponsor the project. They agreed to meet every quarter to review progress – with both sides committing to a strong governance process to make sure this project would succeed.

John summarized the progress at this point in the developing relationship: 'We had built trust with the MD. We had built trust with the operational teams, we had listened really hard, we brought something new they could implement.'

Note the reference to trust (these comments were later endorsed by the MD).

This deepening level of trust led not just to 'sell to' strategies, but also to 'sell with'. Let's take a quick review of some of the collaborations that followed:

- Given the cost-cutting measures, the MD's UK-based organization was open to exploring ways to generate revenues from other sources, perhaps globally. A 'sell with' model was jointly created – the combined expertise of both organizations was used to sell consulting projects. Joint workshops were run to prospective customers, leveraging the professional

services global network – 'so both parties can achieve a win-win'. Their first joint win was consulting on an Indian infrastructure project.
- John's team was also smart on how they leveraged their relationships with cross-party parliamentary groups. They invited the MD's organization to take part in these groups on a zero-carbon project; they also shared initiatives on 'diversity' programmes, something the chairperson and MD were both passionate about.

This is a great example of how John is leveraging the intangible assets of his company to bring value. The beauty about these ideas is that they don't cost anything except a bit of time – so it is feasible to execute on. It is low cost but of high value to his company – these are ideas that came from the solution development grid we looked at earlier in this chapter.

As these ideas developed, the relationships at multiple levels accelerated. The relationship 'capital' built from living these values cannot be compared with the relationships that existed before. John set out to create a new account. He did just that. This had nothing to do with new products and services, and everything to do with aspiring to that highest level of values – tactful audacity.

As one would have expected, the revenues and profitability have increased in spite of the cost cutting; the newly announced measures to stimulate the economy bode well for the future growth.

The customer strategy grid and 3rd Box Thinking™ are tools that helped develop a deep understanding of the customer's requirements, but it must be remembered that without tactful audacity and that first contact, none of this would have happened.

This case study demonstrates the deepening levels of trust once the baseline values of authenticity and client-centricity are lived and shows its power to create value for both parties as it reaches the proactive creativity and tactful audacity levels.

The five key tactful audacity moments

1. Securing the first meeting with the MD.
2. Securing the support of the chairperson.
3. The chairperson asking for the order – going for the single-source option.

4   Developing the 'sell to' and 'sell with' model.
5   Invitation for customer to join the diversity initiative.

This case study demonstrates co-creation and agile thinking. It exemplifies what it takes to create competitive advantage through salesmanship alone and supports the hypothesis that 'emocracy' and 'adhocracy' are a competitive advantage, according to Birkinshaw, in the 'post-knowledge' era.

If tactful audacity is important at the beginning of the sales cycle, it's also important at the end of the sales cycle. Asking for the order, and/or negotiating to close the order, requires tactful audacity. Some negotiating consulting practices suggest that there is no room for fairness in a negotiation – a winner takes all kind of approach – audacity without the tact. But fairness is a subjective word. One's approach at the negotiating table will be driven by one's sense of fairness, effective planning, confidence in the value proposition, and ethical sales practice.

It's clear that the quality of the contract eventually signed is dependent on the ability of the team to build a compelling and differentiated value proposition; it's not just what happens at the end of the sales cycle.

Tactful audacity applied internally

Salespeople are chosen by their customers for their ability to influence the supplier organization – as Chris Burke, the then chief technology officer of Vodafone, said:

> I like choosing a salesperson, I want them to have sales skills but I want them pointing back inside his organization, I want them to leverage my power and weight back inside his organization in order that I can get the benefits of all points of engagement.

Clearly he was seeking salespeople to use this mindset internally. But how often do salespeople challenge their own organizations?

A senior manager of a global manufacturing company with a traditionally hierarchical structure said recently: 'I would always consider a well-considered business case to do something different – the problem is they (the salesperson) don't ask.'

The message here is to use tactful audacity internally to sell new ideas – it is as important a mindset internally as using externally when selling or negotiating with customers.

Recognize wins with your team that are exemplars of bold ideas. When evaluating account plans or sales opportunities, seek internal support for tactfully audacious ideas.

Tactful audacity was described at the outset of this chapter as the art of knowing how far to go without going too far. It is an art, that spur-of-the-moment intervention, that opportunistic chance meeting or that idea that springs to mind in the moment that then challenges the customer. When backed by the science of thoughtful research, collaboration, the testing of ideas, it's much easier to be emboldened, to have the courage to take that idea that no one has thought of to a customer or to internal stakeholders.

Endnotes

1 Collins, J (1994) *Built to Last: Successful habits of visionary companies*, HarperBusiness, New York (Jim Collins is also the writer of the well-known management book *Good to Great* (2001))
2 https://www.cnbc.com/2017/02/07/what-richard-branson-learned-when-coke-put-virgin-cola-out-of-business.html (archived at https://perma.cc/2DCZ-LHT6)
3 https://rework.withgoogle.com/print/guides/5721312655835136/ (archived at https://perma.cc/XX28-C439)
4 Mancera, G (2015) Personal growth leads to business growth, *International Journal of Sales Transformation*, 3, pp 28–32
5 Mancera, G (2015) Personal growth leads to business growth, *International Journal of Sales Transformation*, 3, pp 28–32
6 Mancera, G (2015) Personal growth leads to business growth, *International Journal of Sales Transformation*, 3, pp 28–32
7 https://www.youtube.com/watch?v=fDD0r2zbfpU (archived at https://perma.cc/H5YJ-PK28)

11

Royal Caribbean International case study

Turning a potential disaster into an opportunity

Whilst Chapters 7–10 have focused on each mindset, in this chapter we 'chart' the story of how one account executive at Royal Caribbean Cruises turned a crisis into an opportunity and in doing so displayed all the mindsets in action. We also update this story with their response to the disaster now facing the cruise ship sector.

Royal Caribbean International: how mindsets applied turned 'terminal' decline into 282 per cent growth within 18 months

Over the years Royal Caribbean International (RCL) had developed into one of the world's largest cruise businesses. Russia was never a huge market compared with other parts of the world, but it was significant as the Russians were known for an average higher daily spend on ships than many others.

RCL's Russian market was historically served by one primary international representative who had an exclusive RCL contract to serve the country. This organization went bust in 2011.

Natalya, RCL's EMEA Head of Sales for International Representatives (IR) and responsible for the Russian market among others in EMEA, was tasked to rethink RCL's coverage strategy for Russia. She decided to select five preferred sales representatives (PSRs) to represent RCL – ones that had specialist skills and a complementary market focus. PSR providers work with an extensive network of travel agents who then sell to the public. Each PSR was chosen for different attributes. One was an expert as a 'trade consolidator', another had created an amazingly advanced AI technology-led business that made it easy to link to air travel. Another had a strong loyal customer base, etc.

One might have expected with five partners addressing the same market that they would have developed individualistic and competitive strategies with each other and in addition question their loyalty to RCL given the fact they did not have an exclusive relationship with RCL – their contract allowed them to represent the other major cruise brands. The figures proved otherwise; the five partners had worked hard to grow the Russian market such that RCL saw an 8 per cent growth in passenger numbers in 2016 and 18 per cent growth in 2017.

However, disaster struck.

For many years around 2,000 of RCL's Russian customers took cruises in the Caribbean, enjoyed for its idealistic tropical islands, guaranteed weather and easy access. However, disaster struck when the US Embassy in Moscow announced in August 2017 that it would temporarily stop issuing all non-immigrant visas in Russia and severely curtail visa operations as it slashed its staff to comply with the latest salvo in Washington's diplomatic standoff with Moscow.

RCL did not see an immediate decline in passenger numbers, as most of the bookings and visa applications were made months in advance. In fact, they were seeing a steep increase in Russian passengers in 2018 with advanced bookings. However, it became quite clear within a couple of months that the Caribbean market (served out of Miami) would be decimated.

To get a sense of the scale of the problem is to understand its impact not just on RCL but also on the PSRs. Over the years RCL had steadily increased its passenger numbers and by 2018 had reached second place in cruise market share at approximately 8 per cent, behind the dominant Mediterranean shipping company (MSC) with 50 per cent. Losing and not replacing 2,000 customers per annum (the Caribbean market) would set RCL back many years. This decline would seriously and immediately hit the revenue and profitability of the newly developing PSR community and allow MSC to extend its already dominant market share.

In the weeks following the news, Natalya's immediate action was to see if there could be any way to fast-track the immigration process – she put a significant effort into lobbying RCL's internal government relations department to see what strings could be pulled. In retrospect, Natalya commented that 'this was a fruitless exercise'. It quickly became obvious that there was no way of circumventing the policy decisions made by the US government and in any case, the visa agencies were themselves going through huge turmoil as they had to redeploy hundreds of staff members and set up new processes. They simply did not have the bandwidth to consider the problems of a cruise business.

Natalya realized that the only option was to explore ways of changing their Russian customers' behaviour and ask them to consider completely new holiday destinations with RCL. This was much easier said than done. It required a completely creative and quite radical rethink that would affect all aspects of the 'supply chain': furthermore, time was not on their side. Each day's delay in coming up with a new idea would be impacting Natalya's PSRs' revenue and bottom line. Though loyal to RCL's brand, the PSRs would have no choice but to persuade their customers to consider alternative holidays with or without RCL.

In Natalya's case, the supply chain included RCL corporate, RCL marketing, her EMEA vice president, the ship's hotel directors, the PSRs and even the ports at which ships docked. Essentially, working collaboratively with the PSRs and the supply chain, she had to create a 'new product' for the Russian market – one that could be met with a certain degree of internal RCL support, because although Russia was an important market, compared with other markets it was still small. Trying to get internal sponsorship was a huge task for Natalya. She recognized that trying to sell this internally through a top–down approach would take too long and she was not at all convinced that it would work – *now time was of the essence.*

Typically, the sales team would start with the question: what do we have that we could sell to the Russian market (first box thinking)? This would lead to a review of the current destinations they served with their cruises, then a look at cruise utilization ratios to see what deals they could do to drive Russian customers towards those ships that had the capacity to take the Russian customers.

Untypically Natalya, working collaboratively with the PSRs, started with the question: what *value* do Russian consumers want from a cruise? She linked this to the value that the ship's hotel directors wanted to create for themselves, then finally used this approach to sell more passenger numbers working in close collaboration with the partners. Natalya used third perspective thinking in developing her strategy. Furthermore, this strategy, in Natalya's case, was driven by an authentic passion and desire to provide her PSRs with a sound economic model to thrive in what is a very competitive and fickle marketplace.

The outcome from this approach were some very creative and bold ideas. For example, her 'research' into what Russian consumers wanted surfaced some interesting data. Russians often lack an ability to speak English. English is the spoken language of all the crew on board; furthermore the majority of passengers travelling on the ships often speak English even though it might not be their first language. Menus, food, services and others are in English as well, but they often reflect other nationalities' preferences but not theirs – why not have the option to have Russian food, for example? Why not have menus available in Russian? Why not even have Russian translators on board ships? Understandably Russian passengers felt somewhat less connected with the cruise experience as they felt the on-board services were more tailored for other nationalities.

It was clear that if RCL was to create a compelling winning value proposition, Natalya had to work with the operations teams on the ship, but this meant circumventing the normal practices of working through the global HQ. Unusually Natalya, with the support of her EMEA management, decided to approach certain of the ships' hotel directors directly. If they could not be convinced to work with Natalya in creating a specialized 'product' for the Russian market, the project would fall flat on its face. What she would be asking the ships' teams to do was: invest in Russian waiters; serve Russian cuisine; have menus translated into Russian; contract a translator for the service of the Russian passengers; have a daily newspaper with on-board activities translated and delivered to the cabin each evening; and even have an on-board Russian-speaking guest relations manager to help these Russian passengers with any questions.

So what was in it for the ships' hotel directors?

She knew that in order to convince the ships' directors, she had to educate them as to the typical profile of the Russian passengers, the economic benefit that this would bring the ships, and the reassurance that the passenger numbers would happen. After all, there would be considerable investment required up front to make this happen for the ships that were selected for this 'special' programme. As mentioned earlier, she knew that Russian passengers spend more on ships than other nationalities do: the net ticket spend from Russian passengers is 12.5 per cent higher than the company average. This was extremely important to the ships' hotel directors, who are measured on on-board spend.

However, it's not only about the money. Net promoter scores are also important. By combining this segmented and more personalized consumer approach, Natalya felt that the NPS would improve and loyalty would increase. She also realized that many of the ideas being suggested – such as on-board translators, menus in Russian, on-board Russian-speaking guest relations managers – were relatively inexpensive and would be a cost of sale rather than a fixed cost to RCL. The main expense would be in creating the Russian menus and potentially recruiting Russian waiters.

Working with her EMEA team, she initially targeted two new destinations: the Middle East and Asia. Collaborating with the ships' captains, more creative ideas were added such as a New Year celebration on board *at Moscow time*, Russian evenings with Russian music, vodka bar with caviar and favourite snacks. This was to drive significant increases in passenger numbers to cruises in this part of the world.

In Asia, RCL operated its ship *Spectrum* between Shanghai and Japan to cater for the Chinese market. Natalya saw an opportunity based on the consumer demand from Russia (remember this was a new and emerging market) for extra demand for this route if the ship could dock in Russia. If Natalya could convince RCL and *Spectrum*'s hotel director that this ship could embark and disembark at Vladivostok on route from Shanghai to Japan, this could help drive more Russian passenger traffic onto the ship. This was to be known internally as a segmented cruise.

Why Vladivostok? It's Russia's only Pacific port – it's also served by the Trans-Siberian rail link that connects Vladivostok to Europe and has an international airport hub with routes to the Far East. If Russians were interested in this new route, it would be relatively easy for them to gain access to the ship. Its main economies are fishing and importation of Japanese cars, and its port services Russia's Pacific Fleet. However, Vladivostok is not known for tourism and no ships the size of Royal Caribbean's *Spectrum* had ever moored at the port.

RCL's port agent team then had to sell the idea to the local authorities – they welcomed the idea, anticipating that this would create a tourism economy that previously did not exist. The port was not geared up to have a big number of guests embark and disembark, but the port agent team together with the ship guest services team made it work.

Selling the idea to the ship's hotel director was not 'plain sailing'. Whilst he agreed that the 200 or so predicted Russian passenger numbers might be good for disembarking in Vladivostok and another 200 passengers embarking, he was not at all confident that the process would be smooth as, in addition, the ship had another 4,500 full cruise passengers that would be going onshore. This would severely challenge the ship's logistics capability, could affect guests' experiences negatively, and as a result lower NPS or, worse still, lose the long-term relationships with customers.

Convinced that this project would generate new levels of passenger numbers and open up new markets, Natalya, with the support of her revenue management department, was able to persuade the port agent hotel department team to 'take the risk' on the segmented cruise. In addition, and crucially, the PSRs also agreed to bear the financial risk if passenger numbers were not met. RCL were then completely covered if the 'numbers' did not go according to plan.

As these internal discussions were going on, the Vladivostok authorities worked with the Russian media agencies to ensure that if the project were to come off, there would be significant media coverage that would help drive passenger numbers.

Imagine a ship the size of Royal Caribbean's *Spectrum* entering the harbour for the first time, fully lit up, with a firework display, etc, etc. The coverage as explained later was exceptional and was to play an important role in raising RCL's brand coverage in Russia.

With most of the elements of the strategy in place, Natalya then had to work with the PSRs to promote and market the new plan. Working with the PSRs and the local Vladivostok authorities, they implemented an aggressive marketing and sales campaign:

- It was essential that the PSRs and their supporting travel agents were sold on the idea. Fifty travel agents and their families from all over Russia were invited to join the ship at Shanghai; this was to prove highly successful in driving passenger numbers for that segmented cruise.
- A digital campaign involved paid ads on Instagram, Facebook, Google and Yandex.
- Nine videos were created to break the stereotype thinking in Russia about cruises – there is a high perception that:
    o cruises are boring;
    o cruises are not for young people;
    o cruises are expensive;
    o cruise ships are like the old cruise ships of the Soviet Union era;
    o no internet is available at sea.
- An unprecedented level of media coverage was generated for the Vladivostok initiative, including the main Russian TV channel.

So were all the results of this effort worth it? Natalya reviewed the performance of the initiative at two levels – tangible and intangible.

The tangible results were incredibly impressive – passenger numbers for Asia-Pacific increased by 53 per cent in 2019 and an incredible 282 per cent in 2020. The segmented cruise (Shanghai–Vladivostok–Shanghai) already had 200–300 passengers confirmed for 2020 and demand was growing.

But the intangible results are equally impressive:

- Through this initiative Natalya has built great relationships with RCL's centralized revenue department, who were incredibly supportive of this new venture.
- RCL have now been invited to have talks with the Hong Kong Tourism Board to broaden their activities in the region.
- Singapore Airlines has signed up to be a partner of RCL.
- The all-important net promoter scores have significantly improved by an impressive six points.

Further reflections

It's important to set this huge team effort in the context of what would have happened if Natalya had sat back, done nothing and blamed governmental interference for not reaching her numbers. Table 11.1 shows the passenger numbers if no action had been taken.

These figures are based on losing the 2,000 Caribbean passengers. (As mentioned earlier, the 24 per cent increase in 2018 was partly influenced by pre-bookings in 2017.) The Russian market in 2019 was double what it would have been if no action had been taken.

So what learnings can we take from this?

Authenticity

It is clear that Natalya, being Russian, has a passion about the Russian market. It comes through in the way she excitedly talks about it – she clearly cares about Russian consumers and also her PSRs. Her passion is totally genuine. As a result of being 'authentic', she is highly trusted by internal and external stakeholders. Her enthusiasm and passion for the Russian market

TABLE 11.1 Net benefit

	Actual results Russia market			Potential results if no action		
Year	Results passenger numbers	Increase PA	%	Passenger numbers	Decrease %	Net benefit
2015	3972			3972		
2016	4275	303	8%	4275		
2017	5061	786	18%	5061		
2018	6277	1216	24%	3061	−51%	105%
2019	6600	323	5%	3200	−52%	106%

helped influence the hotel directors, port authorities, revenue teams, etc to want to work with her to serve the Russian market.

This trust is further enhanced by her customer focus.

Client-centricity

Most salespeople would claim to be client-centric. In Natalya's case, she takes this to a very high level. Using what we have previously referred to as the 3rd Box Thinking™ approach, she did not focus on what RCL could sell to the PSRs but used a consumer-backed approach to determine how RCL could serve a new Russian market. Natalya and her team listened to what customers wanted: she considered what she referred to as the Russian stereotypes and how best to shape a communication plan that would sell the programme. The conversations with the hotel directors to convince them to create Russian menus, have Russian waiters, etc, etc. All showed a deep desire to create the right value proposition for Russian consumers travelling on RCL's ships.

She also really cared for the well-being of the PSRs – she was genuinely appalled at the impact Trump's decision to stop issuing visas to the Russian market would have on the PSRs. She carefully worked with all the PSRs to co-market the new routes. They all benefited from the extraordinary publicity. The fact the PSRs also agreed to underwrite the financial risk is testament to the huge levels of trust they had in Natalya, but it also demonstrates how much they believed in the new ideas and strategy. This degree of client-centricity led to very high levels of collaboration and gave anyone in the team, RCL included, the confidence that this was an exciting project to be in.

Proactive creativity

There is nothing like a crisis to get the creative thinking process flowing. This case is full of examples of creative thinking: the Russian menus, translators, waiters, etc. I have observed that salespeople in general terms are deal-makers and therefore potentially creative in the deal-making process – at least the good ones. It's incredibly rare to see salespeople think of ideas before their customers do – unprompted by any external influence.

In this case the degree of creativity showed in developing a new approach to the Russian market was exceptional – particularly the idea that Vladivostok could be added to the Shanghai route. What we can see here is the momentum of new ideas that can flow in a highly collaborative approach. All parties in the supply chain contributed – even the port agencies in Vladivostok. This is a great credit to the vision that Natalya shaped for the account.

The degree of creativity shown is testament also to the lived culture at RCL. At a recent presentation, their vice president EMEA shared the mindset of RCL. They refer to themselves as a challenger company. Challenger is a term RCL use to determine their source of competitive advantage. In RCL's case, their approach to ship design, how they develop new routes, even acquire new islands, are all stimulated by this challenger approach. They have over the years gained a reputation for being a first in many aspects of cruise experience. The 'space' that Natalya was given by her manager to come up with new ideas and to support her in those ideas was a key element of the turnaround success.

Finally, tactful audacity

Salespeople often say that selling internally is more difficult than selling externally. Natalya and her team required bucket loads of tactful audacity. She recognized that a top–down approach would be too difficult, so she had to go it alone; she had the perseverance and drive to create something new, bringing the partners with her, hotel directors to back her plan, negotiating with the PSRs to take the financial risk for the *Spectrum* so that it could dock at Vladivostok – this all demonstrates what I would refer to as audacity. We can see a combination of great sales as well as leadership skills with this case study. Influencing people over whom you have no direct control is hard. Has there been tact as well?

Evidence throughout this process shows there has been a spirit of collaboration and enthusiastic support created by a high level of emotional intelligence. Certainly Natalya has had to argue her case, for sure there have been times when she must have felt the project would not materialize; she must have been disappointed in the apparent lack of bandwidth in and from different RCL departments from time to time as, in her words, the international representative market within RCL is 'not given the same attention' as the direct accounts. But the fact that the vice president signalled this case study at a recent sales meeting as a great example of the mindsets is testament to the tact that Natalya and her team displayed during this most challenging of market conditions.

The element of time

The 'time' dimension is hugely significant in defining what happens in the sales process. Today's world is changing at such a fast rate that super agility is required to deal with the unexpected opportunities and threats that arise.

Natalya literally had to act in the moment to find an immediate solution. Her initial, perhaps almost panic, reaction was to go back and try to fast-track the visa process. Clearly this was never going to work, but it was her first reaction. Recognizing she was hitting 'a closed door', she quickly realized she needed an outside-the-box solution. This did not take her long. The ability to reflect 'in action' and then 'for action' is arguably one of the most important skills in the era of business we find ourselves in. This she also demonstrated.

But how did they respond to the Covid-19 crisis? With cruise ships empty of passengers or stuck at sea unable to dock, with a travel agent network they rely on for much of their business in financial meltdown, what might one expect of a cruise ship organization with the right mindsets? Well, could their ships be offered to New York State and Los Angeles and other major cities around the world to house the homeless or seriously sick people? Could monies offered to them by institutional shareholders or backers be diverted to the less financially strong travel agent network? It's in these crisis times that true values can be seen. These are the kinds of initiatives RCL is looking at right now – whether their ideas transpire or not remains to be seen.

What matters to salespeople in the VUCA world in which we live is less to do with knowledge and more to do with *how 'we' think*. It requires not worrying that we don't have all the answers, but being able to garner great collaborative support as we work with customers and colleagues to find new answers to new problems.

This case may not be the biggest order, may not be the biggest brand to talk about, but it's one of the best I have seen that demonstrates the highest levels of salesmanship – it puts Natalya in that rare and exclusive winner's circle of the top 10 per cent of salespeople. Particularly as we can observe a great range of skills, this is not just about selling but also about leadership.

It involves the active practice of reflecting. It's about reflecting in action, on action and for action. This case study is less about applying a particular sales methodology or process. It goes much deeper than that. Its success is driven by deep-rooted beliefs in her product and her markets. We can conclude that it's Natalya's core values and mindsets that have intuitively led to a set of activities that in turn led to this impressive result.

Whilst the book has addressed the importance of values and mindsets to sales, it is essential to consider the impact that sales managers, and the organizations for which they work, have on developing the organizational and team culture that allows the positive and differentiating values to thrive.

The next chapter explores the typical sales management systems in place that manage the 'business' of selling and questions whether these are appropriate where transformation is required. It also explores other elements of the sales transformation ecosystem.

12

The role of leadership in transforming sales

There is an 'ecosystem' that allows salespeople to live the positive differentiating mindsets. It includes direct line management, senior sales leaders, the board of directors, sales education, professional bodies and, of course, customers.

This chapter focuses on the first three, starting with sales managers. Creating an environment for salespeople to thrive and succeed is key, but do sales managers really care about team performance?

Our research suggests that a significantly high percentage of salespeople miss quota. The range is between 40 and 80 per cent – the average is 60 per cent. The third edition of *SalesForce: State of Sales* suggested that 57 per cent of sales reps expected to miss their quota in 2018.[1]

There could be many reasons for this statistic: targets could be unrealistic, salespeople's skills are not relevant, values are not aligned to those that customers seek, sales managers are not leading and coaching their teams in the right way, sales managers' values and mindsets do not bring out the best in their teams, or they do not have the skills to do their job as a manager. But whatever the reason, the data is not good.

Paul Devlin, a Consalia alumnus and now the chief sales officer of Suse, a German-based open-source software company, said that in his entire 20-year career, he had only three sales leaders that he had really admired. In the same presentation he went on to say that he felt very uncomfortable with the fact that he could do his number, as a sales manager, get feted and lauded, and go to the winner's circle even if 50 per cent of his team failed to meet their quota.[2] How many sales managers would see their role in this way?

Many do not care if, say, 60 per cent of their sales team miss quota, as long as the overall team target is achieved. This is misguided. If the mindset was like Paul's, every attempt would be made for that sales manager to lead, coach and develop all team members to succeed and would result in much greater success in both the short and the long term.

Managers only have to review the great Ernest Shackleton's extraordinary story of survival against all odds to consider the leadership qualities required for success: to have a vision, make the right decisions, achieve success, cultivate the right habits, trust in team members, have individual courage, recognize strengths of the team. Shackleton was driven by a desire that every one of his team would survive. Baz Grey, an ex-marine and now polar explorer, is the only one of a team of five that replicated what Shackleton did (even down to equipment and clothing); he speaks in detail about Shackleton's leadership approach at another of our global sales events. It's well worth watching.[3]

So what mindsets/values are required of great sales leaders?

We started conducting initial research in 2010 with 150 sales managers/leaders to define the mindsets they felt were required for sales leaders as opposed to salespeople. These mindsets are continually reassessed with new groups of managers joining the master's programmes for relevance in the context of the world in which they work.

The research then suggested the following four mindsets are critical.

Vision

Sales managers should have a vision for their team, ideally a purpose-driven vision that goes beyond just hitting the numbers. A vision describes the organization's long-term dream. A vision should stretch the team's capabilities and image of itself. Visions can be inspirational and/or functional.

How many sales managers do this? Informal research at Consalia has shown that less than 10 per cent of sales managers actually have a vision for their team.

It's worth reflecting on Simon Sinek's 'golden circles'. Most companies on the planet, he argues, know what they do, some know how they do it, very few know why they do it.

For those not familiar with his golden circles theory, see the link to his TED Talk in the endnotes.[4] It's our experience that all sales managers know what their targets are, fewer have a plan for how to reach their targets – they just focus on the numbers – and even fewer managers could answer the question: why are 'we' doing what 'we' are doing?

Examples of a vision for sales managers include:

- to lead the team that others want to join;
- to be the benchmark that other teams use to gauge performance;
- to be one of the top five districts in sales in the company.

Desire to be the best

Sales managers should be driven by a desire to be the best: clearly those attracted to sales are competitive by nature, so being the best team performance-wise is key. Sales managers should set aspirational and clear targets, and have the right performance measurement systems to get the best of their teams – focusing on leading, not lagging, indicators.

The desire to be the best goes well beyond sales performance. It's about having a 'growth' mindset, a continuous desire to learn, to look for self-improvement and to encourage others to do the same.

Empowerment

It's well known in sales that it's the top-performing salespeople who tend to get promoted into sales management roles – often, in our experience, with very little training. Yet the roles could not be more different. It's only natural that a super salesperson in a management role will be inclined to step in and take control of the sale, particularly at the end of the sales cycle. Empowerment has much to do with trust and providing the sales teams with the development required for them to do their job. It also requires having a professional coaching mindset. Empowerment mindsets accept that people may make mistakes and provide the psychological safety for salespeople to thrive.

Potential

Finally, it's the mindset of a great sales leader that looks for the potential in people, that spots those with the right attitude, that likes the challenge of, say, taking an underperforming team and believing that teams can be 'changed' or developed to realize higher levels of performance. Or take an underperforming salesperson and find ways to unlock their potential. Those with this mindset are prepared to give people the benefit of the doubt. The impact that managers can have in giving people self-belief can be quite profound.

Given the fast-changing world in which we work, we ask if these mindsets are relevant. To the above list of four we have added a fifth.

Ambiguity

In the 'good old days', life was more predictable; it might have been possible then to have multi-year business plans, but in today's market there is so much more unpredictable change that to set long-term plans is dangerous. David Wilkinson has done much research into this. He argues in his book *The Ambiguity Advantage*[5] that the ability to work with ambiguity is now the predominant trait required of CEOs.

Who would have anticipated the impact that the COVID-19 pandemic has had on global business in 2020? Who anticipated the impact of the global financial crash in 2008? Who can anticipate the impact that new challenger brands and disrupters will have in the marketplace?

How to live and thrive with ambiguity is a mindset, a state of mind. Some can deal with ambiguity well; others cannot function in a less structured environment. Given the context of change, the ability of managers to reflect in action, on action and for action to make considered and informed decisions quickly is arguably one of the most important competencies for sales management.

Sales management systems

So what system of sales management is required to manage sales teams? Let's contrast systems required for managing the business of selling – which we shall refer to as transactional sales management systems – with systems required for transforming sales performance – which are referred to as transformational sales management systems.

Sales management systems typically involve three 'dimensions' to manage sales performance depending on their level of sophistication. They address the setting of targets, sales activities and development. They address the following key questions:

1 What results do we want to achieve?
2 What activities are required to achieve them?
3 What resources and competencies are required?

Results – the what: Sales targets or revenues are set for sales teams, perhaps split by products and services. Sometimes gross profits or gross margins are included. (These are examples of lagging indicators for salespeople – meaning results happen as a result of something happening, an activity, a sales call perhaps.)

Activities – the how: KPIs might be set around sales activities for each salesperson, such as appointment numbers, events, telephone calls, calls to different levels and types of buyer. These sales activities address the 'how'. (They are examples of leading indicators for salespeople, meaning that these activities are most likely to lead to successful sales.)

Resources and competencies – the who: Personal development plans are created to carry out the activity effectively – the 'who'. This could include coaching or training. This addresses the capabilities of salespeople to perform at the right levels the tasks being asked of them.

We refer to those sales managers who implement only a results-focused system as 'managing by fear'. These sales managers literally manage their sales teams by focusing on results, their QBRs (quarterly business reviews), and only look at the deals in the pipeline that can be closed by quarter end. They may adopt a deal-coaching mindset, but it's really short term. They assume that as salespeople are paid well, they are paid to generate the results; if they miss target, they are replaceable.

We refer to those sales managers who implement a results- and activity-based sales management system as 'managing by hope'. Hope, as these managers recognize, is the difference between the leading and lagging indicators, and ensures that they focus on managing the source activities that drive sales results. There is more certainty that targets are reached, as considerable time is spent understanding what actions produce the desired results. For example, it may be that calls to a certain level of buyer are known to be more productive or that calls that include a technical expert with a salesperson generate better results. The timings of these sales activities could be key – at what stage of the quarter or year. Each organization will have its own formula for success, but few have found out what this formula is.

We refer to those managers who implement a results, activity and personal development-based system as 'managing by objectives'. These managers realize the importance of those in the field selling having the requisite skills and attitudes.

The above approaches to transactional sales management systems are based on Peter Drucker's management by objectives framework as described in his book *The Practice of Management*.[6] Jordan and Vazzana's more recent book *Cracking the Sales Management Code*[7] specifically looks at how sales managers tend to focus on the lagging indicators rather than leading indicators and suggests ways that sales managers should develop their sales management system.

The 'sales management system' can be considered as a series of steps within a process as shown in Figure 12.1. The management of results, activities and resources is covered in steps 3–6.

FIGURE 12.1 Sales management system

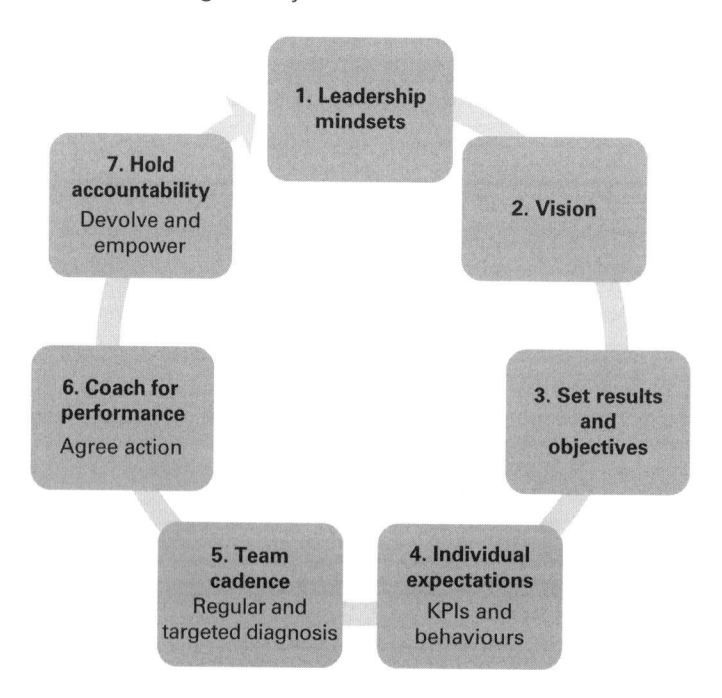

1. Leadership mindsets
2. Vision
3. Set results and objectives
4. Individual expectations — KPIs and behaviours
5. Team cadence — Regular and targeted diagnosis
6. Coach for performance — Agree action
7. Hold accountability — Devolve and empower

1 **Leadership mindsets** – It starts with being clear on your leadership mindsets – what mindsets underpin what you do, and which will you measure yourself by? Whilst our research has suggested what the core mindsets are for effective sales leaders, we encourage sales leaders to develop their own version of the mindsets. It's more authentic.

2 **Vision** – What vision do you have *for your team* that will provide an aligning beacon to the future?

3 **Set results and objectives** – What results (end goals, eg revenue targets) and objectives (means to get there, eg number of prospect calls per week) do you need to achieve to be successful, according to your vision?

4 **Individual expectations** – What individual expectations do you have for each of your team members that will let the team be successful? These may vary by team member. They will be a mixture of KPIs that need to be monitored and kept on track and behaviours (eg sales mindsets and sales activities) that will let the team members be successful in developing sales stars in the future.

5 **Team cadence** – You need to establish a team cadence – a calendar of regular coaching events for the team members, based on the expectations. Prior to each coaching session, evidence-based diagnosis is key to supporting the sales professional's development and performance improvement.

6 **Coach for performance** – Coach each cadence session to exceed sales targets *and* develop your team into stars. The actions should mainly be deliverable in the time period of the next coaching for performance session. For example, if the salesperson needs to improve their client-centricity, you might ask them to show you two examples of call preparation prior to them meeting with the client, focusing on their improved insights of the client needs.

7 **Hold accountability** – *Critically*, hold the team members accountable and follow up on the coaching. The outcome of the coaching for performance reviews is their expectations and you are there to coach, not to do it yourself.

But whilst traditional sales management systems may be fit for purpose – meaning they will meet the sales operations requirements to meet targets – they may not be appropriate for a sales transformation.

It's critical to understand the difference between change and transformation. Does increasing sales by 100 per cent equal sales transformation? Whilst the sales numbers may be 'transformative', is this 'transformation'? Not necessarily so. Transformation is a widely misused word.

So let's define what the difference is between change and transformation. Danah Zohar described how:

> Most transformation programs satisfy themselves with shifting the same old furniture about in the same old room. Some seek to throw some of the old furniture away. But real transformation occurs when we redesign the room itself. Perhaps even blow up the old room. It requires we change the thinking behind our thinking.[8]

Not all change is transformational. Transformational change has unique characteristics:

- It is sustainable.
- It's often subtle but has a profound impact.
- It's not predictable.
- It involves a shift in an individual's perspective/frame of reference, eg transformation involves not only a change in behaviours but also an emotional or psychological change – such as a change in values or mindset.
- Transformation involves a change in both heart and mind.
- Transformation is life-changing. The person now sees the world in a different way.

A caterpillar changing into a butterfly is not transformational. Once a butterfly, it can't change back to being a caterpillar. Its behaviours are very different and irreversible. A chameleon can change its colour, but it's still a chameleon. A snake can change its skin but is still a snake.

Understanding whether or not we need to be a transformational or transactional sales manager requires an accurate understanding of the problem/challenge to be solved. Does the problem/challenge that has be solved require transformation of the team, or just change?

Let's explore this through a case study. A newly appointed sales director inherits a challenge, which he describes as follows:

> My unit represents circa 20 per cent of the total revenue target for the UKI Market Unit (MU). We are a circa €44 million business. We are also the third largest unit globally in my organization and the largest contributor in our region (North EMEA). Although my unit's achievement has stayed steady year-on-year, the lack of growth has meant the business unit has struggled to maintain credibility. Senior leadership rapidly lost confidence in my predecessor's ability to lead the team to success. This lack of trust proliferated to the team, who in turn reacted by adopting behaviours that led to a culture of excuse-making, complaining, blaming others and ultimately resulted in lower motivation and heightened stress.
>
> Currently, as we head into the final quarter, we are tracking to achieve 72 per cent of our annual number. My unit cannot continue to perform to this level. My concern is that unless I can implement transformational change to drive new and improved behaviours in my sales team, my unit will not recover.
>
> In my previous role as an industry sales director I had a team that for several years had been considered one of the most highly performing in the UKI. My role was to move that team from being over-performant to being hyper-performant. To achieve this goal, we implemented new tools, techniques and sales behaviours that enabled me to successfully drive increased performance.
>
> When I reflect on why we were successful in implementing change, I realize that it was all delivered on a foundation of leadership credibility, trust, mutual respect, collaboration, and a belief that the team could influence their own success. Most important was their readiness to accept, and then embrace, these changes. Yes, there was always a level of uncertainty, risk, pressure and tension; however, that co-existed with an understanding and a collective agreement that these changes were being implemented for achieving positive and improved outcomes. I had their buy-in and this eased transition.
>
> Today, however, two immediate concerns exist:
>
> 1 Do I have the leadership credibility to drive change with my new team?
> 2 Is the team ready and willing to accept and embrace the changes that will lead us to success?

What kind of sales leadership approach would be required in this situation? A transactional sales management approach, ie one that focuses mainly on results? Or a transformational sales management approach, where the focus is on changing mindsets, values and beliefs?

It is clear that unless the hearts and minds are won over, the sceptical and cynical team would disrupt and potentially sabotage any attempts to improve the situation. His predecessors certainly tried that route and failed.

He developed a 30-, 60-, 90-day plan.

The 30-day plan

He held a 'get to know each other' team meeting at which he shared the fact that he would like to collectively have their ideas for how they could improve sales for the following year through a survey.

A SWOT survey was completed by all team members and analysed by his five line manager direct reports, for emergent themes and actions.

Focus was also on securing the pipeline for the final quarter – the team ended up with 82 per cent of their annual quota. A slightly better than expected result.

Two of his direct reports volunteered to form a project team and they organized the agenda for the next 30-day transformation plan. They refined the survey results into a team vision.

The 30–60-day plan

At the start of the new business year, a kick-off meeting was held during which:

- The co-created vision was presented – to be the team that others would aspire to join. This was discussed and most of the team signed up to this. The newly appointed director said he would do everything within his power to support this vision.
- They then used a technique called appreciative inquiry to flesh out the details for how this vision would be realized and then sustained.

Cooperrider's appreciative inquiry (AI)[9] theory was developed to take a positive approach to problem-solving to counter deficient models. It requires a belief that people have the potential to solve problems. It was selected as the best change model to develop an action plan – morale was low in the team and there was a belief that by involving the team in AI, hearts and minds would be won.

The appreciative inquiry process was applied as follows:

The objective: How do we become the team that others aspire to join?

Defining – best/good practice: Working with the team, they defined a collective review of the best team experiences they all had, either in current or past teams, and used this to generate ideas.

Dream – pushing the boundaries: The team were encouraged to be aspirational in developing ideas of a future state for that team. This included taking into account business targets as well as the culture they wanted to define.

Design – the future state: This involved taking a reality check on the ideas developed in the 'pushing the boundaries' phase and produced a realistic game plan, one that everyone bought into.

Destiny – empower the team, learn, adjust/improve: The psychological space was created to encourage the team to test new ideas in order to find ways to reignite the growth in this market.

This phase resulted in defining the team's shared purpose, revenue objectives, territory management and account coverage plans. The leading indicators were developed to show the team was working in the right direction. They defined how the team would communicate, how they would celebrate success, how quarterly business review meetings were to be conducted, and how they would celebrate the early wins to show they were on track.

The 60–90-day plan

This phase was focused on coaching, ensuring the team had the requisite skills, pipeline management and demand generation. The newly appointed director ensured that he supported team stakeholder management.

After 90 days they were seeing signs of progress and celebrating successes. Their pride had been restored; their values and belief systems were grounded in a new sense of purpose. By the end of the year the team had become one of the top-performing in the country. What particularly pleased the director was there was no attrition in his team.

So to summarize, a transformational sales manager:

- has the capacity to change their personal core belief systems while at the same time being tactical; they also have the capacity to change the core beliefs of their team;
- has the capacity for transformation and to recognize what is required – which allows for agility, flexibility and adhocracy;

- is also tactical – being tactical is still an important part of the job; it's not either one or the other.

Coaching to the mindsets

It's widely considered that sales managers do not spend enough time coaching. Based on the evidence of more than 100 sales managers now participating in our leading sales transformation master's programmes, we would say that less than 10 per cent of time is spent coaching – many managers simply do not understand what coaching is and what it isn't.

There is a world of difference between deal review coaching and coaching. One is geared to coaching an opportunity; the other is a mindset geared to coaching a person. Deal-focused micro-management is a great promoter of supplier-centric behaviour and, in the extreme, manipulation. If the sales manager is wanting to effect a sales transformation in their team, having a framework and coaching approach geared to changing and shifting mindsets and values is required, one that is focused on the person.

Often managers ask the wrong questions of salespeople. So intent are they to manage the pipeline that their management time has nothing to do with exploring how their sales teams can sell more by being bolder in their ideas with customers.

There are various models that are used for coaching. It's not the intent of this book to cover the topic in detail, but instead to provide a number of simple tools that could be used to help managers and key account managers keep the mindsets top of mind when observing sales conversations in action, or when reviewing account plans for examples of mindsets in action.

So how can sales managers coach to the mindsets? The simple tool in Table 12.1 is one that sales managers can use when observing how their sales teams interact with their customers.

TABLE 12.1 Mindsets for salespeople: coaching checklist

Name:				
Date:				
Authenticity	Green	Amber	Red	Notes
1. Customers find them honest, dependable and trustworthy.				
2. Does not try to sell 'off the shelf' solutions – customers know the solution is original.				

(continued)

TABLE 12.1 (Continued)

3. Through this person customers gain a good impression of the whole company.	
4. Customers are never made to feel pressured to buy.	

Client-centricity

1. Focuses on the specific needs of each customer and on providing the best solution they possibly can.	
2. Believes in developing long-term relationships with customers.	
3. Proactive in progressing the transaction and takes personal responsibility for identifying and solving problems.	
4. Listens carefully to what customers are saying. Explains things clearly and simply so that customers can understand.	
5. Keeps up to date with our own products and services.	

Proactive creativity

1. Enjoys thinking 'outside the box'.	
2. Spends time reflecting on specific customers' issues and what could be offered that would add value.	
3. Ideas challenge customers' thinking and push boundaries.	
4. Customers approach this person and ask for new ideas.	

Tactful audacity

1. Carefully plans and prepares each audacious approach to a customer – to ensure maximum value and impact, and minimum offence.	
2. Customers do not feel offended in response to any bold ideas presented or by the manner in which this person presents them.	
3. Knows the limits for how far to push a suggestion with a customer and does not overstep this.	
4. Self-confident and positive in discussions with customers.	

As many organizations rely on their key accounts for the majority of their business, it's important to consider the multiple touch points within a key account plan that demonstrate evidence of the mindsets in action.

These are summarized in Table 12.2 and could act as a checklist when reviewing key account plans.

A simple scoring mechanism (Table 12.3) can be used to evaluate the plan once completed. To ensure it becomes a living document in this fast-changing world, the plan should be reviewed at regular intervals. We suggest using a 0–5 ranking.

TABLE 12.2 Key account plans: mindsets applied

The mindsets	The behaviour	Multiple touch points
Authenticity	Ethical orientation	Account plan objectives – purpose-driven account planning Client involvement in the process?
Client-centricity	Client 'thoughtfulness' and relevance of solution	Strategy grid; SWOT element Analyst research – cracking the industry code Customer's customer focus Co-creating plan with customer Solution development
Proactive creativity	Out-of-the-box thinking	Strategy grid: strategy element Whitespace analysis
Tactful audacity	Commercial action plans	Win themes Commercial action plans

TABLE 12.3 PACT checklist

P	To what extent are the outputs of your account plan living the value of 'proactive creativity'?	0–5
A	To what extent are the outputs of your account plan living the value of 'authenticity'?	0–5
C	To what extent are the outputs of your account plan living the value of 'client-centricity'?	0–5
T	To what extent are the outputs of your account plan living the value of 'tactful audacity'?	0–5

Organization support for a client-centric culture

Board recognition is hugely important. Some organizations intent on developing an organizational client-centric culture have an annual award for those accounts where the mindsets are best demonstrated and evidenced. It takes a considerable investment of time but will go a long way to elevating the culture internally:

- Managers are invited to nominate exemplar account managers after year-end.
- The account managers submit their nominations, typically as PowerPoints or PDF presentations. Their content provides the context for the account, explains why their account has been nominated and where the evidence is to support the application. This could include client testimonials.
- Business impact is a factor, but not the main factor. An account manager may be doing a great job in an account that is not growing or where the addressable market has not yet materialized.
- Depending on the business size, the winners of different categories are assessed for a final winner 'prize'. Each winner has a ten-minute time slot to present their case and they are asked exactly the same questions. The questions deliberately explore application of the mindsets.
- The assessment board comprises board-level executives, an external assessor and other key stakeholders. This ensures objectivity and currency. The nominees know that considerable effort is made – commensurate with the award's value to the organization.
- At an awards dinner the category winners receive prizes and the final winner a CEO or chairperson award.

In many cases we have seen clients themselves provide testimony (some on video) to the creative and bold ideas and business impact the account team's efforts have made. It's a great way to collect substantive case studies – ones that could be used later for marketing purposes.

A lot of creating the right organizational culture has to do with the level of empowerment given to sales organizations and psychological safety if ideas fail.

The role of the team manager in cultivating a tactful audacity culture is key

Managers need to allow their teams the space to try things out; clearly they will want to see a business case, but if the business case suggests a different tack or an investment to make something work, their job is to find the resources to make it happen.

Concluding comments

This and previous chapters have focused on the proposition that the values that underpin sales behaviour become the operating system of a selling approach. These have been codified into the four positive mindsets and four negative mindsets. We are not sure that it matters what behavioural sales system sits on these – the 'applications', if you will, that connect with the operating system. This could be a future source of research for academics and practitioners who want to test which 'applications' best fit with a values-driven approach. What we do know through the testing of the mindset constructs over the years and the evidence of their application – shared in this book with the case studies and stories of exceptional sales practice – is their power to transform sales performance. So far we have not seen any evidence that they are not fit for purpose.

Furthermore, in this post-knowledge era, the emergent recognition of the significance of customer experience, the research of professors such as Adam Grant and his theories of generosity, reinforce their importance as a source of competitive advantage – a source of competitive advantage, as we know from previous and current research, that less than 10 per cent of salespeople meet customer expectations.

The values are simple to understand but not simplistic to execute. Supporting tools such as 3rd Box Thinking™, customer strategy grid, the tools to support key account planning, etc all help, but it's the 'ecosystem', ie the 'environment' that salespeople work in, that is also a critical factor in enabling salespeople to sell in a manner that fits their personal ethical practice and those of their customers.

The book has to some extent explored how managers, part of that ecosystem, 'manage the business of selling'. We have introduced different systems of sales management – tactical and transformative. If the present and the future are about sales transformation – and we know that transformation involves changing and adapting values and beliefs – unless managers also understand how to shift mindsets, nothing will happen. As we have said before, 'it's like wearing a new suit and expecting transformation to happen'.

The book has so far highlighted the personal and professional bias that influences what we want to see and hear, and suggested the five mindsets/values that are required of sales managers and sales leaders in order to thrive in today's fast-changing and unpredictable sales environment.

Critical reflection is arguably one of the most important competencies of sales professionals. How do we objectively reflect on sales experiences that are subjective so we can better figure out solutions to complex problems? How do we do that in real time, in the moment and intuitively?

This chapter has focused on what organizations can do from a management and cultural perspective to elevate the professionalism of the sales team. There are other important aspects of the sales 'ecosystem' that also help salespeople to thrive and transform their professional status. These are to do with the educational support provided to salespeople and sales managers, respect from other disciplines of a business as to the role sales play in building shareholder value, and finally how professional bodies can elevate the status of salespeople. These topics are covered in the final chapter – looking to the future.

Endnotes

1 https://c1.sfdcstatic.com/content/dam/web/en_us/www/documents/reports/sales/state-of-sales-3rd-ed.pdf (archived at https://perma.cc/ZJ2A-E9UL)
2 https://vimeo.com/consalia/review/182895866/949a1b037c (archived at https://perma.cc/S32L-MQZQ)
3 https://vimeo.com/375649050 (archived at https://perma.cc/MB8H-Q8R8)
4 https://www.ted.com/talks/simon_sinek_how_great_leaders_inspire_action?language=en (archived at https://perma.cc/B9LT-NM42)
5 Wilkinson, D (2006) *The Ambiguity Advantage*, Palgrave Macmillan, Basingstoke
6 Drucker, P (1985) *The Practice of Management*, HarperCollins, New York
7 Jordan, J and Vazzana, M (2011) *Cracking the Sales Management Code: The secrets to measuring and managing sales performance*, McGraw-Hill, New York
8 Zohar, D (1997) *Rewiring the Corporate Brain: Using the new science to rethink how we structure and lead organizations*, Berrett-Koehler Publishers, San Francisco
9 Cooperrider, D and Whitney, D (2005) *Appreciative Inquiry*, Berrett-Koehler Publishers, San Francisco

13

Looking to the future

Having reflected on how the context for selling has changed from 17000 BC, to the opening up of the silk trade routes, and having considered how the sources for competitive advantage in selling have changed through the industrial era, knowledge era and are transforming through the post-knowledge era, how will selling transform as we look to the future?

A 'new' context influenced by changing attitudes to the environment, developing theories of the levers of economic growth, and improvements to how we learn will influence what we sell, how we sell and why we sell, and will encourage new standards of professionalism in sales.

In this final chapter we shall therefore explore:

- the emerging customer experience (Cx) focus: purpose-driven value-creation;
- the future of capitalism and economic theory: implications for sales;
- capitalization of sales relationships: where value and values intersect;
- the professionalization of sales: the final frontier.

The emerging Cx focus: purpose-driven value-creation

BlackRock is the world's largest global investment manager, managing circa $7 trillion in assets.[1] CEO Larry Fink wrote an open letter to CEOs, published on BlackRock's website, in which he says:

> I believe we are on the edge of a fundamental reshaping of finance… In the near future – and sooner than most anticipate – there will be a significant reallocation of capital… a company cannot achieve long-term profits without embracing purpose and considering the needs of a broad range of stakeholders.[2]

The one key theme in this purpose-driven statement is climate change. He argues that climate change is climate risk, one that will impact prices, costs and consumer demand across entire economies. Climate risk is investment risk. BlackRock have openly committed to only investing in those companies that have a purpose-driven strategy.

As part of their commitment, they plan to divest around $500 million out of their coal-producing investments.[3] In addition to climate change, Fink includes diversity policy, data protection policy and business ethics as themes they review when assessing investments. As a warning shot to those many companies in which they invest, he says they will be 'disposed to vote against management and boards' where they feel little progress is being made.

Evidence that organizational boards are measuring and being measured on non-financial criteria can be seen in their corporate social responsibility statements and public announcements. Now non-fiscal measures of performance, such as carbon emissions, women in management, contributions to world health, etc, are gaining more prominence in their being presented alongside fiscal measures.

Take the software giant SAP as just one example: at the same time as announcing their most recent financial results, they also include challenging non-financial targets:

- greenhouse gas emissions reduced for the fifth year in a row, on track for being carbon-neutral by 2025;
- women's representation in the workforce: 34 per cent; women in management: 26 per cent; remains committed to goal of 30 per cent by 2022.[4]

For selling organizations needing to align with the values of the organizations they sell to, they too will need to develop purpose-driven account plans. Procurement will evaluate suppliers on CSR goals they aspire to as well as ethical and supply chain risk.

I agree with Alf Janssen, SAP's sales director strategic accounts based in Holland, who in a recently published research article[5] talks about 'purpose as a profit centre' and posits that purpose-driven account plans will be the new normal. He cites in this article a range of examples that prove purpose-driven organizations create value. These include:

- increases in share price;
- increases in sales;
- increases in employee engagement;
- consumer spending preferences for purpose-driven organizations.

Customers will be less concerned with what you sell and how you sell, but will want to know why you sell. What is the purpose behind you, ie your values and those of your companies? They are interested to know what your intent is and will be informally and formally making a judgement call on these, the intangible assets of your business.

The COVID-19 pandemic will have a profound impact in many ways. Purpose-driven businesses will want to provide their staff with the psychological support to handle crisis, make every effort to keep their employees safe, to allow for different levels of tolerance to risk. They will also seek to develop purpose-driven initiatives and realize the collective responsibility for corporations and citizens worldwide to care for each other.

The future of capitalism: implications for sales

No one, not even former head of the Federal Reserve Alan Greenspan, expected the Wall Street financial crash of 13 October 2008 that led to the bailout of all the major US banks. Just days before the crash, he was saying there was nothing to worry about. A few days later on 23 October, during a live, televised US Senate Committee hearing, he commented defensively:

> I made a mistake in presuming that the self-interest of organizations, specifically banks and others, was such that they were best capable of protecting their own shareholders.[6]

And he went on to say that the crisis had found a flaw and that 'I had been going for 40 years with considerable evidence it (my economic policies) was working well'.

Much of his and other world banks' economic theories were schooled in what Applebaum, in his book *The Economists' Hour*,[7] refers to as the Chicago School monetarist theories. These were made famous by the Nobel Prize-winning economist Milton Friedman (advisor to Reagan and Thatcher), who advocated, amongst other theories, that markets should self-regulate – that government regulation policies would stifle economic growth.

Applebaum argues that traditionally held views on levers for economic management, such as those based on money supply, interest rates, tax cuts, high/low unemployment and self-regulation, are no longer valid. They are no longer predictors of economic performance, and Applebaum cites the October 2008 crash as being the pivotal moment that old theories of economic management were no longer fit for purpose.

Milanovic, in his 2019 book *Capitalism, Alone: The future of the system that rules the world*,[8] also warns that capitalism as we know it must change. That whilst the global economies have thrived, the gap between the wealthy and the poor has widened. The traditional measures of country wealth GDP hide more troubling data. The middle class in particular has been squeezed, with real income levels dropping. He observes such is the inequality in wealth that the 'social contract' is being challenged – the social contract being the acceptance by those being governed and by those governing that the environment in which they live and work is okay.

Examples of extreme 'challenge' can be seen in the Arab uprising that started in Tunisia in 2010 and then spread to Egypt in 2011. Some may consider it unlikely that such uprisings could happen in the developed economies, but the developed world is experiencing large-scale populist movements – particularly on the topics of climate change (Greta Thunberg), equality and diversity, and freedom (Hong Kong) – and is observing how these movements can affect policy.

Questions are being asked of the current economic theories and policies as to how to deal with the COVID-19 pandemic and its impact on a global downturn. Are they fit for purpose? The *Financial Times* in its 'Big Read. Coronavirus',[9] talks of four of the world's leading economic advisors, all who played leading roles in the 2008 financial crisis, now seriously questioning the premises of monetarist economic policy to stimulate growth and confidence. They argue that fiscal policies based on tax reduction and increased government spending are more appropriate measures in the current climate.

The key question as it relates to many of us is this – will the impact that the virus has on the 'demand' and 'supply chain' be temporary? Is this something that will just pass over, or will it make organizations and countries become more nationalistic and more self-contained? What impact will this have on the way we approach our global accounts or sell internationally? To what extent will the virus change people's views on global mobility and travel? What impact will this have on what and how we sell? Inevitably out of the pandemic crisis there will be opportunities and threats. Organizations, with their instinct for survival, will look to find ways around the problem to manage the risks involved and look for opportunities for growth.

Arguably we are in the midst of a significant mindset shift – the short-term focus on quarterly results is seen by many as detrimental to driving long-term shareholder value. The trend to 'private ownership' as opposed to 'public ownership' is perhaps indicative that a new attitude to value-creation is taking place – an attitude that is more conducive for collaboration and a more sustainable future, where salespeople work with customers to innovate and co-create value.

The pressure on salespeople to close deals to meet quarterly targets – current practice in so many organizations – is a reflection of stock market sentiment and is, in many ways, counterproductive (particularly in those organizations that fail to develop sufficient pipelines). Furthermore, customers will either use this pressure to drive down prices, or will avoid working with suppliers who don't pursue client-centric strategies.

Perhaps as the monetarists' theories of country wealth-creation are being challenged, so too might we challenge the traditional levers for increasing sales teams' performance through financial incentives and commission-based schemes. In extreme cases the pressure to close deals can lead to unethical sales practice. Airbus, in the highly competitive aircraft manufacturing business, for example, has recently received a $4 billion fine for a worldwide bribery scheme[10] developed by its strategy and marketing division, responsible for worldwide sales in emerging markets.

The role of regulation in sales and transparency

As self-regulated economic practices are being challenged by leading economists, perhaps questions could also be asked of self-regulated sales practices. It's not until there is a crisis that regulation and legislation emerge.

In the UK, the personal protection insurance (PPI) mis-selling scandal purportedly cost the banking sector over £50 billion.[11] It has resulted in legislation preventing banks from incentivizing inappropriate sales commission. The Financial Conduct Authority (FCA), created in 2013, now has significant power to ensure consumers are protected from selling malpractice. Many banks in the UK have scrapped their sales organizations and invested in systems and people to promote customer service – their example now copied by banks in other countries.

Thus we may be seeing early signs that governance of the sales process is being mandated in certain sectors. To what extent the concept of sales governance will spread to other sectors, only time will tell – much depends on ethics. The more sales is able to improve its brand through ethics, innovation and co-creation, and transparency, the less pressure there will be on regulatory intervention.

Transparency has been an issue partly because the selling systems required to manage the business of selling transparently have been slow to catch on compared with systems that manage the functions for other departments. For example, unsurprisingly the earliest evidence of financial accounting systems dates back to 300 BC to the Persians, Greeks and Romans. The first manufacturing systems date to the industrial era in the late 18th century. The first sales system can be traced to the late 19th century with the development of cash tills!

Whereas accounting started having computerized systems in the 1950s, sales did not benefit from computerization until the late 1980s with digital Rolodex contact management applications. These had extremely limited capability. Arguably it's not been until this millennium, with emerging cloud-based applications such as SalesForce, SAP CRM, Oracle CRM and Microsoft Dynamics, that sales organizations have had access to the systems that enable the sales function to be properly managed. These systems provide deeper insights into the levers that create economic value and that go beyond revenue and sales pipeline management, the traditional focus areas of CRM.

If a values-driven approach is a source of competitive advantage, to what extent can the economic value of relationships that exist between customers and suppliers be measured? Can CRM and technology solutions help provide us with the data now, hitherto unavailable and not transparent, and therefore aid the way *relational economic value* is assessed?

Capitalization of sales relationships: where value and values intersect

Why should we be concerned about this? Some years ago the CEO of a corporate finance company made a passing comment that one of the most difficult aspects of selling a company was in determining the extent to which future revenues could be reliably predicted post-acquisition. He described the prediction process as a 'black hole'. To what extent was the loyalty of customers based, for example, on the key stakeholders of a business? What would the impact be if that stakeholder or stakeholders were to leave? How secure were the current contracts of customers in legal terms? What types of contract does the selling company have with its customers? What churn factor does it have with its customers? What attitudes do customers have towards the selling company, which would determine if sales grow or decline? These questions are pertinent to auditors and the corporate finance world as well as to chief sales officers.

A recent alumnus of ours took on the role of chief commercial officer for a tech company with a large global salesforce. His first task was to do an assessment of sales and the sales organization. The way sales is reported and forecasts made is notoriously unscientific. This makes it very difficult to answer the following questions:

- How is the sales organization currently structured to cover its targeted territory (ie market)?
- Are the right people in the right place to cover the territory?
- Is the cost model correct to serve the territory?
- Have we got the right balance between channel partners, inside sales and the field salesforce?
- To what extent are we currently serving our key accounts? What are our current relationships with these accounts? Who holds these relationships?
- To what extent are we vulnerable to salespeople leaving?
- How reliant are we on existing and new customers?
- What risk do we have in the types of contract we hold with customers?
- To what extent can I rely on the sales revenues of the past to forecast revenues in the future?

Yet the worlds of sales and finance rarely meet. Finance departments often consider their own salespeople to be overpaid with large expense accounts and don't particularly trust those salespeople who sell to them. Salespeople often view finance managers as blockers, lacking in vision, and too risk-averse. It's time to bring the disciplines of these two 'professions' together.

Relationship capitalization is the process of capitalizing the value of client contracts and the network of people and organizations that represent employees' clients, partners and suppliers. It is explained as the value created and maintained by nurturing and managing good relationships. It is therefore a predictor of the current and future value of (key) accounts and as such can be measured.

If the value of relationships is capitalized in an organization's balance sheet, the 'why do we sell', the 'what do we sell' and the 'how do we sell' become important. These questions not only matter to customers, but would also matter to finance.

Let's focus on the finance element first.

It's helpful to understand the core elements that contribute to the valuation of the tangible and intangible assets of a business. These core elements are governed by a number of International Reporting Financial Standards (IFRS). The IFRS is a not-for-profit global body responsible for setting standards for accounting. These standards are set to provide consistency in the way these assets are measured. It provides reassurance, a common language and reference point to both the sellers and buyers of a business.

Valuing the tangible assets of a business such as property, stock, plant and machinery is relatively easily done, but often it's the intangible assets of a business that are the major determinants of company valuation and that are more difficult to assess.

The intangible assets of a business comprise the value of the business's brand, its technology and goodwill.

The levers of value of a brand could include:

- market awareness – how well known is the brand?
- the integrity of the brand – to what extent does the brand deliver on its promise?
- the brand's uniqueness in the marketplace;
- the degree to which customers are satisfied with the brand;
- how much trust exists in the brand;
- how well the marketing and advertising support the brand.

The levers of value of the technology of a company could include:

- patents;
- high entry barriers for competitors;
- licences.

The levers of value of goodwill could include:

- supplier contracts;
- customer contracts.

IAS 38 is the specific accounting standard developed by the IFRS to advise on how intangible assets (not including goodwill) are measured and amortized.

Of the assessments mentioned above, accounting conventions are such that technology and brand valuations are amortized over a period of time. The capitalization of goodwill, though, is fixed – the idea being that the reason company A buys company B is due to synergies coming from customers, lower costs, and that the value of the goodwill therefore should not diminish. Companies, though, are required to re-evaluate goodwill on an annual basis. If the goodwill is reduced, this is termed an *impairment* and the written-down value of the goodwill has an immediate effect on the profit and loss account.

An example of the importance of getting the valuation right can be seen in Hewlett-Packard Enterprise's (HPE) 2011 Autonomy acquisition for $10.3 billion.[12] Mike Lynch, then the CEO of Autonomy, had built the company up to being one of the most successful IT pure play software start-ups in the UK. One year after the acquisition, HPE announced an $8 billion impairment charge, of which $5 billion was attributed to Autonomy, and a legal case was taken against Mike Lynch and his then CFO Sushovan Hussain.

The essence of the allegations is that between 2009 and 2011, Autonomy had inflated its revenues, revenue growth and gross margins. In addition to software sales, the pure play software company was selling hardware and using the hardware revenues to inflate revenues.[13]

The case is still ongoing at the time of writing and no verdict has been made, but even so, the impairment charge has seriously affected shareholders. In the immediate minutes after the announcement, HPE's shares fell by 13 per cent, and by the end of the year had fallen by 55 per cent.

So how are future revenues valued (as an intangible asset) in a company's accounts? Deloitte have identified three critical attributes of an intangible asset:

- Are they identifiable, ie is it capable of being sold, transferred, licensed, rented or exchanged, either individually or together? One of the examples they provide of intangible assets are customer and supplier relationships.
- Are they controlled, ie to what extent can one obtain benefits of the asset?
- Can they produce future economic benefit, such as increased revenue or reduced cost?[14]

On the basis that company A may buy company B on the basis of its client base as well as its technologies/products, clearly the client base and its expected revenue and profit-generation will be considered an intangible asset.

Yet this notion of capitalizing customer accounts as assets as it pertains to an organization's balance sheet is rare; in fact, the only time it tends to be scrutinized financially from a valuation perspective is at the point of a company sale.

According to David Haigh,[15] CEO of the world's leading independent brand valuation consultancy:

> The accountancy profession fully recognizes that customer capital is an asset but is only willing to recognize it in the balance sheet post acquisition, because International Accounting Standard 3 makes it compulsory to recognize all acquired intangible assets in the balance sheet. However, the profession will not allow the recognition of customer capital and other intangible assets in the balance sheet if they are 'home grown' rather than acquired. This is a major reporting failure which needs to be addressed so that these fundamental corporate assets can be recognized in financial statements.

When valuing client contracts, audit companies mostly review revenue trend level and margin level and then use discounted cash flow models to predict the future economic value of those accounts.

This does not take into account two critical and contributing factors that significantly contribute to the future sales. These are perceived sales and service culture of the organization:

- In terms of sales, are the key accounts managers living the positive mindsets?
- What is the quality of the service delivery once contracts have been sold?

If the type of client contracts – with the quantity and quality of client relationships – was explicitly valued on a regular basis, it would drive the right kind of behaviour and create more value at the point of sale, thus linking the principles of key account management directly to shareholder value.

This would also result in a higher degree of ethical sales practice. For example, if sales directors were set key performance indicators that drive higher customer valuations, it would have a direct impact on how they structure their sales organizations, focus the sales teams on the leading indicators required to improve future sales performance, increase customer loyalty and retention, and mitigate risk of losing key accounts through its new business and existing business mix. It would ensure that the highest levels of customer experience were achieved and the manner in which salespeople sell was reflected through professionalism and ethics. How practical is this idea?

It is a well-known fact that in the business-to-business (B2B) world, the 80:20 rule applies to many companies – that is, that 80 per cent of the revenues come from 20 per cent of their customers. We also know that it is easier and more cost-effective to sell existing products to existing customers.

A thorough exploration of how IAS 38 rules could be applied to key accounts is therefore a good starting point for key account strategy, as potentially this could provide an accurate valuation of 80 per cent of a company's revenues.

So what data do we need to review in order to do a valuation of a key account relationship? To take this beyond a sketchily conducted practice to a more structured and systematic approach, we need to combine some of the disciplines of an audit review with what we know to be the highest standards of key account selling.

We believe this involves a review of three broad areas and a ten-point assessment process (Table 13.1).

The good news is that now most of the data required can be automated within a CRM system. Technically it's possible to automate account valuations depending on whether the right fields in the CRM system are set up to do this.

TABLE 13.1 Relationship capitalization chart

	Source
1. Contract Type – Legal Construct	
1. What type of contracts do we have with our customers?	Contacts
2. If so, what period of time do these contracts cover – one year, two years, three years, etc?	Contacts
3. What break-out clauses does the customer have?	Contacts
2. Financial Contribution	
4. What is the gross margin we are making on these contracts?	Finance
5. What is the future cash flow predicted for the account as per the type of contract?	Finance
3. Relational Contribution	
6. Where and with whom do the relationships currently exist? (Is it at the right level?)	CRM
7. How often are we in contact with the customers?	CRM
8. What values do we express in the way we sell to these accounts?	Mindset Survey
9. What relationships do we have throughout the organization, its employees and partners with the client?	Introhive
10. What is our NPS score (or an equivalent) with the customer?	NPS Survey

If the relationship capitalization is officially recognized by the financial community, it would certainly transform the relationships between sales and finance and encourage deeper scrutiny of what constitutes value.

The leading indicators of relationship-building will be more closely measured. How safe is a contract if the customer has no trust in the supplier's sales approach? How safe is a contract if there is relationship risk? How predicable are future sales if contract types are short term? Salespeople could justify investments in relationship-building activities if finance teams could see their impact on improving relationship capital.

The final frontier: the professionalization of sales?

The sales community can be better served by those that teach it. In previous chapters we have reviewed *what* is being taught, we have questioned different approaches and we suggest a new paradigm is required – one based on values. In this section we shall look at *how* sales is being taught and, in a similar fashion, perceptions of what good looks like.

What is the difference between being professional and being a professional?

1. As we explore the idea of the professionalization of sales, it's worth considering the difference between being 'professional' and being 'a professional'.

2. The term 'a profession', as it refers to occupations, is defined by the *Oxford English Dictionary* as: An occupation in which a professed knowledge of some subject, field, or science is applied; a vocation or career, especially one that involves prolonged training and a formal qualification.[16]

3. Many start their career in sales accidentally. It's not currently thought of as a profession (except by those in it perhaps), and for many school-leavers the idea of pursuing a career in sales does not enter their mind. Yet once in a sales role, particularly B2B sales, many consider it a profession. But how legitimately can one lay claim to sales being a profession? Unlike the medical profession or engineering or accounting or law – where educational attainments have to be realized before one can claim to be a doctor, etc – anyone can call themselves a professional salesperson from day one of a sales career.

4 Being professional is acting within a defined code of conduct. It's entirely possible professionals can act unprofessionally, be disbarred from continuing to practise, and in some cases receive a prison sentence. In the case of the sales profession, it's possible to receive a prison sentence or fine for, say, fraud, but it's currently possible to continue the practice of sales in spite of previous misdemeanours. There is no official register of sales professionals currently, but perhaps in the future there will be.

5 Even the best laid codes of conduct will be tested and stretched by unscrupulous practitioners; however, this is not a reason in sales to give up. For selling as a profession to earn the trust of buying customers, it's important that there are initiatives aimed at working towards professional status.

There are two routes to professionalization:

1 One is for that profession to be represented by a not-for-profit foundation, ideally a chartered institute, accountable for the setting of standards and representing the interests of the profession.

2 The other is the attainment of academic qualifications that meet the standards.

Chartered status is considered by many, even those outside the UK, as being the ultimate qualification in a given profession. The term originates from royal charters issued by the British monarch and rights to the award are bestowed by its Privy Council.

Acknowledgement of meeting the strict criteria for chartered status is made by a body outside the profession and therefore arguably more objective. It is a prestigious award and recognizes a strong code of ethics supported by professional education.

There are over 80 professions with chartered status on the Privy Council list – these range from the universally known chartered accountants, chartered engineers and chartered surveyors to the less well-known chartered statistician and chartered town planner.

Whereas the Chartered Institute of Procurement and Supply (for the buying community) was awarded a Royal Charter in 1992, there is no Chartered Institute for Sales Professionals.

To qualify for professional recognition by the Privy Council, four key criteria must be met:

- It must be a unique profession.
- Corporate members should be qualified to at least a first-degree level in a relevant discipline.

- The institution that represents the profession must be commercially viable.
- It is in the public interest to regulate the body in this way.

A reinvigorated drive to professionalize the sales community has led to the advent of more professional representative bodies, such as the Association of Professional Sales in the UK. One might expect the same in the USA. The Sales Association, the Strategic Account Management Association, the Sales Management Association and the Sales Education Foundation are all examples of US-based not-for-profit bodies that represent sales. However, there is no equivalent in the USA of the American Medical Association, a governing body to represent the standards and ethical sales practices of the sales community.

As far as the UK is concerned, it is only since 2018 that all the Privy Council criteria are being met:

- The APS has been formed, now with 2,000 or so members and commercially viable.
- In 2018, the first undergraduate degree was formally launched for business-to-business sales professionals.
- It's in the public interest to protect buyers from mis-selling practices.
- It's a unique profession.

By successfully obtaining chartered status, the sales community would have made a giant step forward as far as professional recognition is concerned – at least in the UK.

According to the US Sales Education Foundation, in 2007 only a handful of US universities offered a sales degree. Now 130 US universities offer a degree. It's been one of the fastest-growing programmes in the USA. Perhaps this is understandable, as sales as a profession is more respected in the USA. Outside of the USA, the chance to do a sales degree is extremely limited. Only a few universities in Europe offer a sales degree; and to my knowledge, none is offered in the Far East.

In 2016 the UK government passed the Enterprise Act (2016), effectively setting up a new government department – the Institute for Apprenticeships (IFA) – responsible for setting the standards and funding for employer-led apprenticeships up to undergraduate and postgraduate degrees.

The first step was for employers to agree the functions in a business that warranted such a standard and this required government agreement. It may come as no surprise to those within sales that the government perception of sales was rather sceptical at first, and surprisingly few realize there is a world of difference between business-to-consumer selling and business-to-business selling.

But working with employers such as British Telecom, Royal Mail, Whitbread, Kimberly-Clark and SIG, and with the support of the not-for-profit APS and a number of UK universities, the sales profession was finally recognized as such by the UK government. With that recognition came the chance to develop a business-to-business sales degree (BSc) and then later a senior sales leadership postgraduate master's degree.

Consalia was enormously proud to be part of the trailblazer group chaired by Graham Davis, then the group sales director of Royal Mail and supported by our own Louise Sutton, academy director.

The apprenticeship programme is part of a government initiative to make university education more relevant to business and to enable the country to be better equipped to meet the challenges that lie ahead. Students are employed on apprenticeship contracts that ensure they have around one day a week for 'academic' study. It's an incredibly practical and relevant way for students to learn and earn at the same time.

Hundreds of 'students' (undergraduates and postgraduates) are now embarking on our two- and three-year sales education programmes – supported by many household names such as those mentioned above, as well as Amazon, Microsoft, Toshiba, Sharp, Aon, E.ON, and many others. The pace at which the degree is being adopted is testament to the latent demand for such an initiative.

Yet still many in sales consider academic studies 'too academic' and therefore not practical. This is misguided but perhaps understandable given the traditional approaches taken by the academic community to how education is delivered. If selling is to be transformed, it could be argued that academic approaches to teaching on the subject require transformation as well.

As one might expect, academic commentary on the efficacy of traditional approaches to sales training is quite well documented:

> It is the unique combination of academic research-led education, consulting thought leadership and business expertise that can create a powerful new pedagogical approach towards the development of the aforementioned selling skills. Despite being a sizeable industry in mature markets, sales training has been found ineffective or less than useful.[17]

Corporate sales education in the past has often been 'prescriptive', 'linear' and content-centred rather than learner-centred. Cron et al (2005)[18] describe traditional sales training programmes as 'standardized (common to all salespeople), top–down (management decides), mandated (nonvoluntary), structured (formal and centralized), and offered in classroom' (p 124), thus potentially out of sync with the evolution of the sales function. The implication of their research is that it is not what salespeople are taught that is the issue; it's they way they are taught.

Since 2006 a number of sales organizations have embarked on implementing a master's-level postgraduate degree on leading sales transformation. Its current iteration has been developed and co-created with SAP, the global software business. Since its inception, other organizations – such as Sony Mobile, Toshiba Tec, SKF, Royal Caribbean Cruises – have participated. The programme has provided a 'unique platform to link research in sales in a mutually reinforcing way'.[19] Unlike traditional master's programmes, 90 per cent of the academic credit is based on learning in the workplace.

Where did the idea of work-based learning with academic accreditation originate? David Kolb, a hugely influential educationalist, acknowledged years later that Dewey was one of the main influences on his ground-breaking 1984 book *Experiential Learning: Experience as the source of learning and development*.[20] Donald Schon was also a key figure. His 1983 book *The Reflective Practitioner*[21] was a core influence in shaping a new approach to work-based learning.

However, it is uniquely in the UK that these ideas have come to life in the academic world.

The pedagogical approach for the master's was developed in the 1990s by Derek Portwood, then at Middlesex University, with Jenny Naish and Dr Peter Critten. Their initiative was funded by a UK government grant with the aim of recognizing learning in the workplace up to doctorate level. Organizations such as Ford were early adopters of the approach. It led to the creation of the National Centre of Work Based Learning and then later the Institute for Work Based Learning, headed up by Professor Jonathan Garnett. It has been a great privilege to have been able to work with Jonathan, Peter Critten and Pro Vice Chancellor Anna Kyprianou in developing these world-class programmes.

Table 13.2 outlines the learning methodology that underpins the master's programme.

TABLE 13.2 New approach to sales education[22]

Learning interventions and tools	Pedagogical strategies	Educational approach
Work-based assignments	Action research	Problems are not separated out from the social context within which they occur, thus the interplay between research in sales and expertise underpins the programme. Organizational change and improving delegates' practice in their sales organizations is encouraged for increased sales effectiveness.
Peer learning sets	Experiential learning	Individual and collective reflective practice is empowered. Reconstruction of experience and paradigm shift are fostered to envision new possibilities in managing the sales organization and to create new opportunities with customers.
Personal development plans	Reflective practice	Enhanced self-awareness and evaluation of outcomes, both organizational (eg sales growth) and personal (eg mindsets), are promoted to help make a difference in own and others' careers.

Following the master's programmes, a fast-growing body of practitioner-based research has resulted and with it the chance to review its impact on organizational business performance and personal sales practice.

This is an example of how one organization, Toshiba Tec, has leveraged an education sales approach to dramatically improve sales performance. Carl Day, the head of sales for Toshiba's indirect sales channel, wanted to embark on a master's and was considering an MBA. Having been impressed by seeing a number of the SAP sales leaders present their master's projects at a sales conference, he approached his dealers with the idea that the owners and senior sales directors jointly go through the master's programme.

Imagine their reaction for a moment. The photocopier sales market is not often associated with academic research. Many in that sector do not have an undergraduate degree. The reasons why they signed up to the programme were varied, but all shared a desire to have a 'stamp', an external accreditation to reflect they had reached a certain standard. Little did they appreciate the business impact this would have.

TABLE 13.3 Control group ROI

	(2012) % of Toshiba business	2012–2014 revenue trends	(2014) % of Toshiba business	2014–2016 revenue trends	(2016) % of Toshiba business
Control Group1 – MSc intervention	40%	↓15%	34%	↑45%	41%
Control Group2 – No intervention	60%	↑10%	66%	↑12%	59%
Total channel sales		↑.23%		↑21%	

The programme involved the sales directors going through seven modules of formal learning intervention in workshops, typically of a two-day duration, followed by peer coaching and a work-based project. The final dissertation was the seventh module.

After two years Carl was able to compare the results of those dealers who participated in a master's (MSc) programme with those who did not.[23] All dealers had the same market opportunity, so the comparison is valid. In a declining market, Toshiba saw a 15 per cent decline in revenues between 2012 and 2014 reversed with those leaders on the programme, delivering a 45 per cent increase in revenue between 2014 and 2016 (Table 13.3). This contributed to a total revenue increase of 21 per cent, with the selected master's group contributing 62 per cent of total revenue growth in this period.

Individual theories of practice have emerged based on academic research, but practitioner-based research applied to many different aspects of sales leadership and sales practice all geared to transform the way sales professionals sell and lead sales practice.

Their research topics include: reviewing the systems of remuneration, coaching, key account practice, relationship management, complex adaptive systems, pipeline management, the efficacy of the challenger sale, change management, winning large deals, emotional intelligence, leadership style, data-driven coaching, leading and lagging indicators, team-building, managing internal stakeholders, developing communities of practice, customer-centric sales management systems, transforming sales performance, sales enablement models, creating new change models, and the positive mindsets in action.

However, many universities themselves currently lack the faculty to deliver the sales content; sales modules are often small parts of a larger marketing programme. Very few embrace the topic, with the result that compared with, say, marketing, little academic research is undertaken in sales.

It makes logical sense, therefore, to find a way to give the sales community the tools to reflect academically and objectively and for the sales community to judge what works and what does not work in sales.

It may be that the approach to academic education initiated by Middlesex University and Consalia is paving the way for other of the more traditional education establishments to follow.

For progress, both sides are required to recognize and respect the functions and capabilities of the other. But progress has been made.

Back in the day when I started my career in sales, preparation for the role involved little more than learning a script and being able to deliver it convincingly. Certainly times have changed since then; we have seen massive growth in the sales training sector to meet demand from industry.

Sales training practices have evolved over the years as consulting organizations have sought to match the content of their programmes to the reality on the ground, taking into account the changing dynamic between customer and supplier, the emergence of new methodologies, and the need for a more consistent approach to sales excellence.

Over the past decade a body of knowledge has emerged that is driving increasing professionalism within the sales community.

In parallel, businesses have been looking for a more strategic approach to sales development with the establishment of in-house sales academies to provide a comprehensive framework across the organization – though admittedly these remain largely the preserve of the large corporates.

Now, however, we stand at a point where traditional approaches to training must be questioned: as we have seen, one-size-fits-all approaches, sheep-dip programmes, do not deliver great results and do not meet today's requirements for flexibility and agility. Perhaps we are witnessing the beginnings of transformation in the way salespeople expect and deserve to be 'educated' (not just attend a few sales training workshops), where salespeople are provided the tools to think and reflect and develop those theories of practice that best suit their particular sales environment.

To summarize, the switch towards sales education offers five key benefits for employees and employers:

1 Sales enablement is becoming much more strategic within a framework that has been built on the expertise of industry, academics, professional bodies and government. The emphasis is not only on providing participants with the relevant skills and a certain level of knowledge, but

also on equipping them with the right mindset to be successful in today's complex, global business environment – the ability to think, explore and reflect.

2 This strategic framework is able to combine with the more tactical, just-in-time learning approaches that are facilitated by technology and are necessary if we are to succeed in an environment where data and knowledge are proliferating so rapidly. Nobody can possibly retain everything they need to know over the course of a business career, but this is not necessary; the important thing is the development of critical thinking skills such that individuals have the wherewithal to find relevant knowledge when they need it, along with the ability to analyse the information, and to communicate and update their analysis.

3 Sales education with recognized qualifications is subject to accreditation, which benefits both individuals and employers. Employees now have an easy shorthand to highlight their capabilities with qualifications that are transferable across roles and companies, while recruitment becomes more reliable for employers who can fall back on a series of benchmark qualifications for comparing applicants.

4 There is now a framework for development during a sales career with relevant qualifications at every level. Individuals can progress along this path as far as they choose. Lifelong learning is becoming a reality for sales professionals.

5 This approach is instilling a mindset change towards professionalization that will ultimately feed into the marketplace to benefit the customer. Using advanced analytics, companies will be able to measure the performance of their sales function not only in terms of revenue and other financial metrics, but also through the lens of improving customer satisfaction and quality of engagement, ie customer experience; in turn, they will be able to cross-reference this with the learning activity and other sales-enablement initiatives happening across their sales organization.

The sales profession is finally coming of age, and sales education is perhaps the vanguard of its transformation.

Endnotes

1 https://www.cityam.com/fink-is-right-to-hail-the-great-reallocation/ (archived at https://perma.cc/FM75-NRJ6)

2	https://www.blackrock.com/corporate/investor-relations/larry-fink-ceo-letter (archived at https://perma.cc/Z3X8-9A3Y)
3	https://www.cbsnews.com/news/blackrock-puts-climate-change-first-in-its-its-investment-strategy/ (archived at https://perma.cc/3LKT-UQ3A)
4	https://www.sap.com/docs/download/investors/2019/sap-2019-q4-statement.pdf (archived at https://perma.cc/8FFP-7E7Y)
5	Janssen, A (2019) Purpose as a profit centre, *International Journal of Sales Transformation*, 5 (4)
6	https://www.youtube.com/watch?v=R5lZPWNFizQ (archived at https://perma.cc/8LEJ-L2CD)
7	Applebaum, B (2019) *The Economists' Hour: False prophets, free markets, and the fracture of society*, Picador, London
8	Milanovic, B (2019) *Capitalism, Alone: The future of the system that rules the world*, The President and Fellows of Harvard College, Boston, MA
9	https://www.ft.com/content/606f1c8c-5f96-11ea-8033-fa40a0d65a98 (archived at https://perma.cc/YG7F-Y7Q9)
10	https://uk.reuters.com/article/uk-airbus-probe/airbus-faces-record-4-billion-fine-after-bribery-probe-idUKKBN1ZR0HW (archived at https://perma.cc/C4EX-6W82)
11	https://www.ft.com/content/606f1c8c-5f96-11ea-8033-fa40a0d65a98 (archived at https://perma.cc/WP5Q-PWZS)
12	https://www.accountancyage.com/2019/06/13/hp-and-autonomy-the-use-of-evidence-in-and-from-foreign-proceedings/ (archived at https://perma.cc/7MK4-R3VL)
13	https://www.theregister.co.uk/2019/08/23/autonomy_trial_hardware_analysis/ (archived at https://perma.cc/D6CU-YWH5)
14	https://www.iasplus.com/en/standards/ias/ias38 (archived at https://perma.cc/N3AX-67E5)
15	Personal correspondence with the author
16	https://www.oed.com/viewdictionaryentry/Entry/152052 (archived at https://perma.cc/RL5Y-3CYS)
17	Salopek, JJ (2009) The POWER of the pyramid, *T+D*, **63** (5), pp 70–75
18	Cron, WL, Marshall, GW, Singh, J, Spiro, RL and Sujan, H (2005) Salesperson selection, training, and development: trends, implications and research opportunities, *Journal of Personal Selling and Sales Management*, **25** (2), pp 123–36
19	Boehm, DN and Hogan, T (2013) Science-to-business collaborations: a science-to-business marketing perspective on scientific knowledge commercialization, *Industrial Marketing Management*, **42** (4), pp 564–79
20	Kolb, D (1984) *Experiential Learning: Experience as the source of learning and development*, Prentice-Hall, Englewood Cliffs, NJ

21 Schon, D (1983) *The Reflective Practitioner: How professionals think in action*, Basic Books, New York
22 Marcos-Cuevas, J, Critten, P, Squire, P and Speakman, JIF (2014) Enhancing the professional mindset of future sales professionals: key insights from a master in sales transformation, *Journal of Marketing Education*, **36** (2), pp 144–55
23 https://www.consalia.com/insight/toshiba/ (archived at https://perma.cc/8T5Y-8V8E)

APPENDIX

Negative/limiting mindsets

1. Manipulative

Attitudes	Behaviours
• Believes that a good salesperson can sell nearly anything to anyone. • Believes that if a salesperson asks enough questions they will always be able to identify a need that can be matched to a product/service they sell. • Tenacious and persistent because they believe the customer can often be convinced or worn down.	• Customer feels pressured to buy and considers the salesperson to be pushy. • Continuously follows up with the customer – even when the customer has said they are not interested. Approaches are often unwelcomed by the customer. • Does and says whatever it takes to get the sale. Exaggerates the product/service in order to gain interest and the sale. • Tries to 'convince' the customer to buy; however, arguments used are often not relevant or of interest to the customer. • Has a 'kitbag' full of 'sales techniques'. These techniques cover most situations that the salesperson will encounter. • The sales techniques and processes used often make customers feel they are being 'sold to' and that a sales process is being 'done to them'. • Does not keep the customer fully informed in order to keep 'the upper hand'. • Can be dishonest and/or unethical in order to get or improve the sale. • Sometimes plays individuals off against each other to get the information required for the deal. • The customer finds that not all of the salesperson's promises are fulfilled.

2. Supplier-centricity

Attitudes	Behaviours
• Higher focus on the immediate deal than on forming long-term partnerships. • Considers that responsibilities finish when the sale has closed. • Targets are short term (eg for the year/quarter) so these time frames are the only concerns. • Does not consider it necessary to have an in-depth knowledge of the customer's company as a whole and their place in the industry.	• Solutions presented only cover immediate or requested needs. • Standard products/services are presented, with very little customization to the needs of specific customers. • Solutions and suggestions are reactive rather than proactive. • Does not think strategically about the customer's company. • Little attempt is made to develop strong and genuine personal relationships with customers. • The customer has difficulty contacting the salesperson once the sale has closed. • Post-sale contact is routine and normally has the objective of trying to sell further products or services. • 'Added value' is at the level of an additional product for free, as opposed to helping the customer to achieve goals beyond the scope of the sale. • Does not 'waste' too much time researching the customer and/or industry.

3. Complacency

Attitudes	Behaviours
• Feeling of contentment or smug self-satisfaction with own abilities. • Excessively favourable opinion of own ability, importance, wit, etc. • Considers own sales practices to be the correct way. • Absence of passion or excitement in relation to the customer. • Is not genuinely interested in or concerned for the customer.	• Does not really listen to the customer and customers feel this. • Rarely strays from own comfort zone. • Does not identify the real issues for the customer in order to match a suitable solution. Customers feel that little or no effort has been made by the salesperson. • Can be seen as lazy. • Little attempt is made to get to know the customer and/or industry better. • Self-satisfied confidence can mean that salesperson does not notice that the customer is responding negatively or that someone else who is more customer-focused is going to win the deal.

Attitudes	Behaviours
	• Knowledge level is low in relation to the customer, the customer's position in the market and the industry. • Information and solutions presented are not always relevant to the customer. • Lacks a sense of urgency on important issues as does not always understand customer priorities. • Solutions lack originality and innovation.

4. Overt arrogance

Attitudes	Behaviours
• Rates self-satisfaction well above customer satisfaction. • Prime focus is achievement of targets and the financial reward. • Believes that salespeople know what is best for the customer as they are the experts in the product/service. • Has not considered that salespeople should be a part of the customer's team.	• Often seen as arrogant and/or aggressive. • Customers do not believe all that they are told, or are suspicious about the accuracy of information provided. • 'Presentations' are delivered, as opposed to having intelligent conversations around a solution. Presentations are often based purely on PowerPoint slides. • Presentations are focused on the salesperson's company and a suite of established products/services – not on demonstrating an understanding of the customer, industry, needs, appropriate solutions, etc. • Does not consider partnerships with other organizations or using products/services of another organization as part of a solution. • Does not inform the customer of all the individuals being spoken with in the customer's organization. • Can be seen as taking over or controlling the customer's environment. • Can be seen to lack respect.

Positive/outstanding mindsets

1. Authenticity

Attitudes	Behaviours
• Is honest and has integrity, resulting in undisputed credibility. • Unpretentious and free from affectation, inflated self-image and hypocrisy. • Does not feel the need to be seen as more important or knowledgeable than the customer. Is confident in own abilities. • Sincere in all dealings with customers, colleagues and partners. • A genuine person. Does not pretend to be someone that they are not. • Feels the need to present information and capabilities factually. • Genuinely believes that each customer requires an original solution, specific to their needs and situation.	• Does not hide things from the customer or try to cover the truth for own or own company's advantage. Ensures the customer does not feel that information is being withheld. • Ensures individuals in the customer's organization are aware of other relationships being pursued/maintained within the company. • Customer is not made to feel pressured to buy. • Does not try to sell 'off the shelf' solutions. Customers 'know' they are getting an original solution. • Ethical behaviours are reflected in both verbal and written communication. • Demonstrates sincerity when rapport-building. Only asks questions where there is a genuine interest or knowledge. Questioning is not forced or interest faked. • Customer gains a good impression not only of the salesperson but also of the whole company. • Data is represented correctly and not manipulated to prove a particular point. All data appears credible and does not look questionable. • Does not make false claims, either in capability or in ownership of material. • Documentation is original and what it claims to be. • Based on behaviours, judged to be dependable and trustworthy by customers.

2. Client-centricity

Attitudes	Behaviours
- Genuinely desires to fully understand the customer's business. Naturally inquisitive. - Believes it is essential to have a good understanding of the company direction and issues confronting the customer. - Focuses on customer needs and providing the best-fit solution – not on finding a home for an 'off the shelf' solution. - Is diligent, dedicated and flexible with each customer. - Passionate about own role and helping customers to improve their business. Positive disposition. - Recognizes that the role is to lead the solution and take personal responsibility. - Believes in building long-term, value-added, equal relationships. Sees this as win/win. - Has energy and a sense of urgency – wants to get things done.	- Researches the customer's company and industry to gain a good understanding of their business drivers, value chain, strategic initiatives, projects, core processes, etc, as well as industry issues, trends and forces. Knows the client's organizational structure. - Uses a variety of research methods, such as books, magazines, analyst reports, government reports, annual reports, attending client briefing sessions, talking to industry leaders, internet and setting up web alerts for news items. - Is available to the customer both on the phone and in person – even at short notice. Leaves internal meetings if a customer phones. - Takes ownership and personal accountability for projects, issues and problems. Proactive in progressing the project and in identifying and solving problems. - Adapts own behaviour to the culture of the organization and the country. Uses the customer's language. - Establishes relationships both inside and outside own organization in order to find the best solution for a customer. - Works together with the customer in joint efforts. Facilitates the development of joint initiatives between companies and partners. - Demonstrates loyalty to the customer and the relationship. - Listens carefully to what the customer is saying and customers feel they have been understood. - Explains things clearly and simply so that the customer can understand. - Adjusts behaviours to adapt to customers' time pressures. For example, skip pleasantries and go straight to the point of the meeting, if culturally acceptable. - Does not use a high-pressure sales approach. - Keeps up to date with features and capabilities of own products and services.

3. Proactive creativity

Attitudes	Behaviours
• Recognizes that clients value creativity highly and that own role is to constantly consider new ways to innovate. • Creative thinker. Strives to invent creative solutions. • Recognizes that creativity is a mindset and relates not only to technical innovation but to all aspects of the role. • Enjoys the opportunity to think beyond the basic solution and consider all aspects of the customer's business. • Enjoys thinking 'outside the box'.	• Time is spent reflecting on the customer's business issues and what could be offered that would add value to areas the customer cares about. • The time spent on reflection and creativity is proactive and in addition to any specific requests from the customer. • Creative ideas go beyond the brief and can be for any area of the customer's business. • Ideas are creative/innovative and surprise the customer. • Ideas challenge the customer's thinking and push boundaries. • Creativity and innovation are included in the deal-making process. • Customers approach and ask for new ideas. • Invitations are received from customers to attend strategic review meetings or innovation workshops. • Processes are developed to ensure that innovation or value review meetings are held to review what went well and what didn't with creative ideas.

4. Tactful audacity

Attitudes	Behaviours
• Fearless and daring when suggesting solutions and collaborations to customers. • Willing to take surprisingly bold risks. • Has a keen sense of what to do or say to avoid giving offence. • Understands intuitively the complexities of situations, discussions and human dynamics and the appropriate behaviours required. • Self-confident and positive in discussions with customers.	• Ideas are proactively put forward to the customer, eg, 'There is something that you might not have thought of yet but because of xyz I think that you might like to explore some new ideas.' • Bold in presentation of ideas, solutions and collaborations. • Suggestions are presented with enthusiasm, demonstrating a genuine desire to add value to the customer's organization. • Customer considers the salesperson forward/audacious and not afraid to stick their neck out. • Audacious conversations are highly positive, clearly highlighting the benefits to the customer's organization.

Attitudes	Behaviours
- Disregard for conventional thought and approaches. - Heedless of restraints imposed by convention. - Self-assured in attitude, does not feel the need to ingratiate self with the customer.	- Offence is not felt by the customer in response to the ideas presented or to the manner in which they are presented. - Carefully plans and prepares each audacious approach to the customer to ensure maximum value and impact – and minimum offence. - Demonstrates diplomacy when suggesting ideas to customers. - Knows the limits for how far to push a suggestion with a customer and does not overstep these.

INDEX

Figures and tables are indicated by page numbers in italics

academic research in sales 45–48
adaptive selling (ADAPTS) model 45, 47
adhocracy 30, 178
Adobe 31
The Age of Discontinuity (Drucker, 1969) 26
agile organizations 30, 31
agile thinking, case study 173–78
Airbus 215
Aleppo, Syria, selling approach in the markets 17–22
Amazon 165
ambiguity, ability to work with 196
Anglo American 103
Apple iPhone 31
Applebaum, B 213
appreciative inquiry (AI) theory 202–03
arrogance 68, 69, 235
Asos 30
Association of Professional Sales (APS), UK 14, 123, 224, 225
authenticity 75–76, 111–23, 236
    assessing your lived values 114–17
    awareness of your authentic self 114–17
    code of ethics for sales people 122–23
    critical reflection 117–22
    cross-cultural acceptance 111
    definition of 111
    explore your personal values and mindsets 115–16
    people's reliance on intuition to make decisions 112–14
    stress caused by conflicts with personal values 123
    workplace values and mindsets 117
autobiographical listening 44

Babylon (healthcare technology business) 31
Bag the Elephant (Kaplan, 2005) 52–53
banking crisis (2008) 2, 213, 214
bartering skills 21–22
Belt and Road Initiative (China) 2, 8
Bezos, Jeff 165
Birkinshaw, Julian 23–36, 113, 178
BlackRock 211–12

boohoo 30, 151–55
books on selling 48–57
Branson, Richard 165–66
British Airways 165
Burke, Chris 40, 178–79
business assets, capitalization of sales relationships 216–22
business-to-business sales, as a profession 14–15
Buyer Approved Selling (Schell, 2003) 54, *54*
buyers' era 2
buying cycle
    importance of values 94–95
    point of engagement with salespeople 94–95

Camp, Garrett 165
Capellas, Michael 82, 85
capitalism, implications of future developments for sales 213–16
capitalization of sales relationships 216–22
case studies
    challenge for a newly-appointed sales director 200–04
    client-centric cultural transformation in a professional services consultancy 137–44
    global mining business 125–29
    Hewlett-Packard (values and sales performance) 103–04, *105*
    impacts of negative values/mindsets (DLC case) 73–75
    Sony Mobile (tactful audacity) 167–70
    Starbucks (impact of positive values) 79–86
    Starbucks (proactive creativity) 147, *148–49*
    Starbucks/Compaq (HP) 79–86
CEB (now Challenger Inc) 32
chaebols in South Korea 160–61
Challenger Sale (Dixon and Adamson, 2011) 54, 55
change, distinction from transformation 200
Chicago School monetarist theories 213

China
    Belt and Road Initiative 2, 8
    Maritime Silk Route 9–13
    opening up of the Silk Road 6–9
Chung Ju Yung 161–62
client-centricity 75, 76, 125–44, 237
    cracking the industry code 129–32
    cultural transformation in a professional services consultancy (case study) 137–44
    customer pulse check tool 132–37
    global mining business (case study) 125–29
    identifying key success factors (KSFs) 131
    knowing your customer 132–37
    knowing your customer's customer 125–29
    knowing your customer's industry 125–32
    meaning of 125
    organizational support for 207–09
coaching to the mindsets 204–06, 206
Coca-Cola 165–66
co-creation case study 173–78
co-creation's era 2
code of ethics for sales people 122–23
Collins, Jim 165
Compaq (HP), Starbucks case study 79–86
competitive advantage
    changing sources over time 23–36
    new selling paradigm 32–35
    sources when selling in the industrial era 23–25
    sources when selling in the knowledge era 26–30
    sources when selling in the post-knowledge era 30–32
complacency 68, 69, 234–35
confidence, distinction from arrogance 69
Consalia 14, 225, 229
    hierarchy of values 99–100
Consalia Mindset Survey 100–03
Consultative Selling (Hanan, 1999) 52, 53
Covey, S 44
COVID-19 pandemic 2, 122–23, 130, 196
    economic effects 214
    response of Royal Caribbean Cruises 190
cowrie shell currency 2, 5–6
critical reflection, core competence for salespeople 117–22
Critten, Peter 226
CRM (customer relationship management) 2, 221, 216
    results of investment in 27–30
cultural transformation, professional services consultancy (case study) 137–44
Customer Centric Selling (Bosworth and Holland, 2004) 51–52
customer experience (Cx), emerging focus on 211–13
customer-orientated selling model 45–46
customer pulse check tool 132–37
customer relationship management *see* CRM
customer strategy grid 155–59

Davis, Graham 225
Day, Carl 227–28
decision-making
    emotional aspect of 113
    reliance on intuition 112–14
    System One and System Two thinking 113
degree courses in sales *see* sales education
Deloitte 219
Delta Airlines, customer strategy grid 157, 158–59
Devlin, Paul 193
Drucker, Peter 198
    The Age of Discontinuity (1969) 26
Dunbar, Robin, Dunbar's number 34–35
Dweck, Carol 106

emocracy 30, 34, 113, 178
emotional aspect of decision-making 113
emotional intelligence 12
enterprise resource planning (ERP) software 130
ethical code for sales people 122–23
European Foundation for Quality Management (EFQM) 133

failure
    approach to 173
    relationship with innovation 166
Financial Conduct Authority (FCA), UK 215
financial crisis (2008) 2, 213, 214
Fink, Larry 211–12
Five Minds for the Future (Gardner) 67
Ford Motor Company 24
Friedman, Milton 213
future developments in selling 211–30
    capitalization of sales relationships 216–22
    effects of the COVID-19 pandemic 214
    emerging customer experience (Cx) focus 211–13

INDEX 243

implications of the future of
   capitalism 213–16
professionalization of sales 222–30
regulatory intervention in the sales
   process 215–16
technology solutions 216
transparency of the selling process 216

Gardner, Howard 67
Garnett, Jonathan 226
generosity, 'otherish givers' 12
Gibbs' reflective cycle 118–22
Gideon Society 25
Gladwell, Malcolm 113
global mining business, using client-centricity
   mindset to win a new account (case
   study) 125–29
globalization 6
Golden Circle Secrets (Ben and Dale
   Midgley, 2005) 56
golden circles theory 34, 194–95
Goldschmied, Nadav P. 69
Google, Aristotle Project 166
Grant, Adam 12, 208
Greenspan, Alan 213
Grey, Baz 194
growth mindset 106, 195

Haigh, David 220
Harrington, Bates, *How 'Tis Done*
   (1879) 14, 25
Hewlett-Packard
   acquisition of Autonomy 219
   HP (Compaq)/ Starbucks case
      study 79–86
   values and sales performance (case
      study) 103–04, *105*
Hill, Samuel E. 25
history
   contribution of selling to economic and
      cultural development 1, 2
   early currencies 2, 5–6
   early evidence of trade 2, 5–6
   how buying and selling were conducted
      in the past 15–16
   how it informs current sales
      practice 5–16
   how long selling has been around 2, 5–6
   locations of historical centres of trade 15
   opening up the Silk Road 6–9
   significant moments in relation to
      selling 2
Hong Kong protests 214
How 'Tis Done (Harrington, 1879) 14, 25

Hussain, Sushovan 219
Hyundai 161–62

IAS 38 218, 221
Iglu 30
industrial era *24*
   bureaucracy 24
   seller-controlled environment 24–25
   selling methods 23–25
   sources of competitive advantage 23–25
industry code, how to crack it 131–32
Innocent Drinks 166
innovation, failure and 166
Institute for Apprenticeships (IFA) 14, 224
Institute for Work Based Learning 226
integrity 111
International Reporting Financial Standards
   (IFRS) 218
intuition, people's reliance on to make
   decisions 112–14

Janssen, Alf 212–13
Johnson, Boris 171

Kahneman, Daniel 113
Kalanick, Travis 165
Kirk, Donald 161
knowledge era 2, *24*
   buyer-controlled environment 26–27
   investments to improve sales
      productivity 27–30
   meritocracy 26
   selling methods 26–30
   sources of competitive advantage 26–30
   technology solutions for sales 27
Kolb, David 226
Korthagen, Fred 58–61, 72, 78
Kotter model for cultural change 139
Kyprianou, Anna 226

leadership, role in transforming
   sales 193–209
LG 160
LinkedIn 27
Lotte SK 161
Lynch, Mike 219

management *see* sales management systems;
   sales managers
Mancera, Gustavo 167–70
manipulation 67–68, 233
Maritime Silk Route 2, 9–13, 15
marketing research, comparison with
   research on selling 13–14

Marks & Spencer 30
McNiff, Jean 57
mental health, stress caused by conflicts with personal values 123
micro-management 204
Microsoft 31
Microsoft Azure 27
Microsoft Dynamics 216
Middlesex University 226, 229
mindsets
    ability to work with ambiguity 196
    coaching by sales managers 204–06, 206
    growth mindset 106, 195
    influence of positive or negative values 67
    see also values
Mitsubishi 161
Modi, Narendra 171
monetarist economic policy 213–15
motivation for selling 106
Museum of Failure, Sweden 166

Naish, Jenny 226
National Centre of Work Based Learning 226
national culture, encouragement to live the positive mindsets 160–63
negative selling values/mindsets 68–75, 233–35
    insights from interviewee statements 70–73
    impacts of (DLC case) 73–75
Nicholson, John H. 25
nine box model 155
Nokia, consequences of not adapting 31

Oracle CRM 216
organizations, support for a client-centric culture 207–09
Outsell Your Competition (Fielder, 2002) 50–51

PACT checklist 206
Park Chung-Hee 160, 162
Pepsi 165–66
populist movements 214
Porras, Jerry 165
Portwood, Derek 226
positive mindsets, national culture and 160–63
positive selling values/mindsets 75–79, 236–39
    insights from interviewee statements 77–79
post-knowledge era 2, 24, 178

adhocracy 30, 178
emocracy 30, 34, 113, 178
importance of agility in organizations 30, 31
selling methods 30–32
sources of competitive advantage 30–32
PPI (personal protection insurance) mis-selling scandal (UK) 215
proactive creativity 75, 76, 147–63, 238
    avoiding supplier-centric bias 150–55
    boohoo 151–55
    customer strategy grid 155–59
    meaning of 147
    national culture and positive mindsets 160–63
    Starbucks (case study) 147, 148–49
    third place thinking from the buyer's perspective 147, 148
    third place thinking from the seller's perspective 147, 149, 150–55
    whitespace analysis 159–60
procurement function, origins and development of 26–27
procurement processes, working with changes in 32–35
professional services consultancy, client-centric cultural transformation (case study) 137–44
professionalization of sales 14–15, 222–30
psychological safety 166
purpose-driven value creation 211–13

questionnaire, Consalia Mindset Survey 100–03

Reagan, Ronald 213
regulatory intervention in the sales process 215–16
relational capital 31
relational economic value 216
relationship capitalization 216–22
relationships
    Dunbar's number 34–35
    trust and 98–99
research on sales and selling
    comparison with marketing research 13–14
    lack of research 13
    reasons for lack of research 13–14
research process 39–63
    academic research in sales 45–48
    adaptive selling (ADAPTS) model 45, 47
    alternatives to the competency approach 43–44

books on selling 48–57
challenging what good selling looks like 44–48
crisis in the sales profession 63
customer-orientated selling model 45–46
effectiveness of sales training 43–44
emerging conclusions 86–87
first attempts at solving the problem 42–43
how to make it into the winner's circle 42–43
identifying the levers that drive sales performance 44–48
influence of values on sales performance 46–48
insights from interviewee statements 70–73, 77–79
lack of effectiveness of many salespeople 39–40
paradigm shift in research approach 58–61
problem that ignited the research 39–40
research demographics 40–42
sales competency approach 42–43
sales orientation-customer orientation (SOCO) model 46–47
sales training spending by organizations 44
selling transformation 58–61
values-based approach 58–61
values for selling 61–63
what enabled a breakthrough 44–48
why customer perceptions of salespeople are so low 43–44
why so few salespeople sell in a way customers want 57
Richards, David AR 69
Royal Caribbean International case study 181–91
application of core values and mindsets 191
authenticity 187–88
client-centricity 188
learnings from 187–90
organizational and team culture 191
proactive creativity 189
response to the COVID-19 pandemic 190
tactful audacity 189–90
time dimension in the sales process 190
turning a crisis into an opportunity 181–91
what was in it for the ships' hotel directors 184–87

Sales Association (US) 224
sales cycle
control of 26–27
existing customers 91
first contact 89–91
gaining commitment 90, 93
handling objections 90, 93
importance of values at each stage 89–94
making a start 173–78
opening the call 90, 91
positive mindsets during 90
post-call review 90, 93
pre-call planning 89–91
product discussion/presentation of solution 90, 92–93
understanding the need 90, 91–92
what the customer really cares about 90, 91–92
sales degree courses 14–15, 224–27
sales education
benefits for employees and employers 229–30
degree courses 14–15, 224–27
new approaches 224–30
traditional approaches 225–26
Sales Education Foundation (US) 224
Sales Management Association (US) 224
sales management systems 196–04
challenge for a newly-appointed sales director (case study) 200–04
managing by fear 197
managing by hope 197–98
managing by objectives 198
steps in the sales management system 198–99
transactional sales management systems 196–204
transformational sales management systems 196, 200–04
sales managers
ability to work with ambiguity 196
coaching to the mindsets 204–06, 206
desire to be the best 195
empowerment of the sales team 195
growth mindset 195
looking for the potential in people 195–96
micro-management 204
mindsets/values required of 194–96
organization support for a client-centric culture 207–09
percentage of missed sales quotas 193–94
promoting a tactful audacity culture 208
role of 193–94
vision 194–95

sales orientation-customer orientation (SOCO) model 46–47
sales productivity, investments in sales training and CRM 27–30
sales psychology, pressure of time 17–22
sales quotas, percentage that are missed 193–94
sales relationships, capitalization of 216–22
sales training, results of investment in 27–30
see also sales education
sales transformation
  meaning of 1
  research process 39–63
  role of leadership 193–209
SalesForce 27, 216
salespeople, environment for positive differentiating mindsets 193
Samsung 31, 160
SAP 31, 212–13, 226, 227
SAP CRM 27, 216
Schon, David 226
Schultz, Howard 80, 85
seller-controlled environments 24–25
sellers' era 2
selling attributes
  Zhang Qian (Silk Road) 9
  Zheng He (Maritime Silk Route) 11
selling methods
  dealing with multiple decision-makers and stakeholders 32–35
  industrial era 23–25
  knowledge era 26–30
  new selling paradigm 32–35
  post-knowledge era 30–32
  working with changes in procurement processes 32–35
Shackleton, Ernest 194
Silk Road 2, 6–9, 15, 162–63
Silla Dynasty (57BC to 937AD) 162–63
Sinek, Simon 34, 194–95
SKF 30
solution development framework 170–71
Solution Selling (Bosworth, 1995) 50
Sony Mobile, tactful audacity (case study) 167–70
South Korea, national culture 160–63
SPIN Selling (Rackham, 1988) 48–50
Starbucks
  impact of positive values (case study) 79–86
  proactive creativity (case study) 147, 148–49
stock market crashes 2

Strategic Account Management Association (US) 224
Summit Group 91
Summit Value Group 150
supplier-centricity 68, 204, 234
  how to avoid 150–55
Sutton, Louise 225
SWOT analysis 155, *156*, 157

tactful audacity 75, 76–77, 165–79, 238–39
  applied internally 178–79
  approach to failure 173
  building a compelling value proposition 170–78
  co-creation and agile thinking 173–78
  conviction required 173–78
  foundation in trust 172–73
  'just do it' attitude 173–78
  meaning of 165
  passion and inspiration 165–67
  solution development framework 170–71
  Sony Mobile (case study) 167–70
  win themes 171–72
tactful audacity culture, role of the team manager in promoting 208
technology solutions for sales 27, 216
TED Talks 194
Thailand floods 130
Thatcher, Margaret 213
3rd Box Thinking™ 150, 188
third place thinking
  buyer's perspective 147, *148*
  seller's perspective 147, *149*, 150–55
Thomas Cook travel agency 30
Thunberg, Greta 214
time dimension, importance in the sales process 190
time pressure, role in sales psychology 17–22
tools
  cracking the industry code 131–32
  customer pulse check 132–37
  customer strategy grid 155–59
  third place from the seller's perspective 150–55
  whitespace analysis 159–60
Top Shop 30
Toshiba Tec 227–28
Toyota 24
transactional sales management systems 196–204
transformation, distinction from change 200

transformational sales management systems 196, 200–04
transparency of the selling process 216
Trump, Donald 171, 188
trust
    bonded trust 97
    categories/levels of trust 97–99
    challenge for salespeople 114
    connection with values 95–105
    creation of mistrust 97
    foundation for tactful audacity 172–73
    hopeful trust 97
    impact of values on 99–100
    personal relationships and 98–99
    progressive trust 97, 99–100
    unstable trust 97

Uber 165
Unilever 103

value proposition
    building a compelling proposition 170–78
    solution development framework 170–71
    win themes 171–72
values
    arrogance 68, 69, 235
    as guiding principles for selling 106, *107*
    assessing your lived values 114–17
    authenticity 75–76, 111–23, 236
    client-centricity 75, 76, 125–44, 237
    complacency 68, 69, 234–35
    connection with trust 95–105
    Consalia Mindset Survey 100–03
    for selling 61–63
    Hewlett-Packard (case study) 103–04, *105*
    impact on trust 99–100
    importance during the buying cycle 94–95
    importance at each stage of the sales cycle 89–94
    influence on sales performance 46–48
    insights from interviewee statements 70–73, 77–79
    manipulation 67–68, 233

negative selling values/mindsets 68–75, 233–35
positive or negative influence 67
positive selling values/mindsets 75–79, 236–39
proactive creativity 75, 76, 147–63, 238
Royal Caribbean International (case study) 181–91
Starbucks/HP (Compaq) case study 79–86
stress causes by conflicts with personal values 123
supplier-centricity 68, 234
tactful audacity 75, 76–77, 165–79, 238–39
Values Based Selling (Bachrach, 1998) 56–57
Values Sell (Thompson and Soper, 2007) 56
Vandello, Joseph A. 69
Virgin Atlantic 165
Virgin Cola 165–66
vision, importance for sales managers 194–95

Wall Street (1987) 69
West, Samuel 166
whitespace analysis 159–60
Wilkinson, David 196
win themes 171–72
    NAB Bank example 172
The Wolf of Wall Street (2013) 69

Xi Jinping 8

Yip, George 42

Zhang Qian 173
    opening up the overland Silk Road 6–9
    selling attributes 9
Zheng He 173
    emotional intelligence and generosity 12
    leadership skills 11–12
    leveraging tangible and intangible assets to create value 11–12
    opening up the Maritime Silk Route 9–13
    selling attributes of 11–13
Zohar, Danah 200